ORIENTALISM: EARLY SOURCES

ORIENTALISM: EARLY SOURCES
Edited by Bryan S. Turner

VOLUME I: READINGS IN ORIENTALISM
Edited by Bryan S. Turner

VOLUME II: THE MOHAMMADAN DYNASTIES
Stanley Lane-Poole

VOLUME III: THE CALIPHATE
Sir William Muir

VOLUME IV: THE RELIGIOUS ORDERS OF ISLAM
Edward Sell

VOLUME V: MODERN EGYPT – PART 1
Evelyn Baring (Earl of Cromer)

VOLUME VI: MODERN EGYPT – PART 2
Evelyn Baring (Earl of Cromer)

VOLUME VII: THE ARAB KINGDOM AND ITS FALL
J. Wellhausen

VOLUME VIII: THE MYSTICS OF ISLAM
Reynold A. Nicholson

VOLUME IX: WHITHER ISLAM?
H.A.R. Gibb

VOLUME X: ISLAM AND MODERNISM IN EGYPT
Charles C. Adams

VOLUME XI: HISTORY OF THE ISLAMIC PEOPLES
Carl Brockelmann

VOLUME XII: THE SOCIAL STRUCTURE OF ISLAM
Reuben Levy

ORIENTALISM: EARLY SOURCES

Volume IX

Whither Islam?
A Survey of Modern Movements
in the Moslem World

H.A.R. Gibb

LONDON AND NEW YORK

First published 1932
by Victor Gollancz Ltd

This edition reprinted 2000 by Routledge
2 Park Square, Milton Park, Abingdon, Oxon, OX14 4RN
by arrangement with Victor Gollancz

Simultaneously published in the USA and Canada
by Routledge
711 Third Avenue, New York, NY 10017

Transferred to Digital Printing 2007

First issued in paperback 2012

Routledge is an imprint of the Taylor & Francis Group, an informa business

All rights reserved. No part of this book may be reprinted or reproduced or utilised in any form or by any electronic, mechanical, or other means, now known or hereafter invented, including photocopying and recording, or in any information storage or retrieval system, without permission in writing from the publishers.

British Library Cataloguing in Publication Data
A catalogue record for this book is available from the British Library

Library of Congress Cataloguing in Publication Data
A catalogue record for this book has been requested

ISBN-13: 978-0-415-20898-7 (set)
ISBN-13: 978-0-415-20907-6 (hardback)
ISBN-13: 978-0-415-51373-9 (paperback)

Publisher's note
The publisher has gone to great lengths to ensure the quality of this reprint but points out that some imperfections in the original book may be apparent.

WHITHER ISLAM?

A Survey of Modern Movements in the Moslem World

edited by

H. A. R. GIBB

PROFESSOR OF ARABIC IN THE UNIVERSITY OF LONDON

LONDON
VICTOR GOLLANCZ LTD
14 Henrietta Street Covent Garden
1932

CONTENTS

Preface   *page* 7

Chapter I. Introduction. By the Editor   9

  II. Africa (excluding Egypt). By Professor Louis Massignon (University of Paris)   75

  III. Egypt and Western Asia. By Professor Dr. G. Kampffmeyer (University of Berlin)   99

  IV. India. By Lieut.-Col. M. L. Ferrar, C.S.I., C.I.E., O.B.E. (Indian Army, ret.)   171

  V. Indonesia. By Professor C. C. Berg (University of Leiden)   237

  VI. Whither Islam? By the Editor   313

Index   381

Map of the Islamic World   *at end*

PREFACE

SOME explanation may seem to be needed for the issue of yet another book on the Islamic world of to-day. Since Lothrop Stoddard published in 1921 his far-sighted study of *The New World of Islam*, the output of books and pamphlets on this subject has increased by leaps and bounds. Not to speak of works in the Islamic languages themselves and in the lesser-known languages of Europe, the student of the Moslem East has an embarrassing choice of books by Jung, Valyi, Meyerhof, Zwemer, O'Leary, Kohn, Hartmann, and many others, together with a host of monographs on contemporary movements in the separate Moslem lands. It is no depreciation of the value of these works that they lay most stress on the political aspects of the problem, and that few of them embrace the whole range of the Islamic world. The papers contributed to the present volume aim rather at analysing the inner currents of thought among the Moslem peoples. For this task no single scholar could claim full competence, since such a study, resting not only upon personal contacts but also upon a thorough acquaintance with the literature produced in each country, demands a knowledge of such different languages as Arabic, Turkish, Persian, Urdu, Javanese and Malay.

The editor counts himself particularly fortunate in having secured the collaboration of four such distinguished authorities as Professors Massignon, Kampffmeyer, and Berg, and Lieut.-Col. Ferrar, in dealing with the four main regions of the Moslem world. Their papers, which are expanded from a series of lectures entitled " Modern Movements in the Islamic World," delivered under the Forlong Bequest at the School of Oriental Studies of the University of London in November, 1931, offer a detailed analysis of the various currents of thought and opinion which are at the present moment occupying the minds of the Moslem peoples from Morocco to Java. The final chapter, resuming the thread of the introductory chapter, aims rather at presenting a composite picture of the main currents on rather broader lines. It is hardly necessary to add that no restrictions have been placed upon the contributors, and that each has been free to express and is entirely responsible for his own opinions.

INTRODUCTION

CHAPTER I

INTRODUCTION

To the world at large Islam stands primarily for a religion, a system of theology, associated with the person of the Prophet Muhammad and the record of his discourses which is preserved in the *Qur'ān* or Koran. We speak of his followers as Muhammadans, Moslems or Musalmans, and our statisticians can supply us with figures in bulk and in detail—rough estimates, most of them, and with surprising discrepancies which run into tens of millions—to show us their distribution, their relative strength, and the place of Islam generally amongst the religions of the world. The most careful of these calculations gives a total of from 240 to 250 millions of professing Moslems, or more than the entire population of the two Americas. Of these there are over 180 millions in Asia (something over 70 millions being in India, nearly 50 millions in Indonesia, about 40 millions in Western Asia, and the remainder in Siberia and China), and over 50 millions in Africa, where indeed the adherents of Islam outnumber by many times those of all other organised religions, and constitute a full third of the population of the continent. In addition several millions of Moslems are still to be found in Europe, chiefly in the Balkan states and in south Russia.

WHITHER ISLAM?

For all these millions the problem of " Whither Islam ? " in the narrowly religious and theological sense of the term, is of vital importance. Nor is it even for us a purely academic problem. We have learned only too well that by their ultimate beliefs are determined the motives, methods and ideals of men in their daily life, and in Islam in particular the place occupied by religious teaching has always been so large that the theological aspect cannot be left out of account in any survey of modern tendencies in the Moslem world. Yet, while religious issues doubtless underlie many modern trends of thought, even though they are not immediately visible on the surface, the developments in " Muhammadan " theology and religious practice form but one aspect (and for the present a secondary one) of a much wider problem.

Islam is indeed much more than a system of theology ; it is a complete civilization. If we were to seek for parallel terms, we should use Christendom rather than Christianity, China rather than Confucianism. It includes a whole complex of cultures which have grown up around the religious core, or have in most cases been linked on to it with more or less modification, a complex with distinctive features in political, social and economic structure, in its conception of law, in ethical outlook, intellectual tendencies, habits of thought and action. Further, it includes a vast number of peoples differing in race,

INTRODUCTION

language, character and inherited aptitudes, yet bound together not only by the link of a common creed, but even more strongly by their participation in a common culture, their obedience to a common law and their adoption of a common tradition.

More striking still is the wide geographical distribution of the Moslem peoples. They stretch in unbroken succession from the Atlantic seaboard of West Africa through the Sudan, and along the southern coasts of the Mediterranean to Egypt and Western Asia, thence by the shores of the Black Sea and the Caspian Sea into the heart of Siberia and eastwards into Mongolia; down the East African coast to the latitude of Madagascar, and across the mountain ranges of Afghanistan into the plains of India. Here for the first time the *bloc* is broken, but after throwing out large isolated communities in Bengal and other Indian provinces, a fresh chain begins in the Malay Peninsula and extends without interruption across the East Indian Archipelago until it ends in the southern Philippine Islands. Outside these areas smaller isolated communities are found in the western borders of China and in South Africa. Looked at on the map, the Islamic world resembles two vast crescents, the horns of which radiate from a common centre in Western Asia. The northern crescent forms a band well over a thousand miles in breadth, encircling Europe almost from end to end, and isolating it geographically from the populous countries of southern and eastern Asia; the slender arms of the southern crescent, broken only by parts of India and Ceylon, embrace the Indian Ocean.

We might reasonably expect that the spread of Islam over such vast areas, covering so many races and older traditions, should have had the effect of preventing the attainment of any real unity in Islamic civilization—that even if religious practice remained uniform, yet the persistence of old-established habits and ways of thought, differing so widely in character as to be irreconcilable, should have exercised so powerful an influence on the culture of the individual regions as to exclude community of tradition and any complete community of feeling, and to create rather a number of regional Islamic cultures. That something of this kind should actually have happened was inevitable, and, as the chapter headings of this book have already indicated, we may certainly distinguish in each main area some characteristic features which to a certain extent mark it off from other areas of the Moslem world. It is not surprising that this should be so; the surprising thing, on the other hand, is that, notwithstanding the presence of so many factors which made for division, the underlying civilization and intellectual outlook should have remained on the whole so uniform. For this phenomenon we can distinguish three main causes.

INTRODUCTION

In the first place, the present territorial expansion of Islam was not the result—save to a minor extent—of a steady process of widening from century to century, but came about in a series of rapid bounds. The conquests of the Arabs between 630 and 750 carried the territorial domination of Islam from Spain and Morocco to Central Asia, and within these boundaries it remained confined for some two and a half centuries more. Between 1000 and 1100 Moslem rule was extended on four fronts—in West Africa, Asia Minor, Central Asia, and Northern India. After the lapse of two centuries it experienced another wave of expansion, thrusting out arms between 1300 and 1400 into the Balkan peninsula, the steppes of Russia and Siberia, the rest of India, and Indonesia. Thus by 1400 the map of Islam was very much the same as it is to-day, only minor advances having been made since, chiefly in Africa. Among the most important consequences of this spasmodic expansion was the fact that, during the building up of its civilization, Islam was not exposed simultaneously to the competing influences of a number of divergent cultures. The two and a half centuries between 750 and 1000 were the formative period during which Moslem civilization in its evolution received the distinctive stamp which it was not to lose again down to our own time.

At this point we must turn aside for a moment to investigate a little more closely one question which has a very considerable bearing on the whole problem of Islam. We are so accustomed to think of Islam as an oriental religion and of its culture as an oriental culture that we are apt to overlook the real character of Moslem civilization and to miss its true place and significance in the history of human society. The old view that Islam issued from Arabia in a complete, fixed and unalterable form has long been recognized as a fallacious half-truth. Even in the narrow field of religious doctrine Islam remained for at least two centuries relatively plastic. Its fundamental principles were doubtless fixed once and for all, but they were not finally developed into a theology until after a long period of controversy. Now the religion of Islam itself is a branch of that group of religions which includes also Zoroastrianism, Judaism, and Christianity, and shares with them the same ultimate postulates. From the very first it belonged, in consequence, to what we may call—in contradistinction to the Indian and Chinese religious groups—the western group. This western character was, moreover, intensified in the sequel. The outer world into which Islam issued from Arabia was the Hellenistic world, the heir of Græco-Roman civilization, and almost all its early conquests were made within this Hellenistic world. Thus it came about that the external influences which moulded Moslem civilization were Hellenistic and Persian. Its intellectual life was penetrated through and through by Greek culture; its very theology is in debt to Aristotle. The whole culture of Islam was thus essentially a culture of the western type, and stands much closer to us than the cultures of India and the Far East. To call it " oriental " is a misnomer; it is oriental not in the absolute sense, but only in its local extension, as the eastern branch of western civilization, and it has at all times been shared by Jews and eastern Christians as well as Moslems.

By the year 1000 this evolution of Islam from a simple creed into a complex society was complete. When subsequently it overleapt its old boundaries and established itself in regions with other cultural traditions, it did so, not in its primitive plastic state, but as a fully developed and coherent culture, which it carried with it wherever it went. Islam in India and Indonesia was thus the spiritual heir of Alexander and the standard-bearer of Hellenism, albeit in assimilated form. (It is perhaps symbolic that Islam alone among western religions raised Alexander almost to the status of a Prophet.) In spite of adaptations in practice to local usage, especially among the lower classes, it refused to compromise with its new environment or to revise its outlook or its character. On the contrary it held high the banner of theism as against Hindu speculation and pagan animism, and the effect of the contrast was rather to stiffen its opposition and to strengthen its hold on its own culture.

Combined with this was a peculiar feature which is associated with the spread of Islam, and was the second cause of its cultural uniformity. This was the power possessed by the developed Moslem culture of weakening, in some cases even of obliterating, the memory of old cultural traditions amongst its converts, and replacing them with its own background of history and tradition. In almost every region of the Moslem world the peoples forgot their pre-Islamic past—the Egyptians their Pharaohs and Ptolemies, the Turks their Khagans, and so forth—and looked back to Arabia and the early Caliphate for their spiritual ancestry. It is not in contradiction with this that elements of the older cultures were caught up and linked on to the local Moslem culture, for their old functions and associations were lost and they were harmonized with the common Moslem tradition. By such concessions, indeed, Islam strengthened its power of appeal and gained a new means of propagating its own tradition and outlook.

Nevertheless there was more than a possibility that as Islam spread ever farther afield and increasingly adapted to its own purposes practices which were essentially foreign to its real nature, the ideal unity which it sought to maintain might be endangered and its real message weakened or perverted. A third factor stepped in, however, to offset this danger. This was the constant intercourse which was kept up

INTRODUCTION

between the various regions of the Moslem world, and more especially between the outlying countries and the central lands of Western Asia and Egypt. The most powerful agency which promoted this intercourse was the *Hajj*, or Pilgrimage to Mecca, which is incumbent on every able-bodied Moslem, who is possessed of the requisite means, at least once in his lifetime; and we shall see that, as a means for reviving religious zeal and strengthening the conviction of Moslem unity, the institution of the Pilgrimage still retains its ancient virtue. Second only to the Pilgrimage in their influence towards spiritual unification were the missionary labours of the mystical or Sufi fraternities, whose devoted adherents in every country strove to maintain and extend the flame of personal religion in the lives of the people. For all their extravagances of ritual and the base alloy in many of the lesser local orders, the fraternities as a whole played, especially in the outer regions which were of more recent acquisition, a fruitful part in spreading the teachings and practices of Islam. Among the secular agencies which also co-operated to this end special mention should be made of the contacts resulting from the operations of mediæval commerce, and maintained in later centuries by the more developed means of communication created by European enterprise. Thus the pure Islamic tradition and cultural influences in the more recently converted areas were continually reinforced both by immigrants from the centre and by local scholars who, after spending years of study at Mecca, in Cairo, and elsewhere, returned to their native lands with the determination to purify the local practice of Islam from abuses and inconsistent accretions.

The net effect of these causes was to create and maintain throughout the Moslem world a solidarity of culture and tradition which, though never quite complete, was truly remarkable in view of its widely scattered constituents and the variety of their racial stocks and languages. It received outward expression in the common use of the Arabic script, and to a lesser extent in the sharing of Arabic cultural terms and even of the Arabic language as the common medium of scholars, as well as in the common conception of one all-embracing *Dār al-Islām* (" dwelling-place of Islam "), in perpetual warfare, spiritual and material, with the rest of the world. The sharing of a common religion, a common law, and a common culture created along with this a feeling of social unity—not to be understood (as it has sometimes been misunderstood) in the sense of social equality, for the democratic ideals of Islam have never succeeded wholly in overthrowing distinctions of class and caste, but in the sense that the Moslem peoples as a whole were conscious of their kinship with one another, and gave practical effect to that conviction in their social life. The Moslem of North-west Africa was, except for language, as much at home in India or Java as in Morocco ; he might come and go, marry, and settle down as he pleased. The whole *Dār al-Islām* was his country ; other country he had none. His affections might centre on his native land, but his loyalty, and all the other sentiments which we associate with patriotism, were given to the Moslem world and its religious culture as a whole. Persia alone, especially from the sixteenth century, stood out as an exception, and there largely because the national feeling was doubled with a special sectarian divergence from the Moslem majority.

Islam of our study is thus not so much a religion, in the modern detached and private sense of the word, as a fully-rounded society on a religious basis which comprehends every aspect of human life. The circumstances of its growth from the very first led, as we shall see shortly, to the linking-up of religion and politics, nay even of theology and politics, and the subsequent working-out of Islamic law and social organization confirmed this inherent tendency. The men of our own early Middle Ages would have understood this—did in fact understand it—perfectly, and we must bear in mind throughout that we are dealing with a society at the heart of which this " mediæval " conception still strongly beats. Indeed, in Islam this development went much farther than it ever reached in Europe, though the characteristic lack of outward organization which marks nearly all Moslem cultural institutions often obscures the interrelations between different sides of life and activity. We find, for example, that political administration has at times seemed to stand completely outside the common framework of Islamic culture, yet the alliance between government and religious and social life was so vital a part of the Moslem view of the world order that the disturbance of this connection was one of the primary causes of the modern crisis in Islam. Conversely, political activity may be, and often is, the outward and visible sign of a disturbance which has its roots in religious sentiment, economic status, or any other field of communal life.

Given the " mediæval " constitution of the Islamic society, it scarcely requires lengthy demonstration that the result of the intrusion of new ideas and new tendencies in any one field was inevitably to bring about, sometimes with startling suddenness, a whole chain of movements, social, political, economic, and religious, by which its intellectual and material outlook was profoundly stirred. The rapidity with which these movements have manifested themselves of late years, and the violence with which they have at times reacted against old traditions and old customs, have produced throughout the Moslem world a condition of unsettlement and psychological strain which

INTRODUCTION

involuntarily recalls the crisis through which Europe passed during the Renaissance and the Reformation, though, of course, with many special features of its own. It is this unsettlement which constitutes the present-day problem of Islam and poses the question to which the following chapters aim at giving a provisional answer.

. . . .

In order to understand the nature of the crisis through which the Islamic world is now passing, and the full significance of these modern movements, we must clearly go back behind the perplexities of the present generation. The object of the following pages is, in the first place, to isolate in brief outline the general causes which have led up to the crisis, and in doing so to investigate the equipment with which the Moslem peoples have been furnished, in order to meet the new problems, by their age-long contact with the religious culture of Islam. We must see what ideals they have absorbed, by what influences they have been moulded, what elements of strength or weakness are afforded by their historic background. Only in the light of these facts will it be possible fully to appreciate the importance of the various local developments, and of the factors by which the course of events is influenced in the four main regions of the Moslem world dealt with in the ensuing chapters.

The manner of its expansion gave Islam from the

very first the character of a conquering religion. While the faith itself was not spread by the sword, it was under the wing of Moslem dominance that its missionaries found most favourable conditions for their activities of conversion. This view of Islam as a conquering religion was universally held by its adherents ; the theologians found justification for it in the Koran, the jurists made it the basis of their expositions of Moslem law, and the mass of the people accepted it as self-evident fact. Its expansion by this means was regarded as having been divinely ordained, and as the supreme proof of its divine origin.

But this process of expansion was hindered by several persistent obstacles, chief amongst which was the resistance offered by the Christian states of Europe. Already in the lifetime of Muhammad the Moslem warriors had begun to cross swords with the Christians, and they have continued to do so ever since. So it came about that, however friendly the relations may have been at different times between individual Christians and Moslems, or between specific Christian and Moslem groups, not Christianity itself but European Christendom has ever been the sworn foe of Islam. To their own Christian subjects the attitude of the Moslems was different. These performed useful services, as cultivators, taxpayers, and officials in the administration, and being powerless, were tolerated, but with a kind of aristocratic disdain which relegated

INTRODUCTION

them to an inferior status, and proved in the long run more pernicious to both Moslem and Christian than downright intolerance. The Moslem state remained for ever debarred from assimilating its non-Moslem subjects, and the day was to come when the Ottoman empire would be called upon to pay the penalty for the narrow exclusiveness of the mediæval Moslem conception of citizenship.

Even such a grudging tolerance, however, was not extended to the Christian world outside the boundaries of the *Dār al-Islām*. Even when no active hostilities were carried on, the latent antagonism bred an irreconcilable spirit of suspicion and distrust, which any minor incident might at any moment fan into flame. Perhaps too, as it has been argued, the opposition to Europe was an organic element in Islam, was one of the historical causes of the Islamic movement in Asia and Africa, when the Arabs gave the long-awaited signal for the liberation of the eastern peoples of the Roman empire from the pressure and persecution of the European hierarchy and administration. It is only to be expected, of course, that this hostility towards Christendom was strongest in the broad northern crescent which faces inwards towards Europe. On the other flank of Islam the chief obstacle in its way, and therefore its most bitter antagonist, was Hinduism. Where Hinduism was weak, as in the East Indies, it was (politically speaking) swept away; but in the greater part of India it resisted all assaults and, like the Christian states of Europe, bided its time until in the eighteenth century it felt strong enough to open the counter-attack. Yet it must not be overlooked that Islam in the Indian Ocean remained in close touch with the nerve-centres of the Moslem world in Western Asia, and that under their influence it was animated by the same suspicion of Christendom as prevailed in the old provinces of the Roman empire, a suspicion which increased, with good cause, when the south-eastern flank of Islam came into direct contact with the representatives of Christendom after the sixteenth century.

Yet in the Middle Ages the cleavage between Islam and Christendom was infinitely less than it has subsequently become. One cause of this was that both societies were built on much the same foundations, the ruling ideas in both were roughly parallel, and both shared to a large extent the same "theocentric" outlook on the world. They might be mortal enemies, but at least they understood one another, and fought with the same spiritual and material weapons. Another, and most important, cause was the softening influence exercised in the background by their commercial relations. Here the two societies met, not only as equals, but as co-operators, and even during the tense struggle of the Crusades both sides did their best to safeguard the interests of their mutual trade. The

INTRODUCTION

geographical situation of the Moslem world conferred on it great economic advantages. Lying athwart the great trade-routes of the Old World, it commanded both the land and sea routes between Europe and Asia. In the Indian Ocean its coastwise expansion and the enterprise of its sailors and merchants gave it the monopoly of sea-borne commerce. It took its natural place in the economic life of the world, and built up a flourishing commercial connection with the countries round about, partly by the exchange of its own products, both natural and industrial, but largely also as the carrier and *entrepôt* for the trade of the Indian Ocean. It not only enjoyed, in consequence, what may be called a normal economic life, but by regular intercourse with other peoples and cultures was enabled to remain abreast—in some respects even in the van—of the progress of economic and artistic technique and of material civilization in general.

But this healthy state of affairs was destined to be succeeded by a progressive economic decline. The first blow to the commercial prosperity of the Moslem world came from within. First industry and then commerce were subjected more and more to the exactions and arbitrary measures of the Moslem rulers; by monopolies and exorbitant import and export duties they were gradually strangled, until at length it seemed as if only the demands of Europe kept any appreciable current of trade moving at all.

The expansion of European industry had already narrowed down the foreign markets for the products of Moslem workshops; and the wealth of Egypt in the later Middle Ages was drawn mainly from the Indian *entrepôt* trade. The second and mortal blow was given by the discovery on the part of Europe that the Moslem world could be circumvented, both physically and economically, by the opening up of the sea route to West Africa and India. The effect was not only to dry up the main artery of economic prosperity, but also to isolate the Moslem world from effective contact with its neighbours and condemn it to economic stagnation, with all the consequences that economic stagnation has on the intellectual and moral life of a people.

Impoverished by internal misrule and the armed competition of its rivals, Islam would, by these causes themselves, have been hard put to it to maintain an equality with its adversary, whose material advantage increased with every year. Its weakness was long concealed, however, by the imposing military strength of the Ottoman empire, the Persian Shahs, and the Grand Mughals in India, which preserved it from feeling the immediate effects of the new situation. Yet their existence served only to intensify, by self-imposed insulation, the effect of the blockade from without; cut off from the fertilizing flow of new ideas which might have enabled them to meet the changing

INTRODUCTION

circumstances of the time, these empires merely carried on the politico-religious traditions of mediæval Islam and pushed them to their ultimate consequences. Looked at from our historical point of vantage, we can see now that the whole system was in an advanced state of decay behind the imperial façade, and that it could not indefinitely maintain itself in a changing world.

Meanwhile, the economic offensive of Christendom proceeded apace. The European trading companies, under the stimulus of national rivalries, did not stop at monopolizing the carrying trade of the Old World. Where the weakness of the local political organization invited intervention, they substituted their own direct rule and so began gradually to extend their political control over various Moslem territories. Simultaneously they began to force an entrance for their own products into the Moslem lands in competition with the local industries. The struggles between Portugal, Holland, France, and England in India and the Persian Gulf, ending in the establishment of the Dutch in the East Indies, and of the British in India, are too familiar to need recapitulation, but it is not always realized that these struggles were carried on mainly at the expense of Moslem states. Nor has sufficient attention been generally given to the economic penetration which went on side by side with these political activities, and which affected areas far beyond those which were the objects of direct political ambition.

WHITHER ISLAM?

This aspect of European intervention is so important that I may quote one illustration which serves to show two different methods by which it was carried out. When, in the sixteenth century the Portuguese occupied Hormuz, in the Persian Gulf, they obstructed all intercourse by sea between India and Persia in order to gain a monopoly of this route. The story is best told in the words of the traveller Chardin : " Now when any Persian merchants went to Hormuz, to desire a passage of the Portuguese, the chief of them at Hormuz would ask them what they would go to the Indies to do ? and what sort of merchandise they wanted to buy ? and when they had told them they would lead them to the magazine of the place, and there showing them great quantities of those goods, would say to them : there is what you want, buy that first, and then if you have any money left to lay out, I'll order you a passage to the Indies. With this severity did the Portuguese oblige foreign merchants either to return without doing anything, or else to buy the goods they wanted of them, at what rate they pleased." In consequence of this the Persians made a treaty with the English to deliver a joint attack on Hormuz, on condition that the pillage should be shared, and that the English should be allowed to bring in goods of all kinds free of duties at Bandar Abbas, and have a half-share in the customs and duties on all imported goods. Hormuz was eventually

INTRODUCTION

captured in 1623, and English goods were duly admitted duty free. The provisions of the treaty were, however, constantly infringed, and in 1670 an English mission laid a formal complaint before the Persian government on that score. It failed to gain its object, but, as the honest Chardin remarks : " To speak the truth, there is no excusing the Persians on that head, for treaties ought always to be observed in their full extent, but it must nevertheless be owned, that they are to be commended for letting the English trade throughout their empire free from all manner of duties, and to pay them every year fifty thousand livres for a service done fifty years before; for which one may say they were even then superabundantly paid."

In the competition between the relatively disorganized local industries and the organized effort to capture the eastern market for the factory-made products of Western Europe the issue could not long be in doubt. The opening up of the direct European carrying trade may have given at first a temporary stimulus to some local industries, but the reverse movement was bound to lead in the long run to their decline or extinction. The economic loss of the Asiatic countries would have been enough had it stopped there. But by stimulating the production of raw materials for their own manufactures the Westerners geared the economic life of these lands with that of their own, and fastened upon them an economic weakness and dependence which could not easily be shaken off. The Moslems did not escape the common injury, and though it was not until quite recently that they began to realize the full implications of their economic situation, the fact, once brought home to them, has naturally embittered still further the resentment and hostility which were first aroused on political and socio-religious grounds.

Down to the end of the eighteenth century, this political and economic penetration of the Moslem lands had been concentrated mainly on the southern crescent, and its progress was relatively slow. There is little evidence to show that the Moslems of Western Asia and Turkey were seriously exercised over the fortunes of their brethren in India and Indonesia. Their own political life was at too low an ebb to permit of their taking an active interest in political movements elsewhere. In the nineteenth century, however, beginning with Napoleon's expedition to Egypt, the pace of European intervention suddenly quickened ; it began to invade the northern crescent as well, and the spectre of Christian domination rapidly materialized with what, to Moslem eyes, appeared almost brutal aggressiveness and rapidity. Can it be wondered at that Moslems of every class were outraged in their deepest feelings as they saw province after province passing into the hands of their hereditary foes, and as they realized that it was only the

INTRODUCTION

mutual jealousies of the European powers that prevented the last vestiges of Moslem independence from disappearing altogether? It must be confessed, too, that the attitude of Europeans themselves, the privileged position which they enjoyed under the capitulations, and the misuse of these privileges by many unscrupulous persons, were scarcely calculated to reassure their fears. Rightly or wrongly, they felt that they themselves, their religion, and everything that they held dear, were regarded as belonging to an inferior civilization, however the fact may have been dissimulated in outward intercourse. It is not pleasant to have to recall these facts, and we should gladly set off against them many notable examples to the contrary, but honesty compels us to admit that lack of charity and sympathy contributed to make the blow harder than it need have been.

The general reaction of the Moslem world to this reversal of what had always been regarded as the normal state of affairs was one of bewilderment and sullen resentment. The world had turned topsy-turvy—why it had done so was a mystery. With this came the natural tendency to withdraw still more into itself, to turn its back on the intruders, to live its own life, and hope that things would right themselves in the long run. In doing so, it was reaffirming a traditional characteristic of Moslem political life. For more than ten centuries the doctors of Islam have taught—in season and out of season—the duty of submission to authority, whether legally constituted or usurped, and the lesson has been reinforced in no uncertain manner by the holders of authority themselves. Political quietism seemed to be ingrained in the Moslem peoples, and the stoical endurance of oppression and misrule which filled western observers with amazement was put to the charge of the fatalistic creed of Islam. But this was never more than a half-truth. Fatalism in this absolute sense is not so much a cause as an effect, and the apathy which the bulk of the population displayed towards political changes was due mainly to physical causes, of which economic poverty was one of the most potent.

If, however, fatalism and political apathy marked the attitude of the Moslem masses, there were other elements in the Moslem world which reacted to European pressure in a widely different manner, and with different motives. The ruling classes feared for their power and the advantages which it gave them, the rich livings which they enjoyed at the expense of their dependants, the prestige of authority; the religious leaders feared for the safety of the Faith. The danger was manifest to both, and it might have been expected that it would inspire them to join together in common action in defence of their heritage. The Moslem political leaders, at least, had the wisdom to realise that if they could mobilize in their support the religious

INTRODUCTION

sympathies of their subjects they would be able to oppose a formidable barrier to the encroachments of Christendom. The first symptom of this tendency is to be found in the very treaty in which for the first time a Christian state forced a powerful Moslem state to break with the traditional religious policy of Islam towards Christianity. By the terms of the treaty of Küchük-Kainarji concluded between Russia and Turkey in 1774, the Porte definitely undertook " to obstruct in no manner whatsoever the free exercise of the Christian religion, *and to interpose no obstacle to the erection of new churches and to the repairing of old ones.*" It seems perhaps a small matter, but by these provisions Russia drove a breach into the fabric of Moslem religious law, which, while guaranteeing the free exercise of the Christian religion, had expressly prohibited " the erection of new churches and the repairing of old ones." At the same time, however, the treaty recognized the right of the Sultan as " Sovereign Caliph of the Muhammadan religion " to protect the interests of Moslems wheresoever they might be, and to legislate for them in so far as they were bound to conform to " the regulations which their law prescribes to them."

This reassertion of the political functions and rights of the Caliphate in favour of the Ottoman Sultans was destined to play so important a part in the subsequent history of the Islamic world that it is worth our while to go into it a little more fully. In essence, the claim was a throwback to an earlier period of Moslem history and an attempt to refurbish for modern use a weapon and an institution which had been discarded centuries before ; though, with characteristic conservatism, it had never disappeared from Moslem expositions of political theory.

The Caliph, by position and function, is the temporal embodiment of the Sacred Law of Islam ; he is the person who is charged with the duty of maintaining its supremacy both against external enemies and internal rebels. Being himself bound by the Law, he may neither modify it nor interpret it on his own responsibility, but is concerned solely with the task of applying it, and in the carrying out of this purpose he is entitled to claim from all Moslems the same unhesitating obedience as they owe to the Law itself. His office is thus essentially a political one, but the sanctions upon which his authority is based are primarily religious. Consequently, the elements of the population on whose support he is entitled to count most securely are the religious leaders and teachers, and this fact, it is safe to say, was not absent from the minds of the advisers of Sultan 'Abd al-Hamīd I when the treaty of Küchük-Kainarji was drawn up.

Nevertheless, there were several factors which stood in the way of the full success of this plan. The great days of the seventh and eighth centuries, when the

INTRODUCTION

entire length and breadth of the Islamic world was ruled by a single Caliph, had left their mark on the ideal polity of Islam, but in the succeeding centuries the divergence between the ideal and the actual state of affairs became more and more accentuated. The duty of absolute obedience laid upon the citizens ministered to the appetite for autocracy on the part of the rulers, and a time came when the autocratic power passed from the hands of the Caliphs into those of secular sovereigns. The duty of submission to established authority was still based in theory on the religious principle that power is the gift of God, but the old religious veneration was replaced by a grudging acquiescence in the actual conditions. The religious leaders more especially maintained a somewhat distant attitude to the holders of temporal power, and when the historic Caliphate foundered under the blows of the Mongols in 1258 the general opinion was that the Caliphate as an institution was now extinguished. Thus for more than five centuries there had been no Caliphate in any real sense of the word in the Moslem world, and the feelings of loyalty and religious veneration which it inspired had gradually died out.

Yet the reassertion of the Caliphate ("ghost" though it may have been) was in itself by no means an empty or an unhopeful move. The conviction of the essential unity of the Moslem world which had underlain the historical Caliphate remained, as we have

WHITHER ISLAM?

seen, a potent element in Moslem thought, creating a sympathetic bond between the Moslem peoples which political disintegration had failed to destroy, and which under the right kind of leadership might serve as the basis for rousing a common effort in the cause of Islam. By diligent propagation of the Ottoman claim, backed up by the story (which seems to have been put into circulation about this time) that the last shadowy representative of the ancient Caliphate had transferred his rights to the Ottoman Sultan in 1517, it might be hoped to revive the old associations of the office, and to invest the Ottoman Sultanate with such religious prestige that under its leadership the whole moral, and if need be physical, force of Islam should be enlisted in the defence of its heritage against Christendom.

Such a project, however, was faced by very serious obstacles inherent in the political structure of Islam itself, without taking account of any external factors. It may have been remarked that in describing the unity of the Moslem world, all the emphasis was laid on religious and cultural ties, and no mention at all was made of political associations. And for good reason. The political history of the Islamic community has followed rhythms of its own, which have seldom or never harmonized with its inner life. It would take us too far afield to enter here upon this point; some of the main causes will be apparent from

INTRODUCTION

what has been said elsewhere in these pages. It is with the results that we are concerned at the moment, and the results at least are unmistakable. The most important fact for us is not so much the repeated disintegration of Islamic empires as the gradual division of the Moslem world into distinct zones, between which the political rift became ever wider. Already before the fall of the Caliphate it was tending towards the separation of a Perso-Turkish zone (Turkish in leadership, Perso-Islamic in language and culture) in the north and east from an Arabic zone in the south and west, with a corresponding restriction of political movements to one zone or the other. This separation was accentuated in the following centuries, when the pressure of the Mongols at the centre contributed to the political expansion of Islam by the extension of the Perso-Turkish zone on either wing. The tendency at this time therefore was all towards decentralization rather than the vain pursuit of a new political unity.

Early in the sixteenth century a fateful realignment was brought about by the rise of a new Persian empire, which not only cut off the Ottoman Turks from contact with the East and India, but also by adopting the Shi'a faith as the state religion blocked the way to any restoration of a common political organization. Almost simultaneously the Ottoman empire absorbed the greater part of the former Arabic zone, and with it the characteristic features of the Arabic Moslem culture. The main lines of demarcation now consequently ran north and south : in the west was the Ottoman empire (Morocco in the extreme west remaining independent), in the centre Shi'ite Persia, in the east the Mughal empire and Indonesia ; and this division has persisted down to our own times. The attempt, therefore, to create an Ottoman Caliphate, as a means towards more effective political unity, could in the circumstances hope for success only in the western zone ; to its further extension Persia placed an impassable barrier.

On the other hand, the Pan-Islamic policy, as it came to be called, might count at least on mobilizing public opinion in support of its aims, and might hope that the force of public opinion would itself issue in organized action. But here again the political traditions of the Moslem world stood in the way. A thousand years of jealous autocracy, which had deliberately adopted the policy of suppressing by the most drastic measures any symptom of political activity amongst its subjects, a thousand years of political quietism, which in the name of religion bade the Moslem render unquestioning obedience even to a depraved ruler as a lesser evil than civil strife and anarchy, had made away with the machinery to enable common action to be organized in defence of common interests. The time was indeed to come when, by the influence of the very forces which Pan-Islamism sought to exclude, the

INTRODUCTION

capacity for political organization was recreated, but only when the Ottoman Pan-Islamic policy was at its last gasp. In the meantime it could act only through the existing administrative machinery, responding mechanically to orders issued from above, and so lacked the essential element of spontaneity.

The chief factor in favour of the Pan-Islamic movement was that the Moslem world was everywhere on the defensive, and eager to find a means by which it might regain control of its own destinies. What was more natural than to seek for it first in what, after all, was the strongest common force, the sentiment of religious unity? It was the need, perhaps even more psychological than material, for mutual support that threw the religious aspect into the foreground. Pan-Islamism appealed to ideals and sentiments familiar to, and shared by, all Moslems outside the Shi'a fold, and sanctioned by the immemorial teachings and traditions of the Faith. Had it been pursued consistently, and with absolute disinterestedness in the cause of Islam—if, more especially, those who directed it had possessed a thorough grasp of realities and had been prepared to adapt its policy and methods to the new forces which were sweeping over Islam—it might indeed have proved successful in the long run, and by restoring the self-confidence and self-respect of the Moslem world have brought about not merely a political recovery, but even renewed economic prosperity. The famous despatch of Prince Metternich to the first Turkish reformers was perhaps less inspired by cynicism and more by real insight than has sometimes been credited to it: "Establish your government on respect for your religious institutions which are the basis of your existence as a power. Move with the times and consult its needs. Bring order into your administration, reform it, but do not turn it upside down by substituting for it forms which do not suit you and which expose the ruler to the reproach of knowing neither the value of what he destroys nor what he puts in its place.... We counsel the Porte not to imitate states whose basic legislation is in opposition with the customs of the Porte, and to avoid with care the importation of reforms which can only react on the Moslem lands as dissolvents, because they must, under the circumstances, be devoid of all creative and organizing force."

As it was, the Pan-Islamic plan, though never lost sight of, and fitfully pursued throughout the nineteenth century down to its climax in the reign of Sultan 'Abd al-Hamīd II, was destined to founder on two rocks. The first was the personal character and ambitions of those who claimed to be Caliphs, and their corrupt administration. No more need be said on this point than that the great protagonist of the movement in the latter half of the nineteenth century, the Perso-Afghan Sayyid Jamāl ad-Dīn, was himself outspoken

INTRODUCTION

in denunciation of the tyranny and misrule which he found rampant in the independent Moslem states, and not least in the Ottoman empire. Yet the ideal was too alluring, the interests and feelings to which it appealed were too strong, for Pan-Islamism not to rouse a sympathetic response in every section of the Moslem community. Though in its fullest form it was most ardently accepted by those who had least personal experience of the government of the Ottoman empire, and more especially amongst the Indian Moslems who, after the suppression of the Mughal dynasty, were conscious of the need for external support against the menace of the Hindu revival, it had the effect of reawakening and strengthening the sentiment of Islamic solidarity to a hitherto unprecedented degree. The formation of " Red Crescent " medical units for service with the Turkish army, the construction of the Hijāz railway with money subscribed in all parts of the Moslem world, were so many material evidences of the success of the Ottoman propaganda. Probably it would not be going too far to claim that the psychological effect of the movement is to be seen in nearly all the subsequent activities of Moslem societies, even when their objects were opposed to the strict policy of Pan-Islamism. For—and herein lay its radical weakness in a world where the balance of forces was distributed as it was in the nineteenth century—in so far as Pan-Islamism put forward a deliberate programme for the Moslem world, it was guided by reactionary and absolutist aims. But any movement in that direction was already impossible ; no matter how earnestly Moslems might strive to exclude new trains of thought, how vigorously they might oppose their spread, it was a desperate and a doomed cause. The intellectual and material preponderance of Western Europe, to say nothing of its economic supremacy, was so enormous that it must inevitably have forced its way into the life of the Moslem community against all resistance. Thus the political doctrine of Pan-Islamism was destined to prove a discordant and a weakening element, rather than a strengthening force, in the task of readjusting the outlook and realising the aspirations of the Moslem world.

This was, in fact, the second rock upon which the Pan-Islamic policy split. Beginning almost at the same time, an opposite current of thought was also making its way in the Moslem world. Amongst the political leaders in Turkey and Egypt, in the first place, and subsequently in other countries as well, a new idea was steadily gaining acceptance. At the back of it was the question : how is it that the nations of Western Europe have so suddenly outstripped us in all fields of activity—in the organization of political and economic life, in knowledge, in power of invention, in all the arts which bind a nation together and develop its willpower ? They looked around for an answer and

INTRODUCTION

believed that it was to be found in western political and military institutions and in the organization of education. They resented the assumption commonly made by European students that the ultimate cause of the decline of the East was an unprogressive religion, and held sincerely to the belief that Moslems could remain Moslems and yet remodel their institutions to conform with the practice and the needs of the modern world. The ideal which the reformers set before their eyes was not a revolution in doctrine, morals, and social institutions, but the introduction of such external and material features of western political life and technical organization as would restore strength and prosperity to the Moslem states. This was the aim which was pursued with varying fortune by the Turkish statesmen between 1839 and 1878, and on its military and economic side by Muhammad 'Alī and his grandson Ismā'īl in Egypt. But so far as political and economic organization were concerned—in the very fields, that is, in which their energies were chiefly engaged—the result was a disastrous failure. Absolutism seemed more firmly entrenched than ever when Sultan 'Abd al-Hamīd II sat on the throne of Turkey, and the economic situation of both the Ottoman Empire and Egypt was by 1878 infinitely worse than it had been fifty years before.

The first reason for this failure was that the reformers were never given a fair chance. From the very beginning they were obstructed by the rival programme of Pan-Islamism. Even when the political doctrines of Pan-Islamism were thrust into the background, its basis of Islamic religious law continued to receive the encouragement of the Sultans and the support of the religious leaders ; that is to say, the highest authorities were unwilling to do anything which might alienate from them the support of the mass of Moslem opinion. And unfortunately Moslem opinion, as guided and expressed by the religious leaders, was bitterly hostile to any measures which the reformers might put forward. Did they desire to abolish slavery—the Sacred Law of Islam recognizes it. Did they desire to give equality of status to all citizens—the Law insists on the political subordination of non-Moslems. Did they desire to reform the administration of justice—the Law will not tolerate any code other than itself. Did they desire to create parliamentary institutions—the Law knows nothing of such and admits no right of legislation. And so on ; on every point the reformers were met with a negative in the name of the Divine Ordinances of Islam. The measures which they forced through were a dead letter from the start, for the opposition which they met effectually prevented them from operating, or at least from operating as they were intended to operate. Thus each party stood in the way of the other's programme and prevented either from giving practical

INTRODUCTION

effect to its ideals. So far from recovering something of the lost ground, Turkey kept on falling between two stools, though it seemed at the end of the nineteenth century as if the Pan-Islamic programme had triumphed over its rival.

But the triumph, even within its limited field (for it failed to produce the political results which it was expected to produce), was destined to be of brief duration. Unobserved by the conservative Moslems, and also by the political reform party, though it was the child of their own movement, a revolutionary force was eating into the heart of Moslem society. We have seen that the reformers had made education one of the planks in their platform. First in Egypt, and a little later in Turkey, this policy was slowly translated into action—not so much by the extension of primary education (though that benefited also to a limited extent) as by the opening of technical and higher schools for the professions, the training of military and economic experts, and the officers of the administration. The character of these institutions (like the famous medical school at Cairo) shows clearly the bias of the reformers towards the practical and material sides of western education, but once having taken the first step, it was not within their power to set limits to the effects which might ensue. For how were the schools to be staffed? Obviously by European teachers, or by teachers trained in Europe.

Their desire was naturally to train up teachers of their own, and by so doing they gave wider scope and a stronger impulse to the very influences which they were hoping to exclude. No intelligent student could spend three or four years in a European capital, in daily intercourse with its people, reading their literature, good and bad, without imbibing something more than the mere externals of western civilisation. Individual students and educational missionaries brought back with them not only the fruits of their technical studies but the germs of political ideas—sometimes even of social habits—which were in conflict with their inherited traditions. In the first generation the total impression thus made might be weak; in the second it increased manyfold, and continued to increase in geometrical progression. The movement of reform might fail in its first assault upon the citadel of Moslem absolutism and tradition, but all unawares it bequeathed its task to a more formidable antagonist.

As we look back from this distance we can see just where the weakness of the first reformers lay, and the principal reason for their failure. They had not realized that the western institutions which they coveted were not mere external features of organization—that they were the expression of a definite philosophy, based upon national habits of thought, maturing slowly through the centuries and adapted to the needs and

INTRODUCTION

purposes of a complex social system. They had not realized that while the constitution of Islamic society was still based upon mediæval conceptions and its outlook governed by mediæval ideas, Western Europe had swung right away from its mediæval moorings and that between the two civilizations, once so uniform in spite of religious antagonisms, the gulf had gradually widened until their common elements and principles seemed insignificant in comparison with their differences. Above all they forgot that no institution will work unless it is backed up by the will of the people to work it, and that that collective will is the product of an education in citizenship in the widest sense of both words. Perhaps they were misled by the apparent suddenness of the French Revolution and the violence with which it seemed to have substituted a new set of institutions for those it had swept away; perhaps they thought that the traditional political apathy of the Moslem peoples would suffer the imposition of new institutions without strong opposition. Whatever the cause they were mistaken. Western political and economic institutions could not be transplanted with any degree of success unless they were felt to answer a need, and the first necessity was to prepare the way for them by a corresponding system of education, which could create the need and at the same time form an enlightened and progressive body of opinion to whom the working of the new institutions could be entrusted. But such an education, if it was to harmonize with those institutions, could not avoid implanting a new outlook and a new philosophy similar to those which had created the institutions themselves. It involved a much more serious break with the past than the early reformers realized; modernized Moslems might continue to be Moslems, but they could not continue to share the views of their conservative Moslem brethren as to the constitution of society and the place of religion within it. In the meantime, while apathy itself would have been fatal to the working of the reforms in any case, so long as the control of political education remained in the hands of their reactionary opponents there was no possibility of gaining any popular support for them. In a word, the mistake of the reformers was that they tried to build without bricks; they believed, as many people still believe, that a people can be regimented into carrying out the duties of citizenship, no matter what their beliefs and opinions. They forgot that the material outward form cannot be dissociated from the inward spiritual urge.

Their failure left the way open to a more promising line of approach. Social and political reforms could not be successfully imposed by casual edicts from above; only if they were introduced in response to the steady pressure of public opinion could lasting results be hoped for. A somewhat irregular progress

INTRODUCTION

in this direction is indeed one of the characteristic features of the Moslem world in the last decades of the nineteenth century. We have seen how technical education under the aegis of the reformers was gradually fostering a disposition to adopt a western point of view among a small *élite* of professional men. But this in itself was of little effect. Brought up as they were under the old system of education and in the old social atmosphere, their inclination to western institutions was a thin veneer. The transplanting of new habits of thought demanded a new system of education from the years of boyhood—in primary and secondary schools, before passing to higher or technical studies. Whether it was desirable in the long run to do so is another question, with which we are not concerned at present. In any case the reorganization of education *on these lines* was at that time completely outside the ideas of the Moslem civil authorities, even had they been able to carry such a plan into effect in the face of ecclesiastical opposition and the absence of teachers. But the gap was filled by other bodies. From the middle of the nineteenth century a vast network of schools was spread over the majority of Moslem countries, particularly in Turkey, Syria, and Egypt, mainly by the efforts of various Christian missionary societies. The most numerous probably were the French, Catholic and lay, then the American, Italian, Greek. English schools were fewer in the

Ottoman Empire, but numerous in India ; Dutch schools were confined to the East Indies. Notwithstanding all that may be said against the rivalries, the parochial outlook and denominational character of the schools, and their poor quality in many instances, they exercised an enormous influence in the Moslem world. The education they offered was generally superior to anything to be had elsewhere, and for that reason they were frequented by large numbers of children from the upper and middle classes, including girls as well as boys. They moulded the character and formed the taste of their pupils, and above all imparted a knowledge of European languages which enabled them to enter into direct contact with western thought, and thus to continue into later life the influences which had been brought to bear upon them in their youth. During the latter part of the century, this process was carried still farther by the development of secular education under English control in Egypt and India. The charge sometimes brought against these foreign schools of denationalizing their pupils has perhaps an element of truth in it, though it can hardly be said that the accusation is borne out by the subsequent political developments in Moslem lands. But what they unquestionably did was to foster a reaction against the social and to some extent against the political institutions of their native lands, and by weakening in these respects the hold of the traditional Moslem outlook upon their pupils, to drive a wedge into Moslem society and snap some of the ties which had bound it together.

The conservative Moslems from their own point of view rightly opposed these tendencies—and not only because the spread of western education meant that the influence which they had so long monopolized seemed to be slipping from their grasp. Those who conceived of Islam as an indivisible complex of social and religious and political institutions could not but remain bitterly hostile to those who, in abandoning one custom after another gave evidence of their emancipation from the cultural tradition of the Moslem world and seemed to be even menacing Islam itself. Their opposition often appeared to fasten on ludicrously trifling matters, as when a religious teacher towards the close of the nineteenth century, in expounding the Koran to a class of anglicized young Moslems, commented thus upon one of the many verses describing how the wicked shall be cast into Hell : " The wicked are those who deny God, liars, adulterers, thieves, murderers, and those who do not clip their moustaches." About the same period a young Indian student, listening to a Moslem street preacher in the city of Delhi, took exception to something that he said. The teacher objected, " You have no right to speak on these matters, since you are no Moslem." The young man replied with some warmth,

"I am as good a Moslem as you." "No," said the preacher, "you are no Moslem; look at your trousers," which extended, contrary to pious Moslem custom, below his ankles.

But such instances, and they could be multiplied, would lead us seriously astray if we were to lay them to the charge of mere obscurantism. What they betray is not so much a mind incapable of distinguishing essential and inessential, as a mind so faithful to the heritage of Islam, so intensely convinced of the divine origin of its institutions, that to depart from even the least of its prescriptions means a rejection of some particle of divine grace. Let us beware of putting this down to pettiness. The most clear-sighted and penetrating of mediæval Moslem theologians, al-Ghazzālī, did not disdain to give the fullest attention to just such minutiæ of practice. His modern followers, equally sincere in their convictions, saw in the neglect of these the thin end of the wedge—and, I repeat, from their point of view they were right. The habit of doubt, the exercise of private judgment, needed only a beginning. Where would it end? The rejection of trifles was a symbol of an intellectual revolution which could lead only to the tearing up by the roots of the whole traditional fabric of Moslem culture; and might even lead to an assault on the religion of Islam itself. Remember above all, that all the emotions which we associate with patriotism were to them bound up with the structure of Islamic society, and that they could not help regarding, and to a large extent rightly regarding, the weakening of that structure as the final victory of the forces of Europe.

The increasing sharpness of this inner contradiction was, as we have seen, one of the most important features in the life of the Moslem peoples during the latter part of the nineteenth century. It is, however, difficult to set chronological limits to its influence, since one of the first effects which followed from it was to disturb the old conception of a Moslem world united by a common culture and governed by a common tradition. The bond of sympathy, the common background, the common faith, it is true, still remained; but the admixture in varying degrees of the new ideas derived from the West was already tending to mark each country off from the others. In some they had already acquired such a hold as to modify very greatly the old institutions and to revolutionize the outlook of the intellectuals; in others they were as yet all but unknown. By the end of the century one or two regions were in a fair way towards a solution of the contradiction; at the present day there are still Moslem countries where it has not yet become a live issue. Contemporary observers were naturally inclined to regard the cultural inequality of the Moslem countries and the conflict between the reformers and the supporters of traditional usages as symptoms of the impending dissolution of Islamic unity and the relegation of the traditional Islamic culture to a few " backward " regions at best. We can already see that their conclusion was over-hasty; nevertheless it was and remains true that the one common problem for all Moslems was to a large extent thrust into the background by the emergence of a series of individual local problems which faced each Moslem country separately, and that its final solution must go hand in hand with the solution of the regional problems.

From this point, therefore, we can no longer deal with the whole Moslem world, but must fix our attention upon the individual Moslem countries and their peculiar reactions to the wave of westernization. It would be impossible here to follow up in detail the course of events in each and every region, nor are all of them of equal importance for the present problem. We might draw in this respect a distinction between those countries which were under direct European control and those which were still politically independent, since the latter would appear to have had more freedom of choice and the former to have been forced by circumstances to allow at least a measure of westernization. But this distinction is not, in fact, fundamental, since the neutrality generally observed by the European governments in social and religious questions allowed each Moslem community to meet

INTRODUCTION

the problem in its own way and with its own resources, short, of course, of the use of force; while on the other hand, the pressure put upon the independent states in their effort to maintain their independence (or, in the case of Egypt, to regain its independence) forced several of them into adopting measures which, though not always well conceived or well executed, led directly or indirectly to an even more radical westernization than was apparent in the countries under European control.

The real criterion of the relative importance of each country is the measure of its influence upon Moslem thought as a whole. The outlying lands on either flank had little share in this; North-west Africa, though linked by many ties to Egypt, has generally followed a course of its own, and the local problems of Indonesia, which will be fully dealt with in their own place, were of minor concern to the Moslem world. India, on the other hand, has made some original contributions, which are described in Chapter IV., and will be touched on here only in so far as they set an example to other countries. The Moslems of Russia and Central Asia also formed a community apart, which has come into some prominence only of recent years. But the heart of Islam remains, now as ever, the central *bloc* formed by Turkey, Egypt, and Western Asia, and it has been mainly from these regions that the most vital of present-day Islamic influences have radiated. It is to them, consequently, that we must now devote our chief attention.

Down to the first decade of our present century, the outstanding feature in this area was the deep cleavage between the advanced degree of westernization apparent in Egypt, and to a lesser extent Turkey, and the conservative outlook, coupled with cultural and economic backwardness, of the other countries. The interior of Syria and 'Irāq, together with Persia and Afghanistan, seemed to have remained almost completely untouched by the wave of westernization. In Arabia itself, Islamic conservatism had gone so far as to produce an ultra-conservative revolution, in which not only the new ideas of the modern West were discounted in advance, but even the great bulk of mediæval adaptations embodied in Moslem tradition were thrown on the scrap-heap, and a return to the conceptions and ideals of primitive Islam was actively preached and enforced. Wahhabism seemed to be in direct negation to every tendency which was making headway in the other Moslem lands, isolated by the circumstances of its development and history, and a movement without a future except possibly as an Arabian sect. It was indeed already regarded as a spent force, and not even the most far-sighted observer, whether within or without the Moslem world, could foresee the part

INTRODUCTION

which within a few years it was to play in the thought of Islam.

Thanks to the Pan-Islamic propaganda, Turkey had long been looked up to by the other Moslem countries as the natural leader of Islam. It is less easy to determine at what moment Egypt also stepped into a position of leadership. Both had a fairly long history of westernization behind them, but its character and results were rather different in the two countries. The westernization of Turkey was much more restricted in its scope ; though it may have gone as deep, it was, as we have seen, constantly obstructed in its manifestations by the rival policy of Pan-Islamism. In Egypt, on the contrary, it had been encouraged up to a point by the Europeanizing tendencies of Khedive Ismā'īl, and while enjoying fuller freedom of expression was of a more literary and educational character, and less active in the field of political life. In both, of course, the mass of the people still remained rooted to the old ways, but in movements of this kind —and the point cannot be too often or too strongly emphasized—it is the leaders that count. The most striking outward sign of the new tendencies was the creation in the sixties and seventies of a new literature, and, still more, of a newspaper press. But whereas in Turkey the press was severely controlled and the chief journals were of an official character or subsidized organs of Pan-Islamism, the press in Egypt was for the most part independent of the government and strongly modernist in its views. It was therefore able to lend powerful support to the westernizing leaders in their struggle to enlist popular opinion on their side.

While, however, the press, utilizing and supplementing the general progress in education, was the principal instrument for the spread of western ideas among the mass of the people, there was another institution which in its power to influence the political life of the independent Moslem states possessed a great advantage over it. In discussing the Pan-Islamic programme, it was pointed out that however strongly the sympathies of a section of the people might be engaged in favour of any policy, this sympathy could not issue in an active corporate endeavour, since the capacity for translating feeling into action in an organized and effective manner had been atrophied by disuse. Before the educational movement could produce definite fruits, it was necessary to remedy this weakness by training in the organization of effort for political and cultural ends. But one institution had preserved the machinery of action unimpaired. This was the army, and both in Turkey and Egypt, as later in Persia, the technique of westernization had first been applied to the army. The adoption of European military tactics and weapons, and training in European methods of military organization, had resulted in

INTRODUCTION

making the army the most westernized element in political life, and in giving the military officers a preponderating position in any movements for the reform of political organization. It is not surprising, then, to find the early reformers, impatient at the slow and arduous task of building up an organized body of public opinion, looking to the army for assistance in the achievements of their aims, or that army officers themselves had a large share in promoting the reforms. On the other hand, though it is true that the introduction of western military technique had important results in leading to the organization on western lines of such other social institutions as hospitals, technical schools, and sanitary services, the ideals of reform which were entertained by the military officers were more limited and superficial than those of the western-educated classes, and their methods more violent and arbitrary.

Both in Turkey and Egypt the first attempts to introduce political reforms thus culminated in a military pronunciamento, but the direct objects, the methods of procedure, and the results in each case were different. In Turkey, the success gained at first was turned into failure and the course of development arrested for thirty years by the arts of 'Abd al-Hamīd II. But the victory of absolutism and the repression which accompanied it made the army more than ever a focus of political agitation, to such a degree that military officers have taken the leading part in all the subsequent developments in Turkey, and that no body corresponding to the organized parties with political and cultural programmes which have grown up in other Moslem countries has yet succeeded in establishing itself alongside of the military party in power. This has had its own reactions on the character of the Turkish reform movement; it has, on the one hand, made its progress violent and erratic, and on the other has prevented it from building up a balanced organization in which the deeper forces of reform might co-operate to assimilate what had already been gained and thus form a basis for further progress. Under these circumstances the Turkish movement, even before the era of nationalism, could not be other than purely national or local in its range, and while it set an example which might be applauded or disapproved in other Moslem countries, it had nothing to offer them as a solution of their own problems, which were bound up first and foremost with the problem of the relations of Islam to the new forces from the West.

Egypt itself narrowly escaped from a similar fate. Here too a military movement succeeded for a time in attracting the support of the constitutional reformers, and even of the conservative religious leaders, in an outburst of national feeling, directed in the first instance against Turkey and subsequently against

INTRODUCTION

European intervention. It is probably useless to speculate on the ultimate possibilities of the outbreak led by 'Arābī Pasha, but it is inconceivable that they should have led to results as fruitful as those which were to give Egypt its outstanding influence in the Moslem world of to-day. The suppression of the revolt and establishment of British control, while outwardly a political set-back, in reality caused the westernizing movement to broaden out and to flow into deeper channels. Cairo became the centre where all the active forces in the Moslem world met and, under the restraining hand and watchful if not always comprehending eye of the Residency, fought out their disputes. In al-Azhar, the only college for training in higher Moslem studies which drew its pupils from every corner of the Moslem world, it possessed an institution which expressed with unequalled authority the views and opinions of orthodox Islam. Political refugees from Turkey and other Moslem states found asylum and freedom to pursue their aims. More especially the enterprising Syrian publicists, muzzled by the severe censorship in their own country, flocked into Egypt, and gave an impulse to Egyptian journalism which carried its productions and its views far and wide. The extension of elementary education at the same time widened the circles to which it could appeal at home, and increasing intellectual intercourse with Europe strengthened the influence of the

West among the upper and middle classes. Even Pan-Islamism found its intellectual centre shifted from Constantinople to Cairo before the close of the century. The ferment of ideas touched every aspect of life, modern and traditional, and if contemporary observers could sometimes see little but the froth (and it would have been strange had a natural cynicism not found the fin de siècle atmosphere attractive and congenial), beneath the surface an intense life was moving. Slowly, grudgingly, at times unconsciously, the conservative opposition was forced to yield point by point, and each fresh advantage gained spurred the reformers to further efforts. It is significant that it was only in Egypt that a movement for social reform crystallized out, and that round the problem of women's freedom. Nothing can show more clearly how deeply westernization had struck root, and how radically it was transforming the outlook of the intellectual leaders of Egypt.

Although the Moslem conservatives were thus being reluctantly dragged along in the irresistible current of westernization, it was by no means certain that the course of events would not lead to a radical split between the modernist school and the defenders of Islamic tradition. For many reasons, however, even the most advanced modernists were averse to such a step. The political circumstances, for one thing, demanded the maintenance of unity in the face of the

INTRODUCTION

occupying power (perhaps in the long run this was the greatest service which British control rendered to Egypt), but the ultimate motive was not mere political opportunism. In spite of all their western training and acceptance of western ideas the Egyptian reformers still felt themselves genuinely attached to Islam, and they never weakened in their sympathetic regard for the rest of the Moslem world. The tendency observed in some other Moslem countries towards the formation of new syncretistic sects found no response amongst them; what they desired was to see, possibly in some form of which they had as yet no clear conception, Islam as a whole restated and brought into relation with modern views. Meanwhile they accepted, with inward reservations, its traditional forms and institutions and continued the struggle to evolve a reformed and reinvigorated faith.

In this struggle they were now to be rewarded with perhaps unexpected support. It was inevitable that sooner or later some attempt should be made to reconcile the aims and ideals of the two parties. Here, on the one hand, were the indisputable advances in knowledge made by the new scientific methods of study; here, on the other, the immense moral and religious force of Islam. The separation between them would surely prove fatal to both. Might it not be, so some earnest Moslems argued, that the pernicious consequences feared by the pious from modern studies were due to the non-Moslem influences of the schools in which they were taught, and to the absence of a steadying moral code? If the two could be combined, if scientific study could be carried on in a Moslem atmosphere in Moslem educational institutions, might not both profit, and the student reap the benefit of both disciplines? It was in India that the most ambitious experiment on these lines was made, when Sir Sayyid Ahmad Khan laid the foundations of the " Muhammadan Anglo-Oriental College " (now the Moslem University) at Aligarh, in the United Provinces. This eventful step seems rather to have been due to the founder's outstanding personality than to any communal movement in India itself; yet that it was taken in India instead of Egypt or Turkey is not surprising. Direct contact with Western Europe was not as easy and as frequent for the Indian Moslems as for their brethren in the Mediterranean area; they were still to a large extent unaffected by the more vigorous westernizing agents which were at work in the Near East, and for local reasons they were attracted with special force to the Pan-Islamic ideal. The same causes have probably been responsible for the fact that Sir Sayyid Ahmad Khan's initiative, despite its far-reaching effects in Indian Islam, was not directly followed up elsewhere.

Yet the ideas which underlay the foundation of the Aligarh College were beginning to make themselves

INTRODUCTION

felt in orthodox circles in Egypt as well, and here they took on an aspect of still more general import to the whole Islamic community. This was nothing less than the attempt to reinterpret and restate the doctrines of Islam in conformity with modern thought, not by western-educated laymen, but by a group of professional theologians. If we are to understand the full significance of this movement and its methods, we must glance for a moment at one of the technical features of Islamic theology. We have seen that primitive Islam issued from Arabia in a relatively plastic condition, and that for two centuries or so it was engaged in adapting itself to its environments and working out the details of its theology. This process was carried through to completion by the labours of theologians and legists who were generally recognised to possess the capacity of *ijtihād* (" subjective effort "), the power to give a decisive interpretation on points of theology and law. Once these decisions were made, they were regarded as unalterable, and the " gate of *ijtihād* " was gradually narrowed down to minor points, until with the final settlement of these it was closed altogether. Henceforth, in Sunni Islam no theologian, however eminent, might claim the title of *mujtahid* (in the Shi'a sect, however, the principal religious leaders have continued to be called by this term down to the present day), and for close on ten centuries its religious life has been regulated by *taqlīd*, acceptance of the authority of the " Fathers of the Church."

It was this dogma that was now disputed by the liberal theologians in Egypt. They asserted that the altered conditions of life and the new intellectual tendencies made the abandonment of simple *taqlīd* and the reopening of the gate of *ijtihād* imperative, that the incompatibility of Islam with modern thought was due only to its wrappings of outworn mediæval scholasticism, and that, on the contrary, Islam, rightly understood in its original form, was not only in full agreement with the assured results of scientific investigation but was even in closer harmony with them than any other religious system. They found a notable leader in the person of Shaikh Muhammad 'Abduh (died 1905), one of the most remarkable and respected figures in the modern history of Islam, whose personal character and capacities secured him a large circle of admirers and gained for the movement a widespread following, not only in Egypt but in other Moslem countries as well.

Welcome as this reinforcement was to the western-educated classes, it must not be imagined that the outcome was any radical revision of Islamic doctrine. Shaikh Muhammad 'Abduh's own writings are distinguished more by a certain modernity of spirit than by originality in thought and teaching, and it was perhaps his cautiousness that more than anything

INTRODUCTION

else commended his views to the rising generation of scholars. The importance of his work was twofold : that he formulated a basis for the reinterpretation of Islam without breaking with its historic past, and that, as Rector of al-Azhar, he began the process of reform of religious instruction by the introduction of modern subjects into the curriculum. By these means he contributed greatly to the broadening of orthodox Moslem opinion and demolished the barrier which separated Islam from the modern world, both in his native land and wherever his influence was felt. His work was continued after him by his disciples who, though they may have come short of his heroic stature, have nevertheless by their publications and personal activities carried the principles of his teaching with tremendous effect into all parts of the Moslem world, principally by their monthly journal *al-Manār*, " The Lighthouse."

Unfortunately, there still remained a powerful section of Moslem conservative opinion, especially in India, which refused to be placated, and viewed both the Aligarh movement and the school of Shaikh Muhammad 'Abduh with no less suspicion than they showed the western-educated intellectuals. By this attitude they did much to weaken both Islam and themselves at the very moment when the more radical fruits of western education began to show themselves in the first decade of the present century.

WHITHER ISLAM?

At what moment the modern western doctrine of nationalism first effected a lodgment in Moslem political thought it would be difficult to say. Doubtless the way had long been prepared for it in Turkey and Egypt, and in a certain sense it may be said to have underlain much of the political development of both countries throughout the nineteenth century. The Egyptian risings of 1879-1882 in particular, as we have seen, had a definitely nationalist colouring, yet there was a profound difference between these movements for political independence and the secular western conception of nationalism. We can understand, for example, how the Shaikh al-Islam, the highest religious dignitary in the Ottoman Empire, should have supported the coup d'état in Constantinople in 1876, and how Muhammad 'Abduh and the Pan-Islamic leaders should have joined the movement of 'Arābī Pasha. The issue at stake now was something far deeper. It was not only the political movements themselves, it was even more the ideas behind the political movements, that began to shake and to reshape the modern world of Islam as it had not been shaken for a thousand years. Outwardly, political reform came first, with social reform a poor second; religion and religious doctrine were left alone, of set purpose, since the nationalists naturally shrank from antagonizing religious feeling. In renouncing, as they did, however, the age-long tradition of political

INTRODUCTION

quietism for vigorous, and in some places violent, political activity, the nationalist leaders of the younger generation at the same time threw overboard the greater part of the old Moslem outlook. In its place they accepted the new political thought of Western Europe, the keynote of which was national sovereignty, and with this they were forced to accept also the basic principles and corollaries of national sovereignty, so far as concerned the structure of the state, the nature and function of law, and the rights and duties of citizens. But with that intimate connection which, as we have seen, exists in Islam between theology, practical religion, social ethics and politics, a revolution in political ideas must of necessity affect Islam itself as a system of thought, a philosophy of life, and a religion.

We may take it for granted that few of the early nationalist leaders were consciously aware of these issues. In its first phase their demands were limited to the establishment of constitutions and representative assemblies on the European model, combined in Egypt with the intensive campaign of Mustafa Pasha Kāmil for national independence. The specific question of the relation of these demands to Islam arose only when the constitutions began to operate, and had scarcely time to reach an acute stage before the outbreak of the European war brought that phase to a close. In Persia, where the homogeneity of the population served at first to obscure the problem, it was definitely laid down in the Organic Law that " the laws enacted by the Parliament must not be in contradiction with the principles and regulations of Islam," and a committee of five *mujtahids* was included in the parliament to act as " clerical censors " of all projected legislation.

Though, it is almost needless to say, no such paper guarantees, however strong, could continue indefinitely to hide the fact that the secular organization of the state was bound to bring it into conflict with the old Islamic jurisdiction, down to 1914 the progress of nationalism as an active force in the Moslem world was on the whole slow, tentative, and restricted to a few countries. It had, naturally, gone farthest in Turkey, where a policy of Turcizing the various peoples of the Ottoman Empire had replaced the former Pan-Islamic policy during the last few years prior to the war, and had awakened an opposing sentiment of Arab nationalism in Syria, 'Irāq, and even Arabia. The events of the war itself contributed to the heightening of nationalist sentiment, and still more the lavish propaganda of the allied powers in favour of " self-determination." Even then, however, few could have seen the disruptive and violent forms which the nationalist movements were to assume in almost every part of the Moslem world. The immediate stimulus was given by an anti-European

INTRODUCTION

reaction, due in large part to the bitter anger and dismay roused by the realization that the peace treaties, so far from conceding rights of self-determination to the peoples of the East, actually resulted in the extension of European control to large new areas in the very heart of Islam, as well as to a feeling of revulsion at the sordid aspects of European " civilization " displayed in the war itself and the peace negotiations.

The most surprising, and at the same time most ominous, feature of this reaction is that it did not lead back directly to an increased appreciation of Moslem solidarity, but on the contrary issued in the form of regional movements each independent of the others. The Moslem community in India stood almost alone in its insistence upon the international aspect of Islam, and even there the motive force was largely defensive in face of Hindu nationalism. Everywhere else the idea underlying the movement of revolt was the very idea which had just led to such havoc in Europe—the secularization of the sovereign state, conceived of as a racial and linguistic unity. Islam of course remained; but to the nationalist mind merely as one element in the complex of the national state, perhaps even as the official religion of the state, but shorn of its legislative prerogatives, reduced to the position of the Christian Church in the European economy.

The application of this principle varied, of course,

with the circumstances of each region. Where the Moslem community was but one of several different religious communities which united in the nationalist cause, as in Indonesia, religious questions were naturally thrust more into the background. In homogeneous countries, like Persia, Islam was merely dethroned from its sovereign position. Egypt has followed, with remarkable moderation, a *via media*, and has so far been content to allow the inevitable change to come about by the slow pressure of events. In Turkey the process of secularization, after proceeding steadily during the war, was carried to violent lengths by violent means.

Yet this final victory of western ideas has not been gained without an undercurrent of Moslem opposition and protest against the disintegration of Islam into secular national states. It is, perhaps, strongest in the Arab lands, especially where the weight of European domination is felt most heavily, but it is strong also in India and Indonesia and possibly stronger than appears on the surface even in Turkey and Persia. In this struggle for the realization of Islamic unity lies the crux of the problem which agitates the Moslem world of to-day, and whose regional developments are studied in the four following chapters.

AFRICA (*Excluding* EGYPT)
By PROFESSOR LOUIS MASSIGNON

CHAPTER II

AFRICA (*Excluding* EGYPT)
By PROFESSOR LOUIS MASSIGNON

Introduction

IN ANY discussion of the contemporary movements of Moslem opinion, it is important at the outset to try to reach a definite understanding of the characteristic manner in which such movements of opinion operate in the Moslem societies. The linking up of successive steps in a gradual evolutionary process—to us the more familiar method—is in this milieu the exception. The movements which confront us are rather in the nature of sudden flashes, almost instantaneous shocks, or explosions, momentarily violent but transitory. It is with just cause that the Islamic conception of history is in general atomistic and not cyclic. In Islam the movements of opinion brood secretly and in silence, and suddenly break out without giving, so far as can be seen, any warning indications. In more precise and technical language the process may be analysed as follows. The first stage is that of *nidā*, of the " inward call " which appeals to the social conscience and awakens it, though it remains nevertheless in a state of apparent calm, or, as it is varyingly expressed, of "repose" (*quʻūd*) or "dissimulation" (*taqīya* or *katmān*). Immediately and without transition, the maturation of the *nidā* is followed by the second stage, that of the *daʻwa*, of the "summons," the tribal call to arms, or general mobilization for the struggle which seeks to vindicate by force of arms the neglected rights of the Divine Law. This is the conception common to all the movements called by different groups and at different times "manifestation" (*zuhūr*), "repulse" (*dafʻ*), "coming forth" (*khurūj*), or "sale" (*shirā*, i.e. of one's life for God's sake).

These facts must be borne in mind if we would realize on how precarious a foundation rest the European establishments in Islamic lands. Suddenly, after years of tranquillity, the call to the Holy War may break out when least expected. It would, however, be out of place here to criticize in itself, in the name of pacifism, the conception of *jihād*, of Holy War, although at the present day there are to be found a number of Moslem apologists who are endeavouring to lessen its importance and detract from its force. It is indeed one of the elements of dignity in Islam that it maintains in the world the conviction that as between men not everything is capable of being made an object of bargaining, buying and selling, but that there are some things which are worthy to have the sword drawn on their behalf.

AFRICA

I

If we examine the situation on the map of Africa, the principal transformation which the nineteenth century has brought about in the movements of opinion in Islam lies in a shifting of their main axis. Down till then the traditional East-West axis retained its pre-eminence and guided the passage of currents of thought and opinion from Cairo westwards to the Sūs, in the extreme south-west of Morocco. To-day this traditional axis has been displaced, in the direction south-north, from Gao on the Niger to Algiers. Let us take some statistical examples. Down to the present century, the current of intermigration flowed from East to West and inversely. The Arabicization of North-west Africa was largely due to incoming Arab tribes from Egypt, while on the other hand in Egypt, Palestine and Syria there were flourishing colonies of Maghribines or " Moors " (*maghāriba*). Since 1910 these colonies have been numerically decreasing and their importance has considerably diminished. The same feature is visible in the falling-off of pilgrims to Mecca ; in 1910 there were 18,000 pilgrims, 3,000 of whom came from French West Africa (A.O.F.)—in 1927 only 2,500, of whom 750 were from A.O.F.

During the same period the phenomena of inter-migration on a South-North axis have continued to expand without interruption. It is represented on the one hand by the flow of North Africans to France for employment as manual labourers and workmen, which in 1910 was limited to some 500 dockers at Marseilles and has risen to the enormous figure of 150,000 workmen in 1927. In nearly every Kabyle village in Algeria there are to be found many men who have lived for some time in France. Equally significant is the flow of university students and others, who without support or encouragement from official circles (who would, indeed, prefer that they should go no further than Algiers), have risen in numbers from the insignificant figure of 10 in 1910 to 195 in 1927, 15 of these being from A.O.F.

The sketch maps on pages 82 and 83 show the distribution of the isolated sectors inhabited by Moslem immigrants from North Africa (chiefly Kabyles) in the various quarters of Paris. It will be seen that they have succeeded in insinuating themselves on all sides, and that they are incorporated into the French social life of the city, not shut off in a closed quarter like the Chinese quarter (" Chinatown ") of San Francisco. For the rest, some seventy per cent. of them remain for more than three years, and twenty per cent. appear to be definitely established in France. A fair number have become naturalized.[1]

[1] See for fuller details, *Revue des Études Islamiques* (Paris : Geuthner), 1930, Cahier II., pp. 161-9, and for the settlements of Moroccan Berbers in Paris, ib., 1928, Cahier IV., pp. 477-80.

AFRICA

In order to focus the African social milieu which we are studying in this chapter, it is necessary to recall briefly a few figures. It numbers in all some thirty millions of Moslems, distributed as follows : 14,000,000 in the Maghrib (Tunisia, Algeria, and Morocco), 6,000,000 in A.O.F., 8,000,000 in Nigeria, 1,000,000 in Libya. Of these thirty millions, only 9,000,000 are Arabs (7,000,000 in the Maghrib, 500,000 in A.O.F., 1,000,000 in Nigeria, 800,000 in Libya) ; the remainder is composed of Berbers, Fulas, and Negroes.

2

If we compare this Moslem social milieu in Africa with the social milieu of the Moslems of the east, we shall observe a number of differences, which are not merely on the surface but go fairly deep. From the intellectual point of view, there are no personalities, no outstanding thinkers, such as the eastern lands can often show. There are no societies which exist for the propagation of an idea, like the "Oriental League" —*rābita sharqīya*—in Egypt. The Moslems of the Maghrib have practical minds of the occidental type ; they are, especially those of them in the north, individualists, who set themselves to solve concrete problems in a positive manner and lose little time in academic palaver. In matters of dogma, they have retained an inflexibility which harks back to the early days of Islam when the converted Berbers, out of

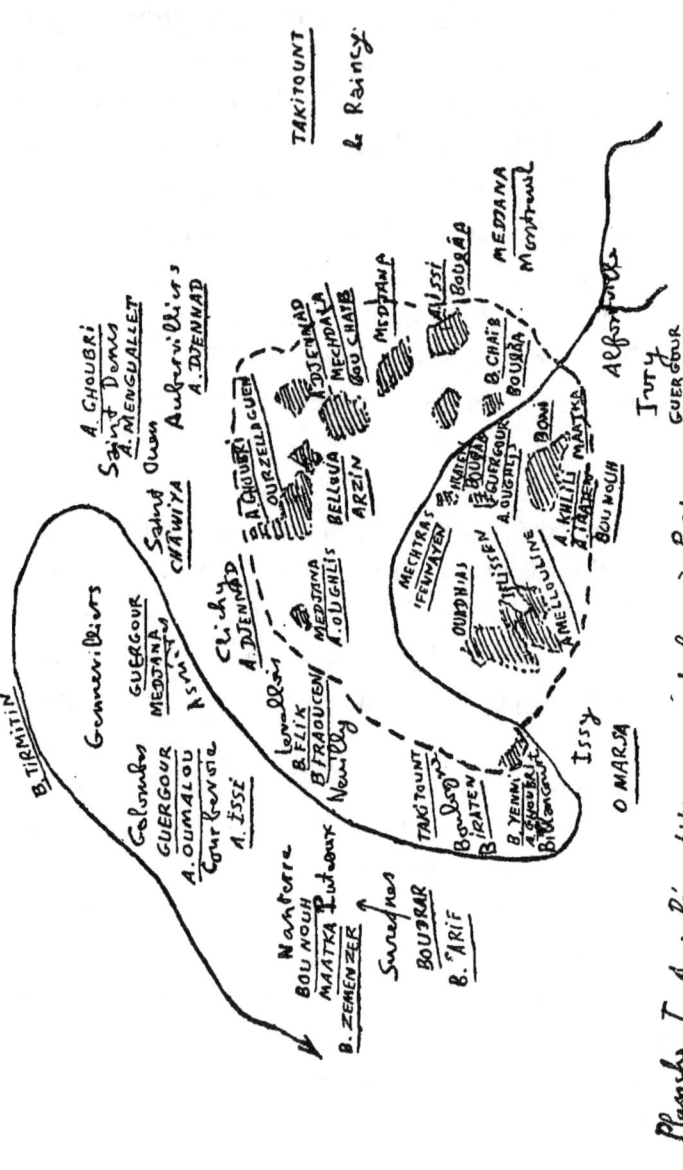

1. Distribution by tribes of Algerian immigrants in Paris.

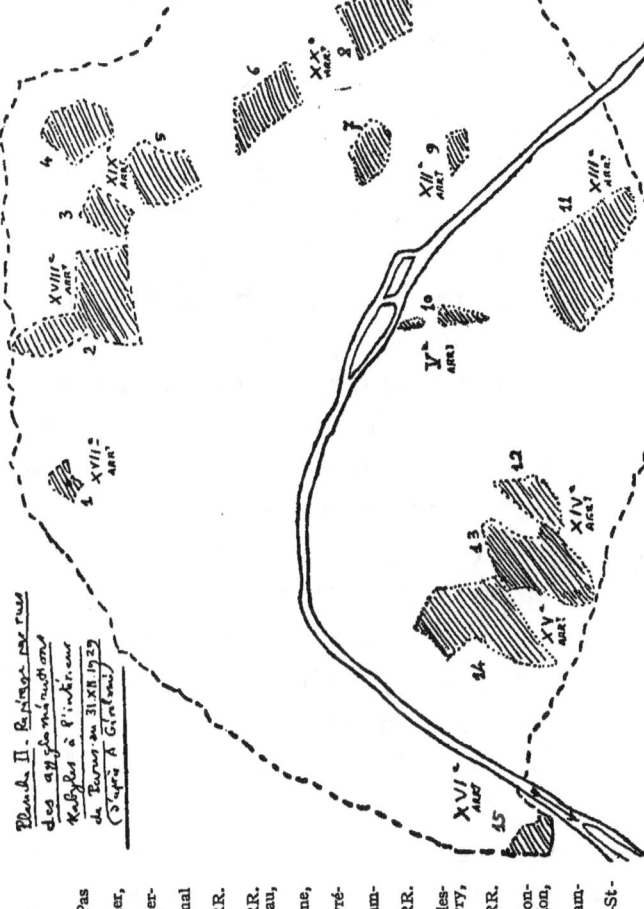

Limites des agglomérations numérotées :

1. Av. Clichy, RR. la Jonquière, Pas d'hier, Balagny.
2. RR. Clignancourt, Pajol, Ordener, BBlv. Ornano, de la Chapelle.
3. Blv. la Villette, RR. Riquet, Aubervilliers, Flandre.
4. RR. Crimée, Flandre, Canal St-Denis, Av. Jaurès.
5. Blv. la Villette, Av. Jaurès, RR. Cavendish, Manin, Bolivar.
6. Blv. Belleville, Av. Gambetta RR. des Couronnes, H. Chevreau, Sorbier.
7. Blv. Voltaire, RR. Charonne, Sedaine, Taillandiers.
8. RR. Bagnolet, de la Plaine, Pyrénées, Blv. Charonne.
9. Blv. Diderot, RR. Crozatier, Rambouillet, gare Lyon.
10. N.: Pl. Maubert. — S.: RR. Mouffetard, Monge.
11. Blv. Blanqui, RR. Château-des-Rentiers, Tolbiac; Av. d'Ivry, Butte-aux-Cailles.
12. Voie ferrée; Av. Maine, RR. Vanves, Alésia.
13. Voie ferrée ; RR. Vaugirard, Volontaires, Procession, Brancion, Cronstadt.
14. Blv. Grenelle, RR. Vaugirard, Cambronne, Croix-Nivert, Violet.
15. R. Petite-Arche, Pl. Porte-St-Cloud, Av. de la Reine.

2. Distribution by streets of Algerian immigrants in Paris.

hostility to the misgovernment of the Caliphs, adopted the puritanical creed of Kharijism, and which was afterwards nourished by their attachment to the orthodox Māliki school. (It is worth noting as an instance of the expansion of the Māliki rite that it is now predominant in the Anglo-Egyptian Sudan, whereas in the fifteenth century we know from Maqrizi that east of Lake Chad was still Shāfi'i). The characteristic quality of the Maghribine on the intellectual side is a certain spirit of decision ('*azīma*), which is too often lacking in the more subtle intellectual equipment of the oriental; and he unites with this a readiness to adopt the technical apparatus of French life, as an auxiliary or instrument for the full realization of the practical aims of life, so long as it is not inconsistent with Islam. This auxiliary westernization is, however, to be clearly distinguished from the tawdry and superficial imitation of French manners which goes by the name of *tafarnuj* in the east.

What are the governing ideas of Western Islam? They are the outcome, in the first place, of a variety of reactions to the intrusion of the three Latin Christian powers which have gained a footing in its area by political control or colonization. In its attitude towards Spain, it is moved principally by regret (*gharām*) for the ancient splendour of Islam in Andalusia, but accompanied by no sympathy for the

Spaniards until quite recently. The new policy of the Spanish republican government has, however, encouraged this sentiment and raised new hopes of rapprochement, by letting it be understood that it is considering a project to establish a Moslem university at Granada, and even (now that the Church is disestablished) a restoration of the ritual services of Islam in the Mosque of Cordova ; but it remains to be seen whether anything will come of these projects.[1] In its attitude to Italy the mentality of the North African Moslem has taken an inverse direction. To the sympathy aroused by the conciliatory policy of the so-called " Statuto " of twelve years ago there has succeeded a violent reaction against the brutal method of summary executions which is at present being rigorously applied in Libya.

The Moslem attitude towards France is less easy to define, because more subtle and more complicated by divergences of sentiment. In Tunisia, and to a small extent in Morocco, there is a tendency which aims at the adoption of a xenophobe policy, and whose programme is imitated from and inspired by the nationalist movement in Egypt. In the centre, however—in Algeria—Moslem feeling is dominated by a very curious sentiment. It is not merely a hope of enlisting French

---

[1] [A School of Arabic Studies was created at Granada in February, 1932, for the primary purpose of " higher instruction in Arabic language and civilization, and the attraction of Moslem youth," for whom special courses are to be provided in a separate building and a hostel established if possible.—H. A. R. G.]

sympathies, but an ambition to conquer a place not only for themselves as individuals, but for Islam, within the mind and soul of metropolitan France. There are a number of Algerian Moslem writers who possess a perfect mastery of French and seek to make use of it to carry on a propaganda in France itself. Nor is this propaganda directed only to reclaiming for Islam those Moslems resident in France who might be in danger of lapsing from their faith, but extends also to wider objects. It is noteworthy that some prominent Moslems have begun to realize the possible influence exerted by the Moslem colonies in France, and do not wish to see them diminished by the return of all Moslems to their lands. To be noted also is the fact that some few Frenchmen here and there have actually become converted to Islam under the influence of North African Moslems, but Frenchwomen less frequently. It is only in Tunisia, where the spiritual impress of Islam appears to exercise a peculiar fascination upon them, that we find Frenchwomen becoming Moslems.

It is an undeniable fact that at the present day there exists between France and North Africa a kind of spiritual interdependence, which takes for some minds the character of a reciprocal intellectual attraction, analogous to that which has been established between England and India, but for the conquered masses shapes itself rather as a need to find the formula of their common aspirations by using even the language and the institutions of their conquerors.

3

There are at present three main directions which can be distinguished in the movements of opinion in West African Islam. The propagandist Ahmadīya movement, introduced and maintained from India, may be left out of account, since its activities are confined to a few coast towns on the Guinea littoral, and some stations in Nigeria, Sierra Leone, and Liberia.

1. The reformist (*islāhī*) movement, which aims at secularizing Islam, a little after the Turkish model. This movement is directed by pupils of the French schools, primary teachers and officials, who possess a very thorough command of French and use it skilfully to organize their activites by means of journals published in French. The measures of control which the government found it necessary to exercise over these organs have for long placed restrictions upon their liberty of expression, and it is one of their aims to gain more and more a fuller freedom in this respect. The principal journals of this group are *La Voix Indigène* of Constantine, directed by Rabih Zenati; *La Voix des Humbles* of Algiers, directed by 'Omar Guendouz; and *La Voix du Tunisien* of Tunis, directed by Shadli Khairallah. Although originally standing for distinct tendencies, these journals are showing a gradual

convergence towards the adoption of a common policy. Another interesting example of this attempt to make French a vehicle for Muhammadan thought, not only in the political but also in the religious field, is a recent translation of the Koran into French by Ahmad Laimêche, which, though not specially skilful, is distinguished by its reverential interpretation and genuine Moslem feeling, conveyed in the French language.

2. The puritan (*salafī*) party, half Wahhabite in tendency. This party, which is an offshoot of the movement in Cairo represented by the journal *al-Manār*, retains a close contact with the corresponding body in Cairo and follows its directives. Though it has only a sparse following as yet in the North African towns, it has already acquired a measure of influence through its programme of reversion to the uncontaminated teachings of the Koran. The principal representative of this party is the journal *al-Shihāb* ("The Meteor"), published in Arabic at Constantine under the direction of 'Abdulhamid Benbadis. There is also a small but expanding nucleus of adherents at Rabat in Morocco.

3. The third group is composed of members of the old mystical fraternities belonging to three distinct congregations :

(*a*) In the first place the reformed 'Alawīya offshoot of the Derqāwī order, directed by Sidi Ahmad ben Aliwa, resident at Mostagānem in Western Algeria, where his journal *al-Balāgh* (" The Message ") is published. This congregation, founded during the war, has gained a very large body of adherents throughout North-west Africa, some of whom are to be found even amongst the Kabyles located in Paris. It is making the attempt to create a modernized Arabic apologetic in French, adapted to the new environment (e.g. in the ethical interpretation of *jihād*), and distributed in the form of tracts.

(*b*) An isolated figure, Ghulām Allah, the head of a Derqāwī congregation at Tiaret (Western Algeria), is at the moment urging a very curious policy of establishing a " concordat " between Islam and the French government, combined with a discreet modernization in his propaganda.

(*c*) The Tijanīya order, or at least its Moroccan branch, which is recruited especially from amongst the high officials and rich merchant class, has of recent years undertaken a propagandist campaign, extending even to the suburbs of Paris. It has set up a mosque at Gennevilliers, in which the ritual *dhikr* services of the order are regularly held. As a social factor, however, this order exercises no extensive action except in the extreme south, but is of importance in the Western Sudan, and even in Nigeria, Bagirmi, and Kanem.

It will be remarked that we have not spoken of the Senussis, who until recently occupied a prominent place in North African Islam. The military action of the Italian government has succeeded, however, in breaking up their centres in Libya, and their present political influence is insignificant. The minor orders in Algeria, the Rahmanīya of Kabylia and the ʿAmmarīya of Guelma, have only a local importance.

4

What are the chief topics of discussion at the present day in Moslem circles in North-west Africa ?

A. The problem of nationalism (*shuʿūbīya*, *ʿasabīya*). This has given rise to three distinct currents of opinion.

1. There is one section, confined for the most part to a few intellectuals, which finds the solution in complete assimilation to French nationality, carrying the full exercise of all civil rights. In Algeria, where the administration has certainly not lent its aid to this policy and the colonists regard it with as little favour, there are scarcely more than 5,000 nationalized Moslems at present; in Tunisia there are some 3,000. Among the chief hindrances in Algeria is the obligation placed upon the naturalized Moslem to surrender his personal statute under Islamic law, including of course, the right of polygamy. In Senegal, on the other hand, where this stipulation is not made, the Moslems of the four " communes de plein exercice " (Saint-Louis, Dakar, Gorée and Rufisque) have since 1848 shared in the election of the municipal council and a representative to the French Chamber of Deputies.

2. The second solution is that of Berberization, i.e. the recreation of a North African nationality based on the conception of an indigenous race, namely the Berber race. This ideal is at present supported in Moslem circles only by a few isolated Kabyles. What are its chances of success? Though of the population of Libya only some five per cent. are Berbers, and in Tunisia only one half per cent., they constitute on the other hand twenty-nine per cent. in Algeria, and these Algerian Berbers already take a deep pride in the fact that they are not of Arab race. The key to the question is to be found in Morocco, where sixty per cent. of the population are of Berber race, but the Arab ascendancy shows no signs so far of weakening amongst them, and as there is no standard Berber dialect they have not as yet become conscious of a common Berber ideal. The French administration, however, by the issue of the *dahīr* (Sultan's rescript) of 16th May, 1930, which gave local validity to the old Berber customary law and personal statute in preference to Islamic canon law, has recently made an attempt to reinforce the racial spirit amongst the Berbers of Morocco. It is on that account that this *dahīr* has roused such vigorous protest and been so violently attacked in every quarter of the Moslem world. It may be that in thirty years' time a Berber ideal will be propagated amongst the Moslems of North Africa. If so, will it prove to be of advantage to European colonization?

It may well be doubted (already the time is foreseen when the French will be "permitted" to become Berbers!), although it is the efforts of European writers which are contributing at the present moment to prepare the way for it.

3. The third solution is Pan-Arabism, which aims at drawing closer the ties between the Arab minority of the North African towns and the Arabic East, whence that minority mostly came 900 years ago. The Pan-Arab propaganda is based upon an educational reform; it urges the restoration of instruction in classical Arabic in all the schools, Koranic and secular. This movement has a large following in Tunis, and is tending to spread in Constantine and even in Fez. It is, of course, hostile to the study and utilization of the colloquial dialects, as a number of European orientalists recommend. All the leaders of the puritan and mystical movements are strong supporters of the Pan-Arab programme.

B. The second subject of discussion is unification, or the establishment of a unified front for common political objects. This aim was at the bottom of the conception of a universal Caliphate, invoked in recent years, and though the idea has collapsed with the suppression of the Ottoman Caliphate in 1924, yet it still possesses a strong attraction in Tunisian circles, who remain loyal to the Turkish claimant. As a means to the creation of a sentiment of unity this ground is not

AFRICA

very happily chosen. In Morocco, the Sultan has for many centuries claimed a quasi-Caliphial status, and the Ottoman Caliphate has never been acknowledged. In Algeria the *Khutba* or allocution at the Friday service, in which by traditional usage the reigning authorities are prayed for by name, has for many centuries included the name of no living ruler; likewise in the western Sudan the *Khutba* has been anonymous since the rise of the Askia dynasty in the sixteenth century.

The Shi'ite conception of the Imamate, once so powerful in North Africa, seems to have disappeared, leaving as its legacy only the latent, but always virulent, ferment of Mahdism, which looks forward expectantly to the coming of a Mahdi, who will vindicate by the sword the cause of Islam.

More modern in its political and intellectual tendencies than the mediæval conception of the Caliphate is the idea of holding an annual Moslem Congress. This idea, which has already proved its value in India as a means of restoring new life to the communal spirit of Islam, is not entirely new to the Moslem world. It is in effect the ancient method of the puritan Kharijite sectaries, and for that reason might well prove attractive in North Africa, in view of its old Kharijite leanings. In this connection it is of interest to find that the modern representatives of Kharijism, who constitute nowadays no more than a tiny minority centred in the Mzab (in Southern Algeria) and Jebel Nefusa (on the boundaries of Libya and Tunisia), had for two years a curious organ, the *Wādi Mīzāb*, published at Algiers from 1926 to 1928, which preached the formation of a Moslem union based upon the congress method.

C. The third point in discussion is that of a reform of the Canon Law (*Sharī'a*) of Islam. On this subject, however, North Africa, with its strong Mālikite tradition, is exceedingly conservative, and the traditional policy of the French government has succeeded only in strengthening this tendency, even in some of its most questionable manifestations. A scheme for the codification in French of Algerian law (the so-called Morand Code) has failed to secure promulgation owing to vacillating administrative action. It could count, however, upon a considerable body of Moslem opinion in its favour, especially among the leaders of the reformist (*islāhi*) movement, and is in accordance with the plan of a concordat, elaborated in 1930 by Ghulām Allah and referred to above.

Among the specific questions relating to law which are of importance as raising wide social issues and which attract a good deal of attention are those of reform of the status of women and the control of religious endowments (called in North Africa *hubūs*, in the East *awqāf*). Not merely in regard to the feminist movement in general, but even in regard to the ordinary status of women, North-west Africa lags far behind other Moslem countries. The most that can be mentioned is, for the former, a recent reformist publication of Tahir Haddad at Tunis, and for the latter an Algerian degree of 19th May, 1931, which seeks to remove some of the more glaring injustices imposed upon the Berber women by the customary law of the Kabyles (who have never in this respect substituted the Canon Law of Islam for their own 'urf). The question of the *hubūs* also presents difficulties; entirely suppressed in Algeria since 1844, their control and utilization by the civil government has given rise to several " incidents " both in Tunisia and in Morocco.

D. The fourth subject of discussion is education, including both education in the narrower sense, i.e. pedagogical reform and the extension of educational facilities, and a reform of Moslem apologetic. The Pan-Arab Moslems are at present concentrating their efforts on this point. In Tunisia the Koranic schools have been reformed, and private Arab schools are being opened up in various parts of Algeria, but here they are handicapped in their struggle with French by the deficiencies of the Arabic alphabet and grammatical structure, which make both writing and the communication of modern thought more laborious than in French. The latter also, favoured by the establishment, some forty years ago, of a series of public primary schools, has profoundly affected the mentality of the Kabyles. Primary education is indeed the ploughshare which Rome needed, but could not forge, in order to leave its imprint upon the mind of Africa.

The primary schools have hitherto been confined to boys ; in the education of girls North Africa is very backward in comparison with Egypt. Nevertheless, the women show in an increasingly marked degree the desire to introduce European social manners and customs.

The development of the Arabic press has already been referred to in section III above ; to what has been said there it need only be added that a number of Arabic journals are published also in Morocco, both in the French and Spanish protectorates and at Tangier. The same inflexible conservatism that exercises such a dictatorship over Moslem opinion in North-west Africa makes it out of the question even to raise here the problem of latinization of the Arabic alphabet, which is already recognized in the East, even the Arabic East, as a subject for discussion.

In the economic sphere there are distinct tendencies towards an assimilation of French methods and institutions. The old industrial guilds and corporations of artisans are in Algeria being reformed as mixed syndicates or trades unions, comprising both Moslem and European workers, and are playing a very noteworthy part as agents in the adoption of French technical methods amongst the town-dwellers. In the country districts the rural centres of technical education are certain to have a similar effect.

The example set by the Banque Misr in Egypt has found imitators in Tunisia, where a few banking establishments have been founded on the same lines. The capitalist organization of industry has also begun to penetrate into Moslem circles in Algeria, where a new class of Moslem capitalists has arisen since the war, notably in the carpet industry at Tlemsen. In Morocco, the industrial preponderance is still in the hands of the converted Jewish families of Fez called the *muhājirīn*.

CONCLUSION

The East still exercises an undeniable influence on the Moslems of North-west Africa, especially in the direction of Pan-Arabism, whether propagated by Syrians, like Shakīb Arslān, or Egyptians, such as Farīd Wajdi. But the curve of evolution is inclining more and more towards Paris, and it is to it and not to the East that the great mass of North Africans are turning their eyes.

The critical question of parliamentary institutions and the electoral representation of the Moslems is clearly impossible of solution by the establishment of a

WHITHER ISLAM?

Chamber at Algiers. A direct conflict would at once break out between the indigenous population and the numerically much inferior body of colonists. There is no possibility of a Dominion in North-west Africa. But it is receiving increasing attention in Paris, along the lines of Moslem representation at Paris.

If we compare the situation of French North Africa with that of British South Africa, it will be seen that in spite of the outward resemblances there is a profound dissimilarity between the two regions. In North-west Africa, there are 800,000 European settlers (forming eighteen per cent. of the total population) in face of five millions of the indigenous population, of whom 300,000 live in the European fashion and 150,000 have been resident in France, twenty per cent. of the latter for two years or more. In South Africa, there are 1,700,000 settlers (forming twenty-one per cent. of the total population), against a native population of 5,300,000. But these natives are of the negro race, often of very low mentality, and they have suffered only a very superficial and partial anglicization, which, for the rest, is leading very rapidly to a xenophobe " Ethiopian " movement, and holds out no possibilities of such a racial hybridization as is ultimately conceivable in North Africa.

EGYPT AND WESTERN ASIA

By Professor Dr. G. Kampffmeyer

CHAPTER III

EGYPT AND WESTERN ASIA

By PROFESSOR DR. G. KAMPFFMEYER

IN THE Islamic World movements have of late begun to spread which until recent years were entirely unknown. Considerable religious and moral forces have been awakened which it is essential to know accurately. The more we analyse, after a detailed study of the facts, the true nature and strength of these forces, the more we may be able to judge of the development which they are likely to have and of the influence which they may possibly exercise in the future. A scientific investigation of this kind may thus prove of practical interest as well.

The countries I have to deal with are these: Egypt, Arabia, 'Irāq or Mesopotamia, Palestine, Syria, Turkey, Persia and Afghanistan. Of these countries the last three have each its own features, and are different both from each other and from the rest of the countries mentioned before. The language of each of them is little understood in the others and in the rest of the Islamic world, nor are there in these countries Islamic movements which exercise any attraction on the others or on any countries of the world of Islam. The case is quite different with Egypt, Arabia, 'Irāq, Palestine and Syria. These countries have a very important common feature : in all of them *Arabic* is spoken. The same language is spoken in North Africa and by numerous Arab colonies scattered all over the world. Besides, Arabic, as the proper language of Islam, is studied and understood to a large degree throughout the Islamic world, from the Atlantic to India and Java, and so facilitates the spread of spiritual movements far beyond the frontiers of the country in which they had their birth. This spread of spiritual movements is aided by various factors. The dominant one is the highly developed Arabic press, especially the press of Cairo, the intellectual centre of the Muhammadan world. The Mecca pilgrimage plays its part too in the spiritual interchange between the different territories of Islam. In the Arabic-speaking Near East, that is precisely in the area covered by Egypt, Arabia, 'Irāq, Palestine and Syria, the vicinity of the countries, the development of the communications, in addition to the activity of the press, are of special aid to the growth of general Islamic feelings and aspirations. If there are serious Islamic movements in one of these countries, one can well imagine the influence they may be able to exercise and the importance they may acquire.

I wish, in the first place, to draw attention to a movement which has sprung up in Egypt and is a better illustration than anything else of the present state of mind not only in Egypt but in a large part of the Arabic-speaking world as well. For the insight which it affords into our problem, it has seemed worth while to devote the greater part of my space to a brief but, as far as possible, comprehensive account of the *Gam 'īyat ash-shubbān al-muslimīn*, literally the " Association of the Moslem Young Men," or, as it may be called, the Young Men's Moslem Association—the Y.M.M.A., to adapt the initials of the Y.M.C.A., the Young Men's Christian Association. The names are most similar ; of course, as will be seen, the Egyptian Moslem Association has important features of its own.

The *Regulations* of the Association were drawn up in Cairo, in November, 1927, and were modified on some points in June, 1928. They are composed of 25 articles. According to Art. 25, there are three articles of these Regulations which may not at any time be modified : the 1st, 3rd and 6th Articles. The 1st Article fixes the establishment and the name of the Association, the 6th the conditions of active membership : the member must be a Moslem, of good conduct and reputation, and must not have any tendencies contrary to the principles of the Islamic faith. The most significant 3rd Article states the *aims* of the Association. These are : (1) to spread Islamic humanization and morals, (2) to endeavour to enlighten the minds by knowledge in a way that is adapted to modern times, (3) to work against dissension and abuses amongst the Islamic parties and groups, (4) *to take from the cultures of the East and the West all that is good, and to reject all that is bad in them.*

The 2nd Article declares that the Association does not under any circumstances interfere with politics.

Art. 4 refers to the foundation of a Club in order to deliver lectures on cultural, scientific and social matters. The Association intends also to issue publications in any language which it may be required to make use of.

The articles concerning the internal order of the Association, the general meetings and so on, may be omitted here. But there are left to us two items worthy of attention. The one is the contents of Art. 23 : " The Association may found Sections in Egypt and Branches in other countries. The relations between the Central Association on the one hand, and the Sections and Branches on the other, are to be determined by the internal regulations of the Association." We shall see to what a large extent this article has subsequently been acted upon.

Secondly we must look at the leadership of the Association. The Board of Directors is composed of twelve members who are balloted for by the general meeting to hold office for four years, according to the modified Regulations of June, 1928. Every two years half of the members retire from office, and the number of the Directors is again completed by a new ballot. Four members have special functions : the President, the Vice-President, the Treasurer and the Secretary-General ; the other eight are simply called Members. The persons who were appointed in 1927 are of special interest : President : Dr. ʻAbd al-Ḥamīd Bey Saʻīd, of whom I shall speak presently ; Vice-President : ʻAbd al-ʻAzīz Bey Shauwīsh, then Director of primary instruction in the Egyptian Ministry of Education, well known for his Islamic interests and publications— he died in 1929 ; Treasurer : Aḥmad Taymūr Pasha, one of the most outstanding figures of modern scientific life in Egypt, who died on April 26th, 1930 ; Secretary-General : Muḥibb ad-Dīn al-Khaṭīb, editor of a monthly magazine *az-Zahrāʼ*, and a weekly *al-Fatḥ*. The former publication is a well directed magazine of more general contents, something like *al-Hilāl* or *al-Muqtataf*, but on an Islamic basis ; the latter is a journal, much appreciated by Moslems, dealing with Islamic politics, ethics and religious matters. The other members are : (5) Professor Muḥammad al-Khiḍr Ḥusayn, teacher in al-Azhar, Section of Special Instruction; (6) Professor Shaikh Aḥmad Ibrāhīm, teacher in the School of Law; (7) Muḥammad Bey Aḥmad al-Ghamrāwī, who studied at London University ; (8) Yaḥyā Bey Aḥmad ad-Dardīrī, who studied at Geneva University, Doctor of Laws, Licentiate in Political Science; (9) Dr. ʻAlī Mazhar Bey, Graduate of Vienna University; (10) Professor Mahmūd Bey 'Alī Fadlī, teacher in the Higher Training College; (11) Muhammad Effendi al-Hahyāwī, Egyptian journalist; (12) 'Alī Bey Shawqī, Secretary of the Under-Secretary of State in the Egyptian Ministry of Education.

It is important to note the high standing of this Board of Directors. The eight Members, fairly young men, represent important sides of Egyptian national life. There is an official of the Ministry of Education (12), there is a representative of the Egyptian press (11), there are teachers of higher schools, such as the Higher Training College (10), and the School of Law (6), and even the famous al-Azhar University (5); there are three young men, personally known to me, who acquired a solid instruction at European Universities, the one in London, the second in Geneva, the third in Vienna—so there is represented, besides the national Egyptian education, English, French and German science.

These young men have gained the support of so eminent a personage as Ahmad Taymūr Pasha, and of Islamic leaders like the Shaikh 'Abd al-'Azīz Shauwīsh and Muhibb ad-Dīn al-Khatīb. Above all, the President, Dr. 'Abd al-Hamīd Sa'īd, is well known to those who are occupied with the politics of Egypt. He is one of the most fervid and most active Egyptian nationalists and a member of the Egyptian Parliament.

It is characteristic of the mind of the young men of the Association that they chose this man to be their President. But there is another fact even more characteristic : they offered to him, by resolution of June, 1928, the presidency *for lifetime*, as long as he would keep to the aims of the Association. It does not matter that he declined this offer and agreed only to be President for four years like the other Directors. The essential thing is that this offer of presidency for lifetime was made, and that it was made on the aforesaid condition. With this we may compare another fact. When the Regulations of the Association were debated on, the question was asked whether the Association should not be called " Association of *Egyptian* Young Men," instead of " Association of *Moslem* Young Men." The latter name has been adopted, and the answer is interesting as well as the question. There is undoubtedly nationalism, and a very strong nationalism, in the minds of these young men, but there is Islam too. They decided, in adopting the name of the Association, to be Moslem young men, and the condition imposed upon their president meant that he had to keep to the religious and ethical aims of the Association. But there is not simple juxtaposition of nationalism and Islam. It is evident from the facts referred to, as well as from other facts to be dealt with later on and from facts known to me personally, that for the men who founded the Association the point of departure was to serve their country and the East. To be sure, in the Islamic world Islam is part of the national past and of the present individuality of the East, and he who wishes to keep to national life may be disposed to keep to Islam too. But there has been another moving idea. The leaders of the Y.M.M.A. were and are still persuaded that for the East the development and maintenance of a strong and sound national life is impossible if people do away with religion and morals, which by contact with western civilization may easily occur. So, it is argued, the young men in Egypt and the East must be restrained from doing so, they must be religious and of moral conduct in order to serve their country. Religion, or Islam, as we are in an Islamic country, must be the basis of national life.

It is important to bear in mind this starting point of the Y.M.M.A. in order to understand fully all its different aspects which I am bound to lay before the eyes of the reader.

Starting from this point, the Association has had, from the time of its first steps down to the present day, an extraordinary development. I dare to say that the Y.M.M.A. is the one great movement of the Arabic-speaking world of to-day, and that its importance and influence, at the present time and in future, can hardly be overestimated. It seems that the young men of Cairo said the right word at the right time, that minds were prepared, so that what had been latent was at once put into effect.

I shall speak presently of the further activity of the centre of the Association in Cairo and of the Sections founded in Egypt. First let me say a few words about the Branches established outside Egypt.

Numerous such Branches have been founded, in Palestine, Syria and 'Irāq. As early as in April, 1928, at the Congress of the Islamic Associations held in Jaffa, the Regulations of the Young Men's Moslem Associations to be founded in Palestine were discussed and agreed upon. They are essentially the same as those of Cairo.

At this Congress different resolutions were passed, two of which I have to mention, as we shall meet with the subjects of them again. The first was to distribute a publication exhorting the Moslems to promote the native schools and to put the Moslems on their guard against the Missionary schools ; the second, to develop more intensively the movement of the Moslem Boy Scouts.

In connexion with this Congress an Islamic Association existing already in Jaffa was transformed into a Y.M.M.A., and soon after, in May, 1928, other Associations were founded in Jerusalem, Acre and Haifa. The Association of Haifa more especially gained the support of men of mature or even old age. The Arab newspaper *al-Karmel* has expressed discontent at this fact. The young men in Palestine, it says, are too much under the control of older persons ; it is to be hoped that they will free themselves from the interference of their elders and will claim for themselves complete freedom of thought, and that they will be guided exclusively by the social and moral commandments of Muhammad.

Other Associations followed in Palestine, and their number seems now to be between ten and twenty.

In 'Irāq, the Associations of Baghdād and al-Basrah have shown great activity. That of Baghdād held its second general meeting in February, 1930. That of al-Basrah published several pamphlets addressed to the Moslem young men, in which it emphasized the most urgent moral obligations incumbent upon Moslem young men, expounded the grave disadvantages which result from failure in these duties, and encouraged youths to join the Association. Space does not allow me to render the full arguments of these interesting documents ; I can only briefly enumerate the items of two of them. The one urges the Moslem young men (1) to renounce wine; (2) to abstain from unlawful sexual intercourse ; (3) to avoid gambling; (4) to forsake the theatres and to save their money for hard times; (5) to overcome laziness and avoid frequenting coffee-houses; (6) to love their country and to make use of its products and manufactures. " Do you know," it is asked in the seventh place (at the end of the pamphlet), " that there exists in al-Basrah a Y.M.M.A., that it has taken upon its shoulders to spread morals, to overcome vices, and to propagate the lofty Islamic culture, and that it is delivering lectures on religious, ethical, literary, hygienic and social matters every week? Will you not attend these lectures, and join this Association and grant it material and ideal help ? "—The items of the second pamphlet are : (1) Give up lotteries ; (2) encourage the native schools and benevolent societies ; (3) take care in guiding your son, let him keep out of the way of bad company, plant in his heart the love of virtue, you are responsible for him to God; (4) guard against the foreign schools ; (5) recommending others to do good and prohibiting what is disapproved of (by God) are among the primary principles of Islam ; (6) stealing and unfaithfulness are amongst the meanest actions, you must keep clear of them; (7) do not send your son to European schools until you have provided him with the force of Islamic faith and loyalty to his country.

All the Associations outside Egypt as well as the different Sections in Egypt itself, are independent in themselves ; there is not, as far as I can see, any central leadership or organization. But the Branches and Sections are in close connexion with the Central Association of Cairo, and there is the institution of a *Congress of the Boards of Directors* of the different

Associations, according to the internal regulations of the Central Association. Such a Congress was held in Cairo on July 10th and 11th, 1930. There were represented, by delegates, Associations of Palestine: those of Haifa, Acre and Selwān, er-Ramle, Liftā (near Jerusalem) and Khān Yūnus (near the Egyptian frontier); and Associations of Egypt: those of Alexandria, Sōhāg, Kafr ash-Sheïkh, and, of course, Cairo. Other Associations, for instance those of 'Irāq, several of Palestine and even of Egypt, were not represented. At this Congress problems were discussed and resolutions passed.

In importance and influence, the Central Association of Cairo is the most outstanding, and I propose now to give, as far as possible, an accurate idea of its further development.

The Association has its accommodation in a very fine Club-house opposite the House of Parliament. If you cross the garden which is in front of the building, you may see young men doing gymnastics or various sports. You ascend a flight of outside steps leading to an open platform, to which the rooms of the first floor are contiguous. Here, on the platform and in the adjoining rooms, you may see other young men taking light refreshments—no spirits—or playing chess or similar games. If it is evening you may attend a musical entertainment, in European or Oriental music, and be struck by the zeal and the skill of these young musicians. You are shown a great number of rooms, amongst them the library filled with plenty of valuable books in Arabic and European languages. Upstairs are situated large rooms, in which meetings may be held and lectures are regularly delivered. Almost at every hour of the day the rooms are crowded. You see no hat, if it be not the hat of a European guest, or if it be not, by chance, the hat of Maḥmūd 'Azmī, the only man of letters in Egypt, as far as I know, who wears a hat. You see the common tarbūsh and also the 'amāmah (the turban) of the shaikhs. There are young men and men of mature age, professors of al-Azhar University as well as of the Egyptian University, men of letters, teachers, officials, merchants, young men of every class of society. You may meet here, as I did, the "Emir of the poets," Ahmed Shawqī, and other celebrated men of Egypt. Very often also you may meet foreigners, renowned Moslems of other parts of the Islamic world, you may listen to their conversation and attend their lectures.

When I was in Cairo, in March and April, 1928, I went to the Association almost every day. I had many conversations, and attended many lectures. Ever since leaving Egypt, I have read in the Arabic newspapers about the lectures of the Association and very often I have found extracts of the lectures, or even the full text of some of them, published in the newspapers. So there is abundance of material at hand for judging of the activity of the Association. But the best source of information on it is the *Review* published by the Association.

The first article of the first number (October, 1929) is characteristic of the movement. The article is entitled : " Our need of *reform*—Our starting point and our line of action." The author, Dr. Yaḥyā ad-Dardīrī, who is also the editor of the *Review*, says that the state of decomposition and weakness which has affected the social life of the Islamic nations must make every thinking man enquire into the causes of it and the remedies for it. He finds that the moral anarchy in which the community of the Moslems is involved is due to a multitude of causes, of which the most important are these :

1. The common ignorance.
2. The fact that the Moslems are imitating what is bad in the western civilization.
3. The fact that the educated classes of the Moslems are neglectful of their duty to fight against the abuses which are spreading in the body of the nation as a fever spreads in the body of a sick person.

Then the author gives particulars about the moral state of Moslem society and indicates the remedy for it.

He says that for Moslems there is only one remedy, that is, to return to the *Koran*, and to draw from the moral commandments of the word of God their own morals. The Koran must be the basis, the guide and the source of the moral revival of the Moslems, and without the moral revival no other revival movements can be of any use, be they social or economic or other movements.

It is well to observe that it is not one of the old conservative shaikhs who traces this line of action, but a Doctor of Laws and Licentiate of Political Science of Geneva University.

Dr. Dardīrī expounds the reasons of his pleading for the Koran as the basis of the moral culture of the Moslems :

1. The moral culture of the Koran is based upon the call to *reform* and to *do good* to everybody.
2. The moral culture of the Koran is based upon the *freedom of science and thought*, and this freedom of science and thought is the basis of all true revival.
3. The moral culture of the Koran impels to mutual indulgence and to the solidarity of mankind.

Thereafter, in support of his statements, Dr. Dardīrī proceeds to quote in full text, and to comment on, a number of verses of the Koran.

In another article, in the number of May, 1931, entitled " Our illness and our remedy," the same author describes and deplores once more, and very earnestly, the moral anarchy, which reigns, as he says, amongst the Moslems of to-day. Men have no aim, no rule of conduct. God must be their aim, they must train themselves to keep His commandments and to abstain from what He forbids. The man whose aim is God, is doing good, and love of mankind and working for their benefit is his standard of conduct. Nowadays men surrender themselves to their pleasures and cupidity. To this, individuals and Associations must offer strong opposition. History proves that such movements of reform have to confront many obstacles and difficulties ; their leaders must show courage and intrepidity, and direct the minds of the friends of reform and all those who devote themselves to their country and are working on behalf of true life. In support of his arguments, Dr. Dardīrī quotes different Muhammadan traditions and occurrences in the history of Islam.

From what I have referred to we can understand that another article (I. 8) is entitled " Religion above all," and that there are many other articles on religious matters : on the Prophet and his life, the Koran —which is the first foundation of Islamic faith—and the traditions—which are its second basis. There are to be found commentaries on parts of the Holy Book, and a series of five articles on spurious traditions. Religious doubts of the young men on the disagreements of science and religion are discussed in two articles (I. 5, 6), and so on. There is nothing narrow-minded nor narrow-hearted, but a real understanding of the religious needs of modern times, keeping to what is essential, and emphasizing it very strongly, and leaving what is secondary.

Now, as religion is required because of its ethical effects, it is but natural to find in the *Review* of the Y.M.M.A. many articles on pure ethical and psychological topics : such as training of the will, education of the soul, articles on vices like avarice, wrath, suicide, and so on, on virtues like generosity, and what is called in Arabic *īthār*, literally : preferring the benefit of others to one's own benefit, or selflessness in giving to others. There are also scattered all through the different numbers of the *Review* ethical aphorisms and proverbs.

The end for which the Y.M.M.A. is aspiring to religious and moral betterment is to breed a new generation of men who may be capable of the highest deeds to serve their country in every branch of modern life, in social interchanges, in education, in public life, in science, in technics, and so on. Now, what can have more influence upon the determination of young people than the example of great men ? So there are found in the *Review* essays on eminent men of Islam and eastern history : Abū Bakr, the first Caliph, the model of devotion to duty ; 'Omar ibn al-Khattāb, the second Caliph, the model, as it is said, of a democratic just ruler ; Muhammad 'Alī, the great founder of modern Egypt and of the reigning Egyptian dynnasty ; Jamāl ad-Dīn al-Afghānī, the renowned reformer and Islamic politician ; Mustafā Kāmil, the hero of modern Egyptian nationalism. On the other hand, there are the lives of men like Benjamin Franklin, Abraham Lincoln, Faraday, Edison, Carnegie, Henry Ford, and other personages, even of men who are less known but remarkable for the excellent qualities they showed in their life-work.

Besides the fundamental and general articles bearing on religion, ethics and ideals of human activity, many special ones are to be found on various matters. Some of them, which relate to natural history and physics, like the age of the world, mimicry, recent discoveries about electricity, etc., are of general interest or connected with general philosophical views ; but most of the articles deal with the immediate needs of national life in Egypt and the Islamic world. The topics are such as education, law, the condition of women, social problems, medicine and hygiene, technics and manufacturing—there are several articles on spinning and weaving—and economics. Other articles refer to gymnastics and sports, also to Boy Scouts as groups of different Sections of the Association ; it is related, for example, how the Boy Scouts of the Section of Alexandria and those of another Section were received as guests by the prince 'Omar Tūsūn. The Y.M.M.A., of course, attach much value to strengthening the body.

Special attention is paid in the *Review* to social problems. I remember a paper of Alfred Nielsen, who during the years 1924-1928 perused the Arabic press of Damascus and gave a statement of the result of his study. As to social questions, he tells us that in the Syrian newspapers, and in daily life in Syria, we miss a note that is sounded so strongly in the West, the note of mutual help and care in public life. And he adds : " The great question is whether all this can be combined with the spirit of Islam. The future," he says, " will show us whether the spirit of Islam is able to produce and to conserve the common love of the neighbour which is at the bottom of all social undertakings." Well, things here in the *Review* of the Y.M.M.A. are quite different from what Mr. Nielsen found in the Syrian papers. Here, the note of mutual help and care in public life is strongly sounded. Here, social undertakings are strongly recommended. Dr. Dardīrī, who has published a separate book on mutual help, deals in no less than twelve articles of the *Review* with co-operation. He writes on co-operation in France and Denmark, on sickness-funds and burial-funds, mutual help in cases of unemployment, loan-banks, and insists especially on the need in Egypt for agricultural co-operation. A special essay is devoted by him to the great British social reformer Robert Owen (II. 1).

The details hitherto related show the essential features of the Y.M.M.A. and illustrate how the young men have carried out the different points of their

Regulations. But I have not been complete as yet. I have further to deal with a very important part of the activity of the Association which is reflected in the *Review* and seems to be in contradiction to the second article of their Regulations, which runs: The Association does not under any circumstances interfere in politics.

In fact, there is no discussion in the *Review* about the internal political life of Egypt, nor about the relations of Egypt with foreign powers, e.g. about Capitulations, or the position of England in Egypt. Nor is there any propaganda for political aspirations, such as inspire the ideal of a union of eastern countries, e.g. *al-wahdah al-'arabīyah*, the Confederation of Arabic-speaking peoples. There is no political Pan-Islam either, nothing similar to the political ideas of 'Abd al-Hamīd II or Jamāl ad-Dīn al-Afghānī. But these young men are Moslems, sincere Moslems. Moslems are brethren, and the feeling of this brotherhood is in no way confined to the frontiers of states; on the contrary, Islamic feeling is essentially international. So, as these young men are true Moslems and fighting for the influence of Islam, they are deeply interested in any events regarding Islam, and feel deeply moved when there is any aggression against Islam or Islamic communities, or when it seems to them that there is any such aggression, in Egypt or outside Egypt. Then they rise vehemently. And when such an aggression, or

EGYPT AND WESTERN ASIA

supposed aggression, comes from political authorities, then the protestations and actions of the Y.M.M.A. seem to have a political character.

The events and facts which have stirred up the Islamic feelings of the Y.M.M.A. in the last few years are chiefly the following : (1) The criticisms directed in Egypt against Islam in public lectures and pamphlets, especially by Christian missionaries ; (2) The events in Palestine connected with the Wailing Wall of Jerusalem, in 1929 and 1930 ; (3) The French policy regarding the Berbers in Morocco, in 1930 ; (4) Severe colonial measures adopted by the Italians in Tripoli, and atrocities ascribed to them, in 1930 ; (5) Recently the execution of the Tripolitan leader 'Omar al-Mukhtār by the Italians.

As to (1) the critical *attacks against Islam* which gave offence to the Y.M.M.A., resolutions of protest were passed by a general meeting of the Alexandria Section of the Association (May, 1930), and by the Congress of the Boards of Directors of the Association held in Cairo in July, 1930. A lecture delivered by Dr. Fakhrī Mikhā'īl Faraj, at the American University in Cairo, induced the Central Association to send a letter to the Egyptian Minister of Interior, and another letter to the Shaikh of al-Azhar. The subject is further discussed in an article entitled : " The Duty of the Government against the Activity of the Missionaries." In this article it is held that the Egyptian law allows the missionary societies to expound the beauties of their religion, but forbids them strictly to attack the religion of the overwhelming majority of the country by insults and criticism. Such attempts create disorders and undesirable dissensions between the two groups of the Egyptian people. In the letter to the Minister it is added that the movement of reform and revival is disturbed by such attacks on the foundations of Islam, to which the great majority of the people are devoted and in the interest of which they will make the greatest sacrifices.

(2) As to *Palestine*, it is well known that the attempt to establish there a National Home for the Jews has led to serious difficulties. The Arabs of Palestine, as a whole, Moslems and Christians, regarded and still regard the Jewish colonization as a diminution of their rights and as a threat to their future. The Moslems especially apprehended, from certain actions and declarations of the Zionists, the violation of sacred rights they possess on the precincts of the Haram ash-Sherīf, of which the Wailing Wall is a part. The Haram ash-Sherīf, where once stood the Jewish Temple, destroyed in A.D. 70, is since the seventh century after Christ, with its two most venerated mosques, the holiest place in the Islamic world after Mecca and Medina. In consequence of incidents connected with the Wailing Wall, grave disturbances took place in August, 1929, when more than one

hundred Jews and an almost equal number of Arabs were killed. A Commission of Enquiry on these disturbances was appointed a little later. Immediately after the disturbances took place, the Y.M.M.A. in Cairo sent telegrams to the League of Nations, to the British Foreign Office, and to the High Commissioner in Jerusalem. It further sent a letter to the High Commissioner (Nov., 1929), another detailed letter to the aforesaid Commission (Dec., 1929) and a telegram to the new international Commission appointed by the British Government to determine the rights and claims of Moslems and Jews in connexion with the Western or Wailing Wall at Jerusalem (July, 1930). In the first of these manifestos it is stated that the Moslems of Palestine were quiet until they were defied by the Jews. The site of the *Burāq* on the Wailing Wall, to which the Jews lay claim, is a sacred spot to Moslems. " Every Moslem in whatever part of the earth regards himself as a warrior who stands up together with the Moslems of Palestine to defend a pledge put into their hands. Moslems never will allow Zionists to make of a site sacred to them a centre of their national propaganda, as long as there is left on the surface of the earth one Moslem, and as long as there is living blood pulsing in the veins of that Moslem."

After this great disaster, the Association also gathered funds to relieve the families in Palestine affected by the consequences of the disturbances.

WHITHER ISLAM?

(3) As to *Morocco*, there is a general tendency of French policy in regard to it which is well known in the Islamic world and very much disliked by it, and certain measures adopted by France provoked irritation throughout the Islamic world far deeper and more general than any irritation which has affected the Moslems in recent years. The general tendency of that policy is to keep the population of Morocco as far as possible apart and separate from the Islamic world outside Morocco. It is said that Arabic newspapers are not allowed to enter Morocco with the single exception of a Cairo paper well known for its relations to French interests. The French further dislike the development of the Arabic language in Morocco, especially amongst the Berbers. The Berbers, different from the Arabs by race and language, a strong population of about seven millions, inhabit the mountain regions of the country. Of course, they are Moslems, and even played an important part in Islamic history in mediæval times. But they have preserved, with their original Berber language, certain customary laws of their own. Now France made the attempt, in 1930, by reference to these customary laws, to introduce among the Berbers a new jurisdiction, comprehending all civil and commercial matters and including especially also all matters of legal status of persons and rights of succession. The Muhammadan religious law was to be abrogated, and, instead of the

Qāḍī, the chief of the tribe was to exercise judicial power. The organization of this jurisdiction was to depend on the political authorities, that is on France. It was this project, laid down in an official regulation of the 16th May, 1930, which provoked the deep irritation of the whole Islamic world, as it showed clearly the intention to separate the important national group of the Berbers of Morocco from the Islamic community. This irritation was increased by the news of efforts simultaneously undertaken to christianize the Berbers.

The Y.M.M.A. joined with special fervency in the general profound irritation of the Islamic world. They directed a solemn " Appeal," covered with numerous signatures, to " all the kings and peoples of Islam," and sent it to the 'Ulamā' of Mecca and Medina, to those of al-Azhar and the other religious institutions in Egypt, to the Zaytūnah Mosque in Tunis, to the Qarwiyīn Mosque in Fez, to all the different religious institutions and associations in India, ' Irāq, Indonesia (especially in Sumatra and Java), to the *Nahdat al-'ulamā'* in Syria, to the Supreme Moslem Councils in Jerusalem and Beyrouth, to the Association of the 'Ulamā' in Kabul, to the Association for the Advancement of Islam in China, and to " *all the Eastern newspapers without distinction of their languages and dialects.*" They further sent a deputation to the chief of the private Ministry of the King of Egypt and asked him to draw the attention of His Majesty the King to the aforesaid Appeal. Besides this Appeal, which is published in the *Review* (Oct., 1930), numerous articles and documents deal with the same question. Two of them refute attempts made to justify the French measure : the Arabic newspaper of Cairo alluded to already had published an article defending France, and the Minister Resident of France in Cairo had given explanations. In another article is published the full text of the protest made against the French proceeding in Morocco in the name of the Moslems of Palestine by the President of the Supreme Moslem Council in Jerusalem, and handed by him to the Consul-General of France in Jerusalem. The echo which the Appeal found in Java induced the Legation of France there to publish on its side official explanations attenuating the facts, to which explanations the Review *Majallat ar-rābitah al-ʿalawīyah* published a refutation. The author of it concludes : " As to us, we see only one thing, that France is disregarding the Moslems to the point of considering them creatures without understanding or judgment " (II. 4).

It would carry me too far if I were to give more details of the vigorous repulse which the French Morocco policy found on the part of the Y.M.M.A. and in the whole Islamic world.

It is of little use for the purpose of our investigation

to deal here with the events which happened in *Tripoli* and *Barqa*, or which are said to have happened there. Whoever may be interested in them and in the strong impression they produced in the Islamic world may refer to the review published in Geneva by the Emir Shakib Arslān : *La Nation Arabe* (Naville & Cie, December, 1930, and various numbers in 1931). The Y.M.M.A., with which we have to do here, convoked a special meeting, and this agreed upon a declaration to be sent to the League of Nations and to be spread throughout the world of Islam. The text with the signatures of a great many eminent personages was also published in the *Review* (June, 1931). It was also agreed at the same meeting to send a deputation to Tripoli and Barqa in order to ascertain the truth of the facts. In execution of this resolution the Board of Directors of the Association wrote a letter to the Minister Resident of Italy in Cairo asking him to fix an appointment for the visit of a delegation of the Association to him for the purpose of considering the way in which the deputation agreed upon by the meeting could possibly be sent to Tripoli. It was also proposed that one of the Italian scholars resident in Cairo should be a member of that deputation.

To this letter, the Board of Directors received no reply, as is stated in the *Review* (ib.), a fact which added much to the irritation of the Association.

Again the Association gathered relief funds, for Tripoli, in July, 1931.

The deep interest which the Association takes in the general condition of Islam is shown in many other articles of the *Review*. I must abstain from entering into more details. I may only refer to two resolutions of protest (July, 1930) : the one against the closing of mosques in Turkey, the other against the attack of Soviet Russia upon Islam by closing mosques and taking possession of the endowments (*awqāf*) of the Moslem communities (August–Sept., 1930).

It is evident that activity of such a kind, carried on to such an extent, with such energy and such discernment, must draw to itself the attention of the whole Islamic world, attract the best intellects and the strongest wills, and lead to the House of the Association the steps of visitors from all parts of the world of Islam, the more so as Cairo is not only the intellectual, but also the geographical centre of Islam. So we cannot be astonished to find amongst the guests and the lecturers of the Association men like the great Indian leader Shawkat 'Alī, the Tunisian leader ath-Tha'ālibī, who delivered a number of lectures, and Dr. Shinkievitch, the Mufti of Poland. Shawkat 'Alī visited the Association several times, he was a guest in the house of the President of the Association and used their Club as his residence by day ; there visits were paid to him, there ceremonies were held in his honour. If we look further at the contents of the *Review*, we notice there also important contributions of non-Egyptian authors. I may especially point to two articles entitled: "The Intellectual Movement in Morocco," by a writer of whose name only the initials are given, but who is qualified as a member of the Association and evidently is a native of Morocco. These articles are very fine and comprehensive, they show an exact knowledge of things in Morocco and give us information about intellectual and religious movements in that country which we can hardly find in any European publication. We learn from them that there is in Morocco too a movement of religious reform which is occupied with national needs, and which criticizes the European methods of colonization. This movement, which seems to be carried on very prudently and sagaciously, is, of course, supported by young men and nourished with the ideas of the Arabic East. Opposed to this new movement are the *Shurafā'* (the saints, descendants of the Prophet) and the religious brotherhoods. It is curious enough that these groups, who represent the *qadīm* (the old religious fashion) are helping the " new order " (the French colonization), even by verses of the Koran and traditions of the Prophet. They are, it is said, " like mute instruments put in motion, at any instant, to what they are directed to."

We see, as I have said already, that there is no

Pan-Islam in the sense of a political scheme, but there is, in fact, a connexion between Islamic communities all over the world of Islam, and there is a very strong feeling of Islamic solidarity. This feeling is a quite spontaneous one, and it seems that it has grown up gradually in accordance with the different events which have affected the Islamic world. At the Congress of the Boards of Directors held in July, 1930, the strengthening of Islamic solidarity was, as we shall see presently, one of the points of the order of the day ; it was much discussed, and resolutions bearing on the different plans to be realized were passed.

Amongst the contents of the *Review* the proceedings of the *Congress of the Boards of Directors* held in July, 1930, are of special interest, as they do not present selected items, but give an idea of the whole of the interior life of the Association, of all the conceptions and tendencies of these young men, and show which are the predominant and moving ideas of the Association.

The object of the Congress was first to examine the circumstances of the Association and to consider how it might be developed, secondly to discuss different points, chief amongst which were those regarding :

(1) the means of strengthening Islamic solidarity between the different countries,

(2) the training of children and education on true Islamic principles,

(3) the counteracting of movements of missionary work and irreligion.

On two successive days many propositions were discussed and resolutions passed by the meeting in regard to these subjects. I may draw attention to some of the most interesting points.

First some remarks as to the *position of the Association*.

A delegate from Palestine criticized the number of the Sections of the Association in Egypt as being relatively small compared with the Branches in Palestine. To this the President and another of the Directors replied that this number would be more numerous but for the principle of the Central Association of laying more stress on quality than on quantity, and of not allowing a Section to be founded unless its existence were guaranteed.

Dr. Dardīrī reproached some of the Branches for not binding themselves to the Regulations of the Association, and asked them to avoid the suspicion of interfering with politics within the pale of the Association.—The President : Islamic actions such as defending the *Burāq* (the sacred place at the Wailing Wall) and the Mosque al-Aqsā, fall within the articles of the Association ; they are pure Islamic actions and do not fall under the head of political actions.—After debating the matter, the meeting agreed upon the necessity of the Association being on its guard against the suspicion of interfering with politics, in order that its enemies might not be given the opportunity of injuring it, and that the Association might be able to devote itself to building up the renewal of Islamic morals.

Interesting discussions went on as to the financial basis of the Associations and the different means of securing the funds necessary for their existence, and to carry through their actual work and the vast tasks to be undertaken in future.

The Club-House of the Y.M.M.A. in Cairo is not their property, it is taken on lease. A member insisted on the necessity of keeping this house, and if it should be necessary to remove, they must remove to a bigger house, not to a smaller one. The President reassured the Congress as to the future of the centre of the Association, and told them that a Prince of the Royal House had promised to give the Association a house far larger than the present and very much more appropriate, as their own property.

As to the first of the special points to be discussed by the Congress (*strengthening Islamic solidarity*), there were 15 propositions presented and debated upon. Resolutions were passed by the Congress for carrying through at once, or for preparing to carry through, some of the propositions presented to the Congress. We may mention : (1) A Congress of the Board of Directors of the Young Men's Moslem Associations is to be held in different Islamic countries ; (3) Information must be gathered concerning the situation of the Moslems in the different countries by preparing in every Association registers containing the news of the country. Every effort must be made to ascertain the truth of these reports; (4) A " Covenant " (compact, *mīthāq*) of the Association was agreed upon, the text of which is given below; (5) A Commission of experts was entrusted with the study of a plan of founding an Islamic *bank* and Islamic *co-operative societies*, and to present a report on this question to the Central Association in order to put the plan into execution; (8) A Commission was entrusted to study the plan of founding a *daily* Islamic newspaper, and to present a report on this point.—On other points resolutions were not passed, but some of them were declared to be " desires and wishes," the realization of which was to be aimed at *as far as possible*. Of these " desires " we may mention : (1) to generalize the Arabic language in the Eastern countries ; (2) to reclaim the Hijāz Railway for the Moslems; (3) to encourage the Moslems to work for the restoration of the Caliphate (on this interesting question more will be said presently); (4) to establish a League of Islamic Nations for settling Islamic disputes.

The second chief point of the order of the day referred to Islamic *education*, to which the Y.M.M.A. attach the utmost importance. Two resolutions were passed, the execution of which depends on the Associations themselves : (1) to establish in every Association a school for the learning of the Koran; (2) to create in the different Associations sections of Islamic Boy Scouts.—Another resolution recommends that those traditions of the Prophet which are generally acknowledged to be genuine should be made the subjects of sermons and religious instruction. The Y.M.M.A. will work towards the realization of this aim.—There are other points the decision as to which depends on the *Government*. The Y.M.M.A. resolved to invite the Government (1) to make religious instruction and the study of Islamic history general in the schools, and to consider these branches of instruction as fundamental; (2) to keep out of the lectures and studies at the University atheism and everything connected with it; (3) to promote religious preaching; (4) to enact regulations of religious law in order to prevent prostitution, wine-drinking and gambling; (5) to restrain women from displaying their charms, to prevent boys and girls from frequenting localities which corrupt morals, and to take care of morals in summer-resorts; (6) to promote the writing of plays on Islamic subjects, and of stories likely to spread amongst children the Islamic spirit.

The Congress further expressed in regard to education certain "desires and wishes" as it had done in regard to the question of Islamic solidarity. These wishes are: (1) the establishment of Islamic schools; (2) the publication of a Commentary on the

Koran to be written by a Commission of men of merit; (3) a great Islamic Encyclopædia to be compiled by Moslems.

As to the third chief point of the order of the day— *counteracting the movement of missionary work and irreligion*— the following resolutions were passed : (1) to found a scientific Commission to combat atheism and to enlighten people about religion ; (2) to send delegates from each Association to refute the arguments of the missionaries in their meetings ; (3) to invite the Governments of the Islamic states to modify the articles of the penal law concerning freedom of thought and science, so that a distinction might be made between this and the defamation of religion ; (4) to rouse the interest of the proper departments in founding societies of 'Ulamā' whose object is to preach Islam, and to spread religion according to its true nature.

The Y.M.M.A. have also a *badge* and a *flag*, the form of which was agreed upon by the Congress. They have, moreover, a *hymn*, the author of which is the well-known man of letters and poet Mustafā Sādiq ar-Rāfi'ī. The setting of it was put up for competition, and the Association received from the composers of Egypt and Syria more than ten airs, amongst which that of Professor Zakī Muhammad ash-Shibīnī, revised by the Shaikh Hasan al-Mamlūk, was chosen.

The "*Covenant*" (compact) of the Y.M.M.A. is the following:

"I bind myself by a Covenant and engagement with God to exert myself to the best of my powers in order

(1) to revive the guidance of Islam in its doctrines, morals, commandments, prohibitions and language, and to oppose the flood of irreligion and libertinism which threaten this guidance;

(2) to be active as a warrior fighting for the revival of the glory of Islam by restoring its religious law and its supreme chiefdom;

(3) to do my utmost to strengthen the ties of brotherhood amongst all Moslems and to put an end to hostility and dissension between the Islamic parties and groups;

(4) to exert myself to strengthen the Islamic nations by the knowledge of whatsoever raises their scientific, economic and social level, and promotes the Moslem's adherence to the teachings and virtues of Islam;

(5) to work for the realization of the aims of the Y.M.M.A., the enlargement of its sphere of action, the expansion of the number of its regular members, and the strengthening of my acquaintances amongst the Y.M.M.A. in the moral qualities which it is the object of the Association to propagate.

I bind myself by a Covenant and engagement with God to do this to the best of my powers without sparing in this any abilities. And I call God to witness what I say."

In a short notice referring to the general meeting of the Central Association held in Cairo on September 18th, 1931, the fact is reported as a characteristic feature of this meeting that the members recited aloud this Covenant standing the while.

As we have seen above, one of the propositions made to the Congress was to work for the restoration of the *Islamic Caliphate*. The Congress was of opinion that " this question is amongst the questions *upon which it is difficult to take action at present*." But the members agreed upon a declaration that the revival of the Caliphate must be the desire of every member of the Y.M.M. Associations, and that he may work towards its realization whenever opportunity offers. The members, moreover, accepted the proposal of Muhibb ad-Dīn al-Khatīb to insert the words relating to the Caliphate in the " Covenant " of the Association. In fact, Article 2 of this compact, the translation of which has been given above, speaks in rather general terms of the supreme chiefdom (*imāmah*) of Islam, towards the revival of which the members must direct their efforts.

The position taken up by the Y.M.M.A. with regard to the famous Caliphate question is an indication of the present state of opinion in the Arabic-speaking Near East on this question, which, in

WHITHER ISLAM?

consequence of the Turkish abolition of the Ottoman Caliphate, has so strongly stirred up the East. I may here briefly summarize the facts which illustrate this state of affairs.

On the first of November, 1922, the Grand National Assembly of the Angora Republic passed the bill for abolishing the Sultanate. Sultan Mehmed VI, having fled to Malta on the 17th of November, was deposed next day, 18th of November, 1922, and on the same day the Crown Prince, 'Abdul-Mejīd, was created Caliph without temporal power. Although temporal power, according to the religious law of Islam, is one of the conditions of the office of Caliph, 'Abdul-Mejīd accepted the Caliphate in this new form. But only a little more than a year later, on the 3rd of March, 1924, the Grand National Assembly of Angora passed by an overwhelming majority the new bill for abolishing the Ottoman Caliphate altogether. 'Abdul-Mejīd was expelled next day and went to Territet in Switzerland, where, and at Nice, he has continued to live to the present day.

The world of Islam, which had been alarmed by the stripping away of the Caliph's temporal power in 1922, was now, in 1924, being left with no Caliph at all, in the utmost confusion. At once efforts were made to proclaim a new Caliph. When King Husayn, the Shereef of Mecca, visited Transjordania in March, 1924, he was offered, at ash-Shūnah, and he accepted the oath of allegiance taken to him as Caliph by some sections of the population of Transjordania, Palestine, and Syria. But he had no time to obtain a more general acknowledgment of his office as lawful Caliph of Islam. Defeated by Ibn Sa'ūd, he lost Mecca in October, 1924, went to Jiddah and, in June, 1925, to Cyprus, where he remained until shortly before his death at 'Ammān (Transjordania) on June 6th, 1931.

In the meantime, while the practical attempt was being made to establish King Husayn as the new Caliph, the 'Ulamā' of al-Azhar University considered the convocation of a general Islamic Congress in order to examine and settle the Caliphate question according to the regulations of the religious law and having regard to the circumstances of the present time. After many delays the Congress was finally held in Cairo, from the 13th to the 19th of May, 1926. The attendance was not as general as had been desired and expected, and India, for instance, did not send a delegate. The Congress, which was presided over by the late Shaikh Muhammad Abū 'l-Fadl al-Gīzāwī, then rector of al-Azhar, passed a resolution which declared the establishment of a Caliph according to the conditions of the religious law to be possible, but that the appointment of the Caliph must be deliberated on in a meeting at which all the peoples of Islam are represented. This condition not having been fulfilled by the Congress, it recommends all Moslems not to neglect the Caliphate question in future and to work towards the realization of that institution, which is the spirit and manifestation of Islam.

As I write these lines, a new general Islamic Congress is preparing to meet in Jerusalem, on the 7th of December, 1931. Newspapers, both English and Arabic, Zionist and others, had spread the news that Mawlānā Shawkat 'Alī intended to propose to this Congress the election of 'Abdul-Mejīd as Caliph with spiritual powers only. This report has been denied by Shawkat 'Alī as well as by the President of the Supreme Moslem Council in Jerusalem. It is not quite clear from what source the report originated, and whether it had any foundation. The view of the Caliphate question taken in India is different from that taken in the Arabic-speaking Near East. Here, the general feeling will probably be that expressed by a Damascus Arabic newspaper (23.10.1931) at the end of a leading article entitled "The Islamic Caliphate: Has the time come to examine its revival?" The question is answered in the negative: the Caliphate must not be raised from its slumber. Neither Shawkat 'Alī nor anybody else can at the present time establish a Caliph. We must await further developments, as the atmosphere does not favour the raising of a question which has been left untouched for years. Men have forgotten it and are now occupied with other affairs.

It is important, moreover, to notice that *Nūr al-Islām*, the review edited by al-Azhar University, has published at this juncture, in its number 6 of Vol. II. (Jumādah II., 1350 = Oct.–Nov., 1931), a declaration opposing the intention of dealing with the Caliphate question at the Congress of Jerusalem. The declaration says that an affair like that of King Husayn, in 1924, must not be repeated now, and after a reference to the Resolutions of the Congress held in Cairo in 1926, concludes that the time has not yet come to enter into this question.

In the Arabic-speaking Near East the Moslems are convinced that to raise the Caliphate question now would be to stir up dissension amongst Moslems, and the general tendency of the Moslems of these territories is precisely to exclude and remove dissensions.

Thus, as we have seen from the facts set forth above, a " Caliphate question " can scarcely be said to exist in the Arabic-speaking Near East, though, as we have seen as well, the idea of the Caliphate, in its historical and legal conception, is far from dead. Al-Azhar University showed this conception also in the famous case of 'Alī 'Abd ar-Rāziq. This eminent man of letters was one of the 'Ulamā' of al-Azhar and Judge of the Moslem Religious Courts (at Alexandria, al-Gīzah and al-Mansūrah), and has subsequently edited the magazine *ar-Rābitah ash-sharqīyah* (" The Oriental League ") which is devoted to the union of the East without regard to religion and nationality. In 1925 'Alī 'Abd ar-Rāziq published a book entitled *al-Islām wa-usūl al-hukm*, or " Islam and the Principles of Government," in which he declares Islam not to be a theocracy. Muhammad, he says, had not in view the institution of a Caliphate, such as is depicted in the conception of the 'Ulamā' ; he was the Prophet, but when he acted as a politician or a military leader, he did not act as the Prophet. Religion directs only the individual conduct of men. The State stands by itself. Nowadays Moslems must compete with the other nations for social and political science, they must give up the ancient constitution of the Caliphate, and take as the basis of their State and Government the modern achievements of the human mind and the most solid experiences of the nations as to the best foundations of Government.

These contents of the book provoked many controversies in the newspapers, and roused the indignation of the 'Ulamā' of al-Azhar University. According to law No. 10 of 1911 (13th of May), al-Azhar has the duty of censuring all the 'Ulamā' of Egypt for any behaviour not becoming their dignity as 'Ulamā'. After disciplinary investigations, 'Alī 'Abd ar-Rāziq was deprived of his degree and of his position as a judge. The case had even more consequences : the

Minister of Justice, who did not at once, as was his duty, divest 'Alī 'Abd ar-Rāziq of his office as a judge, was himself dismissed.

I have not to deal here with Indian views regarding the Caliphate, but I may mention the book of an Indian scholar of Islamic religion well known in England, Professor Muhammad Barakatullah (Maulavi) of Bhopal, India, who published his book, in 1924, in different languages. The title of the English edition is *The Khilafet* (Luzac & Co., London). On the cover there is printed this summary : " When the Khilafet was perverted Islam was corrupted and the Moslems were ruined, And when the Khilafet will be reformed Islam will be purified and the Faithful will prosper." The author insists on the necessity of there being a Caliph, who must be the *spiritual* leader of Moslems, but only this, without temporal power. " Spiritual organization is a world in itself. It requires people entirely devoted to its service. In these days more than at any time religion must be brought within the reach of every member of the community. Religious organization must be perfected scientifically, and moral and religious culture must be imparted to every child of man in order to protect society from decay and disruption." Starting from this point of view, Barakatullah traces out a whole scheme of organization to be presided over by the Caliph. His Council has to comprise the Ministry of Religion, the

Ministry of Finance or *Bait ul-Māl*, the Ministry of Education and Research, and the Department of Propaganda and Missionary Organization. The question as to who might be, under the present circumstances, such a spiritual Caliph, is for the author a crucial point which he is not able to decide; the place of the Caliphate might be Constantinople or Medina or Cairo.

It is interesting to compare this programme of the Indian professor with the programme of the Y.M.M.A. There is an identical insistence on religion and morals as the basis of social life. But there is, as to the rest, a very great difference. On the one hand, a vast theory far beyond the possibility of being put into effect; for the establishment of one central authority, as provided for in the Indian plan, depends on a multitude of factors which will hardly act together; and if it be established, will it, in an effective way, control its vast domain? On the other hand, immediate action, adapted to immediate needs, in a sphere of action controlled by the individual force of the Y.M.M.A., developing as seeds develop in appropriate soil; various such circles of action, of the same nature, constituted on similar conditions and acting together—so, out of this, a great movement arises, spontaneously and rapidly, a real revival, a real reform, such as could never be produced by the factitious organization of a Caliph with spiritual power.

If we ask what the Y.M.M.A. really means in the Islamic world of to-day, we must make an enquiry into its own strength and the conditions and forces with which it is confronted in its action in that world of Islam. Are there forces which may help it, or are there others which stand in its way?

We must first consider the leaders of the Association. They are men of high education, both European and Eastern. They are young men in the full strength of their vitality. They have a strong will. The source from which this will draws its vigour is a moral one: the love of God and of their country. The aim of these young men is a moral one too: to serve their country and the East by laying the foundations on which alone a real revival and renewal is possible: a sincere and pure religion, sound morals and a thorough education adapted to the needs of their country and the East. Thus in these young men is a tremendous moral force which has the power to surmount the greatest difficulties. And this force, and the aim to which it is directed, are so sound that, by mere contact with the activity of the Association, a powerful influence is brought to bear upon others, provided that there is a disposition to healthy development.

Evidently there is such a disposition in Egypt. The number of the members of the Y.M.M.A. is considerable, though it seems that the Directors have not always been satisfied with it nor with the assiduity of all members. The wide range of the Association is shown by the number of its Sections in Egypt (at Alexandria, Asiūt, Banī Suēf, al-Faiyūm, Sōhāg, and elsewhere). It has gained the support of all classes of Egyptian society and of most distinguished personages, as I have already said. The Section of Alexandria is under the patronage of Prince 'Omar Tūsūn, a member of the Royal family. The Government does not favour the Association officially, out of consideration, it would seem, for the Christian sections of the population of Egypt, who may fear lest their interests should be prejudiced by a strong Islamic propaganda. It is certain too that, as far as the Islamic population of Egypt is concerned, there are also tendencies which do not make in the same direction as the Y.M.M.A. The very existence of the Association which is striving to reach an aim proves that the aim is not reached.

But the question is whether the Y.M.M.A. is an isolated movement, or whether there are other tendencies in keeping with those of the Association, and numerous and strong enough to allow us to speak of a general direction of Islamic thought in Egypt. I venture to say so.

In the general aspects of public life in Egypt, in the Statutes of the Constitution, in parliamentary life, in legislation, in public instruction, and in every manifestation of social tendencies, Islam is maintaining its leading position. And it is characteristic of the development, taken as a whole, that there are combined in it two things : on the one hand, a cleaving to what is fundamental in Islam, on the other, a largeness of view admitting the necessities of modern life, and therefore a readiness for wise reform.

Article 149 of the *Egyptian Constitution* of the 19th of April, 1923, states that Islam is the religion of the State. The Constitution of 1923 was changed and replaced by a new one in October, 1930, but Article 149 has not been modified, as has been the case with a corresponding article of the Turkish Constitution.

In the *Egyptian Parliament* modifications of some details of the religious law (*sharī'ah*) of Islam—regarding the *awqāf* or endowments—have been discussed by the deputies, others have been decreed by legislation of the Government. As to the latter, I may refer to the *Décret-Loi* No. 78, of 1931, dealing with a reorganization of the administration of justice in the Moslem Religious Courts. By this *Décret-Loi* the forensic procedure of the *Mahkamah Shar'īyah* (Religious Courts) has been altered, the jurisdiction of the single judge (the *qādī*) has been exactly determined and restricted to cases of personal statute and succession, and some regulations relating to *matrimony* have been established, e.g., the marriage age has been raised for girls to 16, and for the husband to 18 years. But, in spite of such reforms, the institution of religious jurisdiction is itself maintained, and the religious oath, the origin of which is ascribed to Divine revelation, is also maintained. And in the deliberations of the Parliament on the religious regulations of Islam, the fundamental principles of Islam were highly respected by the deputies, and warm defenders of those principles arose amongst them whenever opportunity offered.

There is, moreover, the sphere of public *education*. When I was in Egypt in 1928, I paid special attention to the character of public instruction. I studied in the Ministry of Education the curricula of all the public schools in Egypt and visited personally the different types of these schools, from the Kindergarten to the primary and secondary schools for both boys and girls, attending the lessons. I was deeply impressed by the high standard of this instruction, by the zeal which the Government, professors and pupils devoted to this instruction, and by the results attained. Well, at the basis of this instruction was religion, the religion of Islam, and the love of country. Also, in order to create a sound and strong generation, a large part of the instruction was given to gymnastics. It is well to observe that the Government is gradually carrying through compulsory education throughout the country. What will be the state of national life when the high intellectual and moral faculties with which the Egyptians are undeniably endowed, are brought more and more into activity by the development of a public instruction of the kind I observed in 1928?

It seems that a new Minister of Education, in 1930, changed the general plan of instruction which I found in 1928, and that he gave less attention to religious instruction and gymnastics than had been given before. But he found opposition, and his ministry was of short duration. The Y.M.M.A., which addressed remonstrances to him in December, 1930, had recently to address thanks to his successor. I cannot think that, the general movement in Egypt being given, any ministry would be able definitively to put aside the sound principles which presided over the programme of instruction described above.

There is, moreover, the movement devoted to women's education and rights, generally carried on with great prudence and discernment. The chief leader of the movement is so distinguished a lady as Mrs. Hudā Shaʿrāwī. I may also mention the excellent school directed by Mrs. Mansūr Fahmī, the wife of the distinguished and well-known Professor of Philosophy at Cairo University. The importance of women's education, in consideration of their influence in the family, is widely acknowledged, and the question has been much discussed in the Y.M.M.A. too. But there is opposition to a general competition of the two sexes and to their free intercourse, in the interest of morals. Girls have been admitted to study at the Egyptian

University. But the two sexes are not allowed to be instructed simultaneously or to mix with each other, either at the University or in the other High Schools of Egypt.

We see, on the one hand, that public instruction is impelled, by the sound elements of the nation, to keep in view religion, morals and bodily health, and, on the other hand, we notice that the Religious Institutes are enlarging their ideas and spheres of activity. There is the reform of the famous al-Azhar University, and the Review founded by it two years ago, *Nūr al-Islām*, which proposes to study earnestly the teachings of Islam and the scientific, ethical, historical and philosophical problems connected with these teachings, in order to arrive at an unbiassed view of them. To this end a special Section has been created which is intended to follow the progress of science and technics and to make for the Review translations from the English, French and German languages. In this way the Review will maintain an interchange of views with the non-Islamic world.

If we look at the contemporary *Arabic literature* of Egypt, we shall find nowadays in the writings of the best authors a general absence of frivolity, minds open towards Western culture often conjoined with religious feeling, a deep sense of moral and social necessities and a growing consciousness of Egyptian and Eastern individuality.

From al-Manfalūtī, who stands at the beginning of the new epoch of Arabic literature and is one of its most appreciated representatives (1876–1924), to the contemporary modernists, we should be able to quote many interesting evidences of these facts. Al-Manfalūtī, says Professor Kratchkovsky, shows to what heights a representative of the Islamic world who adheres to the old faith may rise. In his *an-Naẓarāt* al-Manfalūtī confesses himself, in the most fervent terms, to be, first of all, a Moslem. Now take a modernist, 'Alī 'Abd ar-Rāziq, the same scholar who, as related above, was brought up for trial by al-Azhar University on account of his book *Islam and the Principles of Government*, and was deprived of his degree and of his position as a judge. He believes that Muhammad is the greatest Prophet of God, and in an address he gave at *ar-Rābitah ash-sharqīyah* on November 24th, 1927, he said: " I feel that I am, first of all, an Egyptian, an Arab, an Oriental, and, with the permission of our reverend religious leaders—also a Moslem." This is striking evidence of the evolution in Egypt: al-Manfalūtī, first of all, a Moslem,—'Alī 'Abd ar-Rāziq, first of all, an Egyptian, but *also a Moslem*.

Dr. Muhammad Husayn Haykal, who is the chief editor of *as-Siyāsah*, the organ of the Liberal Constitutionalists, is another typical example of the modern development of thought in Egypt. He is thus characterized in the book *Leaders in Contemporary Arabic*

Literature (London : Kegan Paul, Trench, Trubner & Co., Ltd.), published by Tahir Khemiri and the present writer : " His most characteristic view and the subject to which he refers very often, is what he calls ' the spiritual resurrection of the East.' He believes that the only hope for civilization is a spiritual awakening or ' a new Light,' and that this Light should come from the *East*.—On Religion he has also very definite views. He is convinced that knowledge alone cannot satisfy the human soul, and that religion is a real need, and we cannot dispense with it."

Social feeling too, which is one of the most important features in the Y.M.M.A., is not at all confined to it, but now generally diffused in Egypt and other parts of the Arabic-speaking Near East. When after the death of King Husayn (who died on June 6th, 1931) funds were gathered for erecting in 'Ammān, the capital of Transjordania, a monument to this defunct leader of Arab independence, the editor of a Cairo newspaper, a fervent Moslem and consistent champion of the cause of Arab independence, published from a letter which he had received from 'Ammān, a passage running thus : " But, oh brethren, will the Shaikh of Quraish in his tomb be satisfied by the erection of the monument while there are to be found amongst the Arab nation people who go barefoot and cannot go to school on account of their utmost indigence, and while thousands come to the hospitals of the missionaries to be treated for illness? Why should not the memorial of our great deceased be a Hospital in 'Ammān, or a School in the Shrine of Jerusalem, that people may derive benefit from it?"—We meet frequently similar ideas in the Arabic Press of to-day.

There are various *reviews* as well as *benevolent societies* which are joining in the Islamic religious and moral movement in Egypt. I have mentioned already the weekly *al-Fath* and the monthly *az-Zahrā'*. The Review *al-Manār*, edited by Muhammad Rashīd Ridā, a disciple of Muhammad 'Abduh, is well known. Amongst the societies the *Gam'īyat al-hidāyah al-islāmīyah* ("The Association of Islamic Guidance") and the interesting Islamic Home Mission of *al-Faydīyūn*, directed by Abū'l-Fayd, are notable. You may see members of this latter Association in the railway cars between Cairo and Alexandria and elsewhere distributing to the native passengers religious pamphlets published in Arabic by the Association.

On the other hand, the efforts to develop *national industries and undertakings*, of which the *Bank Misr* (the Bank of Egypt) is a striking example, are being strongly carried on. There are many other examples which it would take too long to enumerate here. The Egyptian Tal'at Harb Bey is very active in this direction.

During the last 20 years, there has been a danger that the Egyptians might lose, by contact with

WHITHER ISLAM?

Western civilization, their individuality, might part with their own past, with religion and morals, and surrender themselves to what is bad in Western civilization without the possibility of taking in what is good in it. This danger seems to have been overcome. National feeling has grown, has deepened and become almost general. With it has grown the understanding of the real needs of the Nation and the East. There is, in fact, a widespread feeling of which the activity of the Y.M.M.A. is a strong and organized expression.

The situation in the other lands of the *Arabic-speaking East*, in Arabia, Palestine, Syria and 'Irāq, corresponds in essentials to the situation in Egypt. There are two typical facts : on the one hand, Ibn Sa'ūd, the reformer both religious and civil, leading back religion to its ancient purity and simplicity, at the same time opening Arabia to the improvements of Western science and technics, settling the nomads, developing the resources of the country, providing hygienic institutions and arrangements, establishing order and security—on the other hand, in Palestine, Syria and 'Irāq, a rising generation of youths to whom Ibn Sa'ūd is the great moral ideal, and who associate with their strong national feeling the revival of Islamic religion. I have already spoken of the Y.M.M.A. in Palestine and 'Irāq. But even apart from these Associations, I can affirm from a close contact of many years with the young Arabs of Palestine, Syria and 'Irāq that there is in these countries a strong movement of the best elements of the educated sections of the nation, whose tendencies are in the same direction, and who, on account of their moral strength, seem to have a vocation for leadership in future developments. In Syria, where many influences are meeting, the movement is more latent and not exposed in public, but it exists and is growing very strongly under the surface.

In Syria, Palestine and 'Irāq the direction of future development is also expressed by the following movements:

(1) The rapid development of Islamic and Arab *Boy Scouts*. These are partly sections of native schools, of the Y.M.M.A. and other Associations, and partly independent.

(2) The growing movement towards the development of *native industries* and the use of the products and manufactures of the country. The addresses given by the Indian leader Shawkat 'Alī on his visit to Syria and Palestine in February, 1931, gave to this movement a further impulse. There are now Commissions and Societies constituted in Syria and Palestine which organize efforts in this direction. Colonial measures taken by European powers anywhere in the East and in North Africa and which stir up Islamic feeling, contribute greatly to turn the populations from buying

merchandise imported by those European nations, and to promote national industry. Interesting too are the attempts to create a national wearing-apparel, especially a national head-dress, in Syria and Palestine.

(3) The special attention paid to Islamic and national *education*. There are many Islamic and native schools in 'Irāq, Syria and Palestine, some of them very active, e.g. the *Madrasat an-najāh* in Nābulus. Most important is the " Association of Arab Education " (*jam'īyat ath-thaqāfah al-'arabīyah*) in Baghdād.

(4) The growing interest in founding and developing religious and benevolent institutions.

This is not the place to deal with the political developments in Syria, Palestine and 'Irāq, nor to show how the Mandate system, by frustrating the expectations and opposing the aspirations of the Arabs, has contributed immensely towards developing and deepening their national feeling, which, as we have seen above, is amongst Moslems combined with Islamic feeling. The political division of pre-war Syria and Mesopotamia into three different Mandate administrations, French and English, and the further dismemberment of post-war Syria into different States —which the Syrians understood to be due to the maxim *Divide et impera*—increased rather the desire for unity. In internal as well as in external political life, the stronger the fermentation of parties, natural under the present unusual circumstances, the more the aspiration towards *ittiḥād* (union) is taking ground. The political difficulties for the Mandatory powers are great. England, by preparing the supersession of the Mandate in 'Irāq and the admission of this country to the League of Nations, has given an example of political sagacity which may be followed by France with respect to Syria. It seems not impossible that, after such a change, a union between Syria and 'Irāq may follow.

In *Palestine*, special circumstances and events are concurring to make of this country a new centre of the revival of Islam. Here, the difficulties connected, as in 'Irāq and Syria, with the Mandate system, are complicated by the Jewish National Home forced upon the Arabs, and the Zionist claims. It is well known to what extent this Jewish question has called out the opposing energies of the Arab population. Jerusalem has played a special part. Here, already, the Missionary Congresses held on the Mount of Olives, were felt by the Moslems to be a general attack on their faith. More recently the events at the Wailing Wall stirred up the whole Islamic world, which regarded, rightly or wrongly, the Zionist claims as an aggressive movement against one of the holiest places of Islam. Their effect has been to strengthen the resolution of the Moslems to make just of that place which they regard as the centre of the aggressions directed against Islam, a central bulwark and rallying-point of Islamic defence. The interment of the great Indian leader

WHITHER ISLAM?

Muhammad 'Alī and of King Husayn in the precincts of the Mosques of the Haram ash-Sherīf, the plan pursued especially by Shawkat 'Alī of founding a general Moslem University in Jerusalem, and the general Islamic Congress convoked by the President of the Supreme Moslem Council in Jerusalem to meet in this city in December, 1931, are symptoms of an evolution which, as it seems to me, in consequence of the strong moral forces engaged, cannot easily come to a standstill.

Whither Islam?

It has been asked, in proposing this question, whether Islam will be able to maintain its inner unity under political dismemberment and the assaults of modern ideas and Western science. Will it prove an enemy or an ally? Or is it breaking up into small national units, each reacting to European influences independently and in its own fashion?

Though no final answer can yet be given as to special points, it seems to me that some general lines of future development can already be distinguished. It is certain, I dare say, that the Arabic-speaking world, especially its great centre, formed by the coherent bloc of Egypt, Arabia, Palestine, Syria and 'Irāq, will play in this development a most important, probably decisive, part. The culture of these territories is highly developed and will tend increasingly, on the basis of the identical literary language and the easy communications which exist between them, to form an intellectual unity. The revival of Islam in these countries is a fact. A change of tendency is impossible. Nothing similar to what happened in Turkey is possible in the Arabic-speaking countries. The Arabs cannot part with the glorious past of their Islamic history and literature; on the contrary, the recollection of this past is one of the factors in the present national and religious renewal. Here, never will the peoples substitute the Latin alphabet for the Arabic; they cannot prohibit access to the rich sources of their literature, nor relinquish the use of an extraordinary instrument which allows them to communicate with the whole Islamic world. Nor, in these countries, can the Islamic revival cease or be stopped, because the peoples are in need of it as the basis of their national renewal, and this national renewal cannot cease nor be stopped, if there really are in these peoples high moral qualities which demand freedom of development. And there are these qualities in them. So the Islamic revival will, in this Arabic bloc, of necessity go on in the direction traced in these lines. Cairo and Jerusalem will more and more become, next to Mecca, the great centres of Islamic life. More and more, as is already the case, students will go from the Arabic-speaking countries of North Africa to Egypt and Palestine, to pursue their education there, and will return to their countries to extend gradually there the revival of the East. A corresponding influence will be exercised on the other parts of the Islamic world, and the general influence of this new Islamic bloc on the whole of Islam will be aided immensely by the mighty instrument of the Arabic Press so highly developed in this Arabic bloc.

Political divisions will never be able to change the common features of national and religious needs.

Will this new Islam prove an enemy or an ally? It depends on Europe which will be the case. It must expressly and firmly be stated that in the Arabic bloc dealt with here, there is no hostility at all towards Europe or Europeans, towards Christianity or Christians. Politically, Christians and Moslems go together in the Arabic East, of which many striking evidences could be given. There are only two things generally and extremely hated in the East, the Arabic expressions of which are: *isti'mār* and *tabshīr* : that is, on the one hand, European colonization and imperialistic domination forced upon the East, and on the other hand, missionary attacks against Islam. The East, at least the Arabic East, cannot bear these two things directed against the basis of its life. But it does not hate the Europeans nor the Christians and missionaries. Nor does the East, or do the Arabs, hate the Jews, as Jews. The East, as things are now, is on the defensive, it does not aggress. As soon as pressure ceases, opposition will cease too. The Islamic world wishes to live in friendship with the West, but *on equal terms*. It is well to remember the motto of the great Egyptian nationalist, Mustafā Kāmil: *Ahrār fī bilādinā, kuramā' liduyūfinā*, "Free in our country, generous to our guests." This is the only possible solution of present difficulties in the Arabic-speaking Near East, also regarding the most difficult problem of all : the Jewish National Home. Pressure and force used against the Arabs can lead to catastrophes. Promises are of no use : of course, the Arabs are distrustful of words. No propaganda, no *Brith Shalom* can help. Only a *free agreement* between Arabs and Jews passed by a National Government (which Government may be of the character suggested by Philby in the *New York Times* of November 24th, 1929) can settle the question.

There is another difficult problem : that of the Christian missionary work in the Arabic-speaking East. We have seen how this work stirs up the feelings of the Moslems, and it will perhaps be useful to make clear the real state of things with which it is to-day confronted in the Arabic-speaking Near East. It is important to note that I now speak exclusively of this bloc formed by Egypt, Arabia, 'Irāq, Palestine and Syria. Of course, things are different in different parts of the Islamic world, though the Islamic solidarity by which these territories are connected with one another must never be forgotten.

WHITHER ISLAM?

There are several undeniable facts which must not be neglected.

First, as I have said above: the Moslems do not hate the missionaries. As to this, I may allude to an interesting article published by an influential Moslem leader, the Emir Shakīb Arslān, in *al-Fath*, the very Islamic weekly edited by one of the Directors of the Y.M.M.A. In this article the Emir Shakīb Arslān praises in the warmest terms the zeal and self-denial of the Christian missionaries (see the *Moslem World*, October, 1931, p. 410).

The second fact, which is very important, is the friendly and intense collaboration of native Oriental Christians and Moslems in the cultural renewal of the East. This collaboration is especially evident in Egypt and Mesopotamia. I may allude to the part played in the Press and literature of Egypt by Christian authors, of which, e.g., the well-known Reviews of *al-Hilāl* and *al-Muqtataf* are striking examples. In Mesopotamia, the Reverend Father Anastase Marie with his review *Loghat al-'Arab* is an outstanding figure. The services which this Oriental white friar has rendered to the revival of the Arabic language and culture are highly appreciated by Moslems as well as by Christians. Thus a latent but efficient influence is exercised by Christianity on Islamic feeling and development, and vice-versa. This state of things is appreciated by the Reverend Father Fr. Tillo

Bannerth, O.S.B., who in a German missionary Review (*Die Katholischen Missionen*, April, 1930) devoted an interesting article to the activity of P. Anastase Marie, looking back upon the fiftieth anniversary of his literary career celebrated solemnly on the 16th of July, 1928, by Moslems and Christians, under the presidency of the famous Moslem poet Jamīl Sidqī az-Zahāwī. As to the friendly relations between Moslems and Christians, the Reverend Father Bannerth relates that at the present time Moslems in Mesopotamia are following the example of the Egyptians and are founding, under the direction of some zealous 'Ulamā', Islamic charitable undertakings, and that the Arabic newspapers are publishing enthusiastic reports thereof without inserting one word of unkindness towards Christians. Fr. Bannerth is of opinion that Western Christianity must welcome a religious revival of Islam, such as is now developing, Christianity being a factor in the new cultural self-expression of the rising Islamic nations. The conception of God, he says, is relatively pure in Islam. As the conversion of the great bloc of Islamic nations to the Christian faith is not to be expected in our century, " *it is*," he continues, " *of the highest value that Islam at least maintains the belief in God in purified forms*. If this refuge of belief in God should vanish, then Western Christianity will be threatened by a new seat of danger. The consequences of the vanishing of the last ethical ties can be seen already in the emancipated Turkey of to-day."

The third undeniable fact is this : There is really, in the Arabic-speaking Near East, a strong religious, ethical and social revival of Islam, and this revived Islam is taken to be the basis of a renewed national life.

The fourth fact is this : Given the tendencies and circumstances stated above, the conversion of this Islamic community to the Christian faith is now impossible.

Now, with respect to these facts, three questions may be asked.

First : Will Christian Missions be content with the friendly and intense collaboration of native Oriental Christians and Moslems in the cultural renewal of the East and with the salutary effects produced by such a collaboration ?

Secondly : Will Christian Missions object to the revival of Islam in the manner described, and to religion, although Islamic, being taken to be the basis of a sound national life ? Given the fourth fact—the impossibility of conversion to Christianity under present circumstances—, the alternative before these Islamic nations is only : either the revival of Islam, or materialism and moral decay. Which of the two will be in the interest of Christian Missions ? Which will be in the interest of the *Islamic nations*, whose welfare will undoubtedly be very dear to true Christians?

Thirdly: What will Christian Missions infer from this state of things? Certainly, there can be no objection to "expounding the beauties of the Christian faith," as was said by the Y.M.M.A., and to showing a true Christian life and true Christian deeds. There may be salutary effects produced in this way. But attacks on Islam are of no use. I am sorry to say that such attacks have occurred, not only in Egypt. It does not matter where they occur, and whether they occur in German or English books, pamphlets, newspapers, reviews and lectures. There are too many Moslems nowadays who understand English, German and French, and who read all that is printed, and hear all that is said at public lectures about Islam. Such attacks will neither convert any Moslem, nor, of course, hinder the revival of Islam—on the contrary, they will strengthen it; but, in addition, they will also poison the atmosphere, create troubles in the friendly intercourse of Moslems and Christians in the East, and deepen the gap between the East and the West—effects contrary to the interest of the Christian Missions themselves, as well as to the desirable general settlement of the relations between the East and the West.

WHITHER ISLAM?

I have now to add a few words about those parts of Western Asia in which Arabic is not spoken : Turkey, Persia and Afghanistan. Having no personal knowledge of these countries, I collect my information from authentic sources and the best first-hand authorities, especially, as to Turkey, from what is to be found in the valuable publications of Dr. Jäschke and from his personal communications to me.

There is no Islamic movement in *Turkey*. The great war and, after the war, the new order of public life, have not allowed ideas of reform like those of Sa'īd Halīm Pasha to be continued ; some other similar ideas which were said to be there in 1928 have not been developed. There is nowadays no basis left in Turkey for religious development. The Turkish Constitution of the 20th April, 1924, declared Islam to be the religion of Turkey (Art. 2) and provided a religious oath to be taken by the deputies and the President of the Republic (Arts. 16 and 38). Another article seemed to admit the possibility of enacting regulations of the Muhammadan religious law (*sharī'ah*). But all these provisions seem to have been a mere compromise, which, only four years later, was given up ; in fact, by law 1222 of the 10th April, 1928, they were abrogated. Turkey is now no longer an Islamic State. There is no Islamic teaching in the schools; there is a kind of moral instruction in the Training College and in the middle classes of the primary schools, but not in the lower or higher classes, and there is nothing of that kind in the secondary schools. Arabic and Persian are not permitted to be taught in the schools, not even optionally. There is one Professor at Stambul University who is allowed to give private lessons in Arabic and Persian, but only up to 3 pupils. More than 3 pupils would be regarded as a " School," which would need the approval of the authorities, and such an approval would not be given. The compulsory substitution of the Latin alphabet for the Arabic makes the reading of the Arabic Koran and religious books in any Islamic language impossible. The *tekkes* or monasteries of the religious orders and the *turbes* or the tombs of saints are closed ; nobody is allowed to enter them. The religious exercises of the *zikr* are forbidden, even at home. Only the five prayers prescribed by official Islam are allowed and are still seen, even in public, although seldom. The authorities in Turkey disapprove of Islam. Mosques are not closed, except in a few cases ; but the number of the religious officials has been greatly diminished. These officials, who are appointed by the authorities, are strictly watched over in their sermons and all their actions ; if they show the least attempt to act against the will of the present Government, they are removed. How, under these circumstances, can any religious movement gain ground in Turkey? The country is, on the other hand, wide open to Western civilization, and to what is bad in it. But Islam is certainly not dead in Turkey. I am told by friends that the mosques are now even more crowded than before the war. But one must be careful in interpreting this fact. There may be in it a good deal of obstinacy against the Turkish Government. Is it a revival of Islam? The Beyrouth newspaper *L'Orient* published in its No. 127, of Saturday, 28th February, 1931, an article entitled: *Coran et Laïcité*, of which a German version has been published in German missionary Reviews, the title being changed to: " The religious awakening of Turkey." The author of the French article points to the fact referred to and derives from it conclusions which have no solid foundation. The author of the German version of this article, giving rather a recast of it than a translation, discovered even more in the original article than it contains. The translation is very inexact, and there are sentences and ideas inserted which belong exclusively to the translator, so that the German article gives, as a whole, a complete misrepresentation of things.

It may be that the present policy of the Turkish Government will not last for ever. What will happen in future, should it be changed, nobody can say to-day.

As to *Persia*, it seems that one cannot speak of modern Islamic movements here either. Certainly, the Persian Government has not expelled Islam from public life, as Turkey has done. The Persian

Constitution of 1906–1907, modified in 1909 and 1925, has a national and religious character; in religious matters it is even conservative. The matrimonial laws of August 15th, 1931, introduce reforms in an important part of religious law, but in a rather prudent and sound way. The Government has also introduced some reforms in public life, and Western science into public schools, but the Persian young men themselves do not seem prepared to make much use of this science. There is now in Persia a kind of intermediate state of mind. There is no great warmth in the Persians' attachment to the old forms of Islamic religion, nor is there a strong impulse towards a new order of things. Baha'ism too seems to be stationary. Perhaps the condition of things in Persia depends to a great extent on racial and historical factors. At any rate, as things are now, it is difficult to say how future development may go on.

Afghanistan was left as the only independent Islamic State of the Sunnite bloc, and its ruler Amānullāh may have been conscious of fulfilling an essential condition for his election as Caliph. He tried to introduce reforms by the Constitution of 1923–1924 and the Penal Code promulgated at the same time. But his country was not prepared for such reforms. After five years of unsettlement and disturbance Amānullāh finally lost his throne. Now, under Nādir Shah, things are more settled. But as yet circumstances do not seem to have favoured the organic growth of spiritual development.

It is a strange fact that from here once came that renowned reformer, Jamāl ad-Dīn al-Afghānī, who went to the West and came to Egypt, where he exercised a great influence. He and his disciple, Mohammed 'Abduh, sowed in Egypt seeds which took firm root, and the crops are now ripening and scattering their seed more and more widely, whereas, in the regions whence the reformer came, sterility seems to reign. But already other Islamic countries partake of the crop which grew in Egypt. Will the time come when also the regions whence the seed was brought will have a share in the fruit and sow some of its seeds in their own ground? Then it may take root all the more firmly. Its vitality has been proved.

INDIA

By LIEUT.-COL. M. L. FERRAR

CHAPTER IV

INDIA

By LIEUT.-COL. M. L. FERRAR

ANY STUDY of the past and present conditions of the Moslems of India must be based on a full consideration of two important factors which from the earliest days of Islam have profoundly influenced their development and modified their characteristics. The first has been their isolation behind formidable physical barriers and the second their Hindu environment. These two factors produced the Moslem India of 150 years ago, but to them must be added two more, the advent of British rule and the contact and influence of the West. Owing to the immense improvement in all conditions of travel and communication this last factor is now the prime one for consideration but must await its turn. We will begin with the first two.

The general distribution of Islam has already been given in the introductory chapter of this book. There is, we were shown, a solid block of Islamic countries having its centre in the Middle East and stretching out strong arms to Morocco in the West and Mongolia in the East. The South-East border line of this block is politically conterminous with the North-West frontier of India although, as will presently appear, there is a sufficiently homogeneous Moslem population along that frontier for the border line of the Islamic block to be advanced to the River Indus. The Central block has an almost completely Moslem population and, with the exception of parts of Northern Africa that have come under Christian rule and parts of Asia that have recently been absorbed into the Union of Socialist Soviet Republics, has remained continuously for 1,200 years under Moslem control, has enjoyed Moslem institutions and retained an unbroken tradition of Moslem culture interrupted only by the great Mongol catastrophe. Very different have been the conditions under which Moslems have lived in India. The Ocean, so dreaded by the Indo-Iranian peoples, nevertheless has been and still remains the safest and most expeditious route for Indian pilgrims to the Holy Places of the Hijaz; the land frontier has offered no less serious an obstacle, and the deserts of Baluchistan and the great mountain ranges of the Sulaimans and the Hindu Kush with their virile robber tribes have ever formed a barrier to be passed only by a successful General and kept open for so long only as he or his descendants could maintain their power. In spite of some centuries of military conquest accompanied as often as not by forcible conversion; in spite of seven centuries of autocratic Moslem rule over Hindustan and other parts of Northern India; in spite of successful, if intermittent, preaching by Moslem missionaries, whose triumphs seem to have been ignored for the most part by Court historians and to have first received adequate recognition from a non-Moslem, Sir Thomas Arnold ; in spite of the friendly tolerance of Islam, which knows no caste but regards all men as brothers and has in consequence attracted millions of humble outcasts and untouchables into its fold, India to-day not only has a non-Moslem Government but a population more than three-quarters non-Moslem. The Government is British and the mass of the population is Hindu.

In the eyes of the early invaders the Hindu polytheists were not *Ahlu'lkitab*, that is to say followers of a revealed religion but *Kāfirs*, infidels, whose country was *Dāru'lharb* and whose lives were forfeit unless they embraced Islam. It is clear, whatever modern Moslem writers may say, that in the beginning there were systematic efforts at forcible conversion, but as I have already said, the invaders' first difficulty lay in the physical bulwarks of the country, which limited their numbers and jeopardized their communications. Thus hampered they would have found any people hard to convert by force, let alone persuasion, but the Hindus were no ordinary people. Their caste system and the penalties it imposed on those who deviated from it and also their outlook on life made any conversion of the better-born Hindus difficult, while their division into many petty States made rapid conquest through the defeat of one principal ruler impossible. Though for several centuries efforts were made by some of the more bigoted of the conquerors to impose their religion on the conquered by force, it was early recognized that the Moslems must in the main be content to be the rulers and to give their Hindu subjects the status of *dhimmis*, to which under a strict interpretation of the *Sharī'at* they could not become entitled. The case of those lower in the Hindu system and those actually beyond the pale was different, and partly through the prestige of the new rulers and partly through a desire to better their state under the more generous and brotherly conditions of Islam and partly too in response to the preaching of Moslem missionaries large numbers of low caste and outcaste Hindus embraced Islam. India nevertheless remains a Hindu country.

If we exclude the Indus valley and Baluchistan there is only one predominatingly Moslem tract in India, that is Eastern Bengal. Even in Delhi, for many centuries the capital of a Moslem Empire, less than one third of the inhabitants are Moslem. Lucknow, a city with similar traditions of Moslem supremacy, contains less than forty per cent. Moslems. Hyderabad, the chief and the only large Moslem-ruled State, had only ten per cent. Moslems, mainly living in the capital of the State. In Southern India Moslems form only five per cent. of the total population. As a rule it is

INDIA

found that where the percentage of Moslems to the total population is low, as in the Deccan, they are found mainly in the cities. Where the percentage is high, as in Eastern Bengal and the Punjab, Moslems are found as agriculturalists. Along the Indus and beyond it the percentage of Moslems rises to over ninety and the people are in many respects a true Moslem people.

Some particulars regarding the principal groups of Indian Moslems may be recorded here. By far the largest block is to be found in Eastern Bengal, where the rural population is almost exclusively Moslem and has been so for a great number of centuries. To these Bengalis religion is a very real thing and signs of religious activity abound. Mosques form a conspicuous feature of the countryside, religious instruction of the young is universal, and from time to time during the past hundred years successive widespread religious revivals have occurred, which have been generally of a puritanical type and which have eliminated much of the taint of Hinduism that formerly existed. Popular preachers draw large congregations and it is the ambition of every self-respecting man to perform the pilgrimage to Mecca. There is no rush to the towns, for the people prefer to live on their scattered homesteads and to till their exiguous patches of rice land, which average only two and a half acres per cultivator. The absence of villages, the difficulties of communication, the general dearth of any well-to-do class, but chiefly the very great backwardness in education, prevent the growth of corporate life and civic responsibility, and so it is that while, as the Bengal census report for 1921 claims, Bengal may be the great stronghold of Islam in India, its Moslem inhabitants do not contribute a share in the advancement of the Moslems of India as a whole which is proportionate to their numbers. At the 1921 census the province of Bengal contained 25,000,000 Moslems out of a total population of some 47,000,000. The proportion of Moslems to others in the province is growing steadily. Next in numerical strength comes the Punjab with 11,500,000 Moslems out of 20,700,000 inhabitants. The West and North-West of the province are almost solidly Moslem. In the U.P. 6,500,000, that is fifteen per cent. of the total population, are Moslem. This low percentage is interesting, for the whole province was under Moslem domination from the 12th century onwards. In Sind seventy-three per cent. and in Baluchistan and the Frontier Province over ninety per cent. are Moslems, but it is in the Punjab and Hindustan, i.e. Delhi, Agra and Oudh, that we must look for the men and the organizations that are necessary to give the Moslems of India the lead that they require.

The average town Moslem can seldom retain an environment of Islam about him. At the best he may live in a Moslem quarter or a Moslem street but as often as not he has only to leave his front door to find himself among people whose every thought runs counter to his, whose clothes have another cut, whose hair is differently trimmed and whose standards and habits and ways of life draw a sharp dividing line between him and them. The village Moslem is somewhat better off, for a village community in the North at least is usually homogeneous. How far is the average stay-at-home Indian Moslem conscious of this loss of full Moslem environment ? To me my first impressions of the North-West frontier 34 years ago are still vividly fresh. My first year of Indian service had been spent at Bareilly in the United Provinces, where only one man in five is a Moslem. Serving there in a regiment of local Indian Moslems I studied Moslem languages and read books on travel in Moslem lands. The regiment was suddenly transferred across the Indus to Kohat, where I found myself still in British India but as though in a foreign Moslem land and the full Moslem flavour of it all gave me a thrill of pleasure and excitement that I have never forgotten. If these were the emotions of a Christian it can be realized what the Moslems of my regiment, born and bred in Hindu India, must have felt and what a realization of loss thay must have experienced. Some observers, on the other hand, deny that isolation in a pagan land has been detrimental to the Indian Moslem and even hold that it has been to his benefit ; that he

WHITHER ISLAM?

has thereby held the more firmly to the essentials of Islam and is a better Moslem than his brethren in the true Islamic countries, but few within or without the ranks of the Indian Moslems will accept this assertion.

Let us next consider the numbers of the Indian Musalmans. The country in which they form a scattered minority is so vast that their total by the census of 1931 comes to 77,000,000 and they therefore form one quarter of the entire Moslem population of the globe. To see how they are composed it is necessary to refer to the details of the census of ten years ago when they totalled 68,000,000. Of this total it was estimated that less than 5,000,000 were of foreign origin, descendants of Arab, Persian, Turk or Afghan immigrants. The remainder, 63,000,000, were converts or descendants of converts from Hinduism and its satellite creeds. More than half of this large number were of humble origin but some of the higher castes of Hindus must long ago have also supplied many recruits. Thus in 1921 of the Rajputs no less than seventy per cent. were Musalman while forty-seven per cent. of the Jats were also Moslems. It is significant that the Moslem population has increased its strength by no less than thirteen per cent. in the last ten years and thus continues to exhibit a much quicker rate of growth than that of the Hindus. " Fifty years ago," says H.H. the Agha Khan, " the Moslems were one-fifth of the population, to-day they are one-fourth and before our children are middle-aged men they will be one-third." This estimate must be discounted by the fact that the Hindus have increased by ten per cent., but nevertheless the Moslem proportion is steadily increasing. This rapidity of increase in India is probably being paralleled in other parts of the Moslem world which are under alien government or control and is in sharp contrast with the more stationary conditions in autonomous Moslem lands. A point of general application not to be lost sight of is the difference in reaction to Western influences that may be expected from autonomous and non-autonomous Moslem populations. In the latter there is more contact with the West but there is more individual freedom and the Moslem subject may use his own will in adhering to or modifying his thoughts or his ways. In the former there is an autocrat who decides for the people whether they shall retain a narrow outlook as in Arabia or proceed to the other extreme as in Turkey and place religion entirely on one side. To return to India. The size of the Moslem population, the rapidity of its increase and the closeness of contact of its educated members with Western civilization and Western influences give the community a very special importance in the Moslem world generally, an importance which has only in 1930 received due recognition in the shape of Dr. Titus' comprehensive handbook entitled *Indian Islam*. This work and Dr. Kraemer's recent article "Islam in India," which appeared in 1931 in the *Moslem World*, form valuable contributions to the study of their subject. Dr. Kraemer's interpretation of the psychology of the Indian Moslem appears to have particular value.

One-third of the Indian Musalmans live in Eastern Bengal in a state of considerable isolation. Their language is Bengali and few know any other. Of the rest the great bulk speak Urdu as their mother tongue or as a *lingua franca*, though there are communities in Sind, Gujarat, Malabar and elsewhere who resemble the Bengalis in their linguistic isolation. For the Musalmans of India generally the Urdu language comes second only to their religion as a bond of unity generally and is in daily use by the entire mass of Northern Moslems, who, having a tradition of rule and having the most bodily and mental vigour and the most cohesion, lead the way in all religious, educational and social progress of the present day, and whose reactions to Western influences are the more likely to be followed by the rest of the community.

It is advisable therefore to study the trend of thought and the activities of these men of Hindustan and the North if we are to understand the lines of advance that are likely to be followed and the nature of the developments that are likely to occur.

Far away in the Deccan there is another focus for inspiration and leadership—Hyderabad, the last of the old Mughal provinces. On this state and its Moslem ruler and his determination to stimulate Moslem culture through an Urdu medium rest the hopes of many Moslem patriots.

Examining once more the census figures for 1921, we find that of the 68,000,000 Moslems in India about 63,000,000 were Sunnis and the rest Shi'as. Of the Sunnis, 48,000,000 were Hanafis and another 10,000,000 were described as Wahhabis. Of the five and half million Shi'as less than ten per cent. were Ismailis. The Ismailis are split up into two branches, the Bohras and the Khojas. The leader of these last is the Agha Khan and it is significant of the necessity for united action that the general body of Indian Moslems should gladly accept as one of their chief leaders a man whom they must regard as a religious schismatic. Among the masses of the Hanafi Sunnis there is almost universal saint worship and great numbers of the same sect belong to various orders of Sufiism. These practices are not confined to India and need little comment.

Most observers hold that saint worship still retains its old fascination as something more satisfying and more conducive to the peace of mind of those who practise it than the more orthodox religious observances enjoined by the *Sharī'at*. Christian writers find in this a proof of their contention that the average Moslem needs a more personal relationship with God than they consider he can obtain through the conception of God as an impersonal, supreme and all-powerful Being. A Moslem friend of mine who holds high Civil rank and is thus a dispenser of patronage tells me that he finds that the *Pirs*, or religious leaders, who occupy some of the shrines in Northern India are beginning to find their spiritual hold on the people is slackening. Accordingly they have begun to ask for temporal forms of power such as honorary magistrateships.

Peculiar to India is the reaction of Islam to its unyielding pagan surroundings. I do not allude to the well-known efforts of the Emperor Akbar and some of his courtiers and later of his great grandson Dara Shikoh to find common religious ground with the Hindus on a basis of mysticism of which there has been a recent echo in the pronouncements of Mirza Ghulam Ahmad, nor yet to the definite borrowings from Hinduism of some of the Sufi doctrines and practices, but rather to the tolerance which arose from social contacts, to the assumption in a minor degree of the Hindu caste system and to the very mixed religious observances of large groups of Moslems whose conversion from Hinduism in ages past must have been summary and incomplete. It has been explained that the Moslem conquerors of Hindustan very soon discovered that to uphold Islam as a rigid polity, as an all embracing Church-State in which infidels had no place, was impracticable on every ground. Compromise was inevitable. The earliest contacts with the Hindu population were made through the institutions of marriage, concubinage or slavery. There were also the necessary dealings between the Moslem rulers and the Hindu shopkeepers, artisans and cultivators, following on the latter receiving a definite status as *dhimmis*. Later came admission to the army and to office, until under the Mughal Emperors periods of extreme tolerance and severe repression alternated. Long before the accession to power of the British the *jizyah* (poll tax) had been abolished and superficially at least the two communities lived at harmony with each other.

The polytheistic all embracing tolerance of the Hindu engendered something of a contemptuous tolerance in the Musalman. One hundred years ago the communities displayed a grudging politeness to each other which could progress no further. Real social fusion was impossible. The necessities of the situation produced one interesting modification. The tolerance which Moslems found they must display towards the Hindus was also exercised towards followers of other religions and in India there has never been that open contempt for and abhorrence of the non-Moslems which has been so much in evidence until the most recent times in the autonomous Moslem States.

With regard to caste there are three main manifestations. There are in the first place agricultural tribes proud of their origin and their genealogy and found in the greatest purity in Northern India. A member of one of these will say he is of such and such a race and such and such a clan. His name, his personal law and many of his customs may all show clear signs of Hindu origin. At the other end of the scale are the men who follow lowly occupations or whose ancestors were imperfectly converted. These will adhere to their vocational name or their old Hindu caste. In a third category may be placed the social climbers. For them is employed an arbitrary four caste Moslem scale analogous to the Brahman, Kshatri, Vaish and Sudra scale of the Hindus, the converts from among whom make much use of it. This table of precedence is perhaps most popular in the United Provinces and was even adopted mistakenly by the Army forty years ago with mildly humorous consequences. Hindustani Moslem recruits found to their surprise that they must enlist as Sayyids, Mughals, Pathans or Shaykhs. No one dared to style himself a Sayyid who had not been born one, but there were dubious Mughals to be met with in the ranks, while hundreds of Ahirs, Gujars and other simple folk had to choose, much to their own embarrassment, whether they would be called Pathans or Shaykhs.

On the subject of incomplete conversion I will quote Dr. Titus. He says:

" In a land like India, where the majority of the

Moslem population has been recruited from Hindu caste and outcaste groups by mass conversion, whether from fear of military power, or to attain some desirable object, or because of persuasion, complete Islamization of the converts has not been accomplished. There are great sections of the Moslem community, here and there, which reveal their Hindu origin in their religious and social life almost at every turn, constituting a curious mixture of the old and the new. There is little wonder that this should be so. The Moslem armies moved over the country in wave after wave for centuries, from Peshawar to Dacca and beyond, and from the Himalayas to the southern end of the peninsula. It often happened that hastily converted peoples were left behind after the army moved on. These had been given but scant instruction in the new faith, and were left to remember and practise what they could. The pressure of the old idolatrous surroundings upon them was great. Not only their neighbours, but many of their relatives in other places were still Hindu. Little wonder that the worship of the village godlings went on as before, that animistic beliefs continued, that Brahman priests were still employed, and Hindu festivals observed. The wonder is, not that these hereditary customs and beliefs were adhered to, but that any belief in Islam remained at all."

Other observers such as Risley and Crooke, in census reports, gazetteers and elsewhere, have given a mass of information on the subject of the Hindu beliefs, rites and customs followed by these large communities of semi-Moslems, some of whom are so equally divided in their leanings that they have recently become the object of solicitous attention by reformers on both sides. There are castes which not only neglect the five cardinal observances of Islam but worship Hindu deities, great and small, avoid eating beef, employ Brahmans as their family priests and follow a hundred and one superstitions of Hindu or animistic origin. These communities are for the most part backward and uneducated. Their condition has excited the attention of reformers and it can be safely assumed that through the efforts of the latter and through education and increased contact with purer forms of Islam they will tend to become more orthodox, or, if orthodoxy is a word to be avoided, we may say that they will tend to come into line with general Moslem thought and practice.

Another source of confusion for the more orthodox Indian Moslem is the regard paid to Moslem shrines by Hindus. At two shrines of which I have personal knowledge, that of Sālār Mas'ūd near Bahraich and that of Sakhi Sarwar near Dera Ghazi Khan, Hindu pilgrims are extremely numerous and their alms form a source of considerable income to the *mujāwirs* or keepers of the shrine. One cannot imagine a Zoroastrian or a Christian being allowed to enter a Moslem shrine in Persia or 'Irāq and make his intercession. The religious revival among the Sikhs which accompanied the Akali movement ten years ago led to the casting out of Hindu

INDIA

images from many of the older Sikh shrines and it may be that communal tension has led to the exclusion of Hindus from Moslem shrines of a similar catholic type.

Thus far I have endeavoured to give an account of the numbers and composition of the Indian Moslems and to draw attention to the special modifications arising out of their environment without reference to the effect produced by the assumption of power by the British and the levelling results of the restraint that they imposed. The historical facts are well known but must be mentioned here briefly. In the eighteenth century the Mughal Court at Delhi ceased to wield any power. Two great provinces, Oudh and Hyderabad, remained under Moslem rulers who feigned allegiance to the Delhi Emperor and yet were bound by treaties to the British. Moslem Sind was under its own rulers. Elsewhere bit by bit the Marathas, the British and the Sikhs assumed control. The Emperor found himself first the prisoner of the Marathas and then a pensioner of the British. The Moslems steadily lost ground until a little over a hundred years ago they found themselves in a position of inferiority and humiliation. For the next thirty years they received shock after shock. First came the unpalatable fact that from having been masters of the Hindus for 600 years they were now but their fellow-subjects under rulers so pledged to neutrality as to appear indifferent to the result of the struggle between the two communities for wealth and for the loaves and fishes of minor office and the influence that office carried in its train. Then came Macaulay and his momentous decision to introduce English as the medium for higher education. Soon there followed the abolition of Persian as the language of the courts and of the general administration. About the same time Macaulay's Penal Code was introduced and the *Qazis* who administered the *Sharī'at* had to make way for law officers who thereafter might be of any religion and would apply the *Sharī'at* to Moslems only in matters concerning personal relations such as marriage and inheritance and then only to the extent permitted by the alien ruler. The Musalmans found their prestige gone, their laws replaced, their language shelved and their education shorn of its monetary value. Then came more palpable blows —the annexations of Sind and Oudh and the crowning catastrophe of the Mutiny, which ended in the suppression of the last shadowy vestige of Imperial Mughal rule at Delhi and in extensive confiscation of Moslem property. This final disaster brought the Musalmans to the lowest depths of broken pride and black despair from which they seemed powerless to extricate themselves.

In his work on the influence of English on Urdu literature S. Abdu'l Latif writes of this period:

"There was now no place left in North India to which the Moslems could turn for help or support. Bereft of power and wealth they presented a pathetic spectacle. The gradual disintegration of their religious and social life in no small measure contributed to their political downfall . . . they disdained the pursuit of trade, commerce or industry. Their mainstay was administration and as they began to lose their political power their economic condition grew steadily worse."

During the early part of the nineteenth century there had been several notable movements which had grown mainly through the feeling of wounded pride and a desire to hold aloof and to remain on the defensive. As few of these movements have survived to the present day they need not be described here in detail. It is sufficient to say that they were of a simple puritanical " back to the Koran " type but they were accompanied by a mental outlook which helped to intensify the misery of the community after their collapse in 1857. Prompted by their bigoted spiritual leaders they refused to make use of the opportunities given them by the British to acquire Western learning. To give one instance out of many, there was for long a determined refusal to make use of the English classes started in the Delhi college in 1827. The Hindus, except for a few of the orthodox, had no scruples of this nature and by eagerly acquiring the new learning left their Moslem fellow countrymen still further behind. With a few exceptions like Hāfiz Nazīr Ahmad and Munshi Zakāu'llah the Moslems maintained this attitude for several years after the Mutiny, but their salvation was at hand. In their dark hour of despair they had need of a man to lead them out into the sunshine and to reconstruct their shattered world for them. They found him in Sir Sayyid Ahmad Khan. This pre-eminent champion of the Moslems was born at Delhi in 1817. Rather than take up a sinecure at the effete Mughal Court he entered the British service in 1836 when nineteen years old. Early promotion had secured him a responsible position when the Mutiny broke out. In its course he rendered loyal and valuable service to the British and at its conclusion he redoubled the efforts he had already started for the rehabilitation and advancement of his community. As the years pass and a truer perspective is obtained the greatness of this great leader becomes more apparent. Simplicity, straightness, tenacity of purpose, a cultured mind, imagination, fervour, personal magnetism—all these and many other qualities he possessed and put to good use. He saw that his community must first be acquitted of the charge of being the chief culprit in the Mutiny and then, having regained its good name, must accept the new order and find its salvation through the new learning. Accordingly he set to work and in 1877 after seventeen years of effort he succeeded in opening the Muhammadan Anglo-Oriental College at Aligarh, which ten years ago became as he had hoped a University. He had early realized that his community required a band of leaders whose education would have dispelled the illusory traditions of the past, removed baneful prejudices, inspired practical energy and made them good appreciative and therefore loyal citizens. His purpose, he declared at the opening ceremony, was to leaven the whole community by training and sending out men who would, said he, " preach the gospel of free enquiry, of large-hearted tolerance and of pure morality." The success of his aims has been immense. The leaven has spread and there is a wide school of men who have freely acquired the new while holding to all that is vital to them in the old. From this school come all those who are working to bring Islam into line with modern Western learning, ethics and economics, or as I think they would prefer it put, to show that Islam is not a confined and unprogressive faith but has a universal applicability and has in times past shown its power of adjustment to change and once more is doing so. To return to Sir Sayyid. His second foundation was the *Nadwatu 'l'ulamā* of Lucknow and its college, the *Dāru' l'ulūm*, for the better instruction of the Indian '*Ulamā* in the Arabic sciences in the light of modern requirements. These two institutions have also succeeded in their rather limited field. In addition to the University at Aligarh there are also Moslem Universities at Dacca and Delhi. There are also colleges in various places such as the Islamiya Colleges of Lahore and Peshawar, the Calcutta Madrasa and a Shi'a College at Lucknow and many High Schools throughout India. Another concrete result of the Aligarh movement has been the founding thirteen years ago of the Osmania University at Hyderabad by His Exalted Highness the present Nizam. This institution has taken its own line by imparting all main instruction in Urdu, and relegating English to an ancillary position. In connection with the University there is a special translation bureau which supplies by translation or otherwise all the Urdu text-books required for the University courses and incidentally produces standardized Urdu equivalents for all the original ideas or technical terms met with in the originals. The service performed by this University to the Urdu language and to the Moslem community for which that language forms so strong a bond of union is very great. Other institutions for the development of Urdu are the *Anjuman-i-taraqqi-yi-Urdu* of Aurangabad and two similar societies in the United Provinces. Other visible results of the Aligarh movement have been the starting all over the country of societies pledged to protect the interests of Islam and its followers. I will quote again from Dr. Titus. He says:

" Another organization of note is the All-India Muhammadan Educational Conference, which was founded in 1886, by Sir Sayyid Ahmad Khān, and has for its object the promotion of Western learning among Moslems. It has its permanent headquarters

INDIA

by the side of the Moslem University at Aligarh; and the conferences are held annually in different cities of India, usually in the north.

" The All-India Moslem League was organised in 1906, for the purpose of giving special attention to the political interests of the community, inasmuch as men had come to feel that the policy of Sir Sayyid, in abstaining from taking an active part in the political life of the country, had caused Moslem interests to suffer. With the exception of a number of years during the period of the Great War and after, when agreement on policies could not be reached, the league has functioned regularly through annual meetings, and through the establishment of provincial leagues, which are affiliated to the central organisation. Besides these, there is a veritable host of other anjumans, each seeking in its own way to serve the community, both locally and nationally. The learned theologians are served by the *Jamʿīyat-ul-ʿUlamā-i-Hind*, with provincial branches. The Central *Jamʿīyat-i-Tabligh-ul-Islām* (Society for the Propagation of Islam), with headquarters in Ambala City, Punjab, is a strong growing organisation of India-wide character, with not only provincial but district organizations as well. Its twofold task is said to be (1) to prevent apostasy by seeking to counteract the efforts of the Ārya Samāj Shuddhī Movement, and the work of Christian missions; and (2) to send missionaries to teach backward Moslems. Also in almost every important town there is an *Anjuman-i-Islāmīyah*, looking after the local Moslem educational interests,

One of the strongest of these is the *Anjuman-i-Himāyat-i-Islām*, of Lahore, which undertakes a variety of duties, such as the refutation of objections to Islam, the care of Moslem orphans, and the employment of preachers. It has established schools and orphanages, and maintains a college affiliated with the Punjab University."

Another very important sequel to Sir Sayyid's efforts was the birth of a new school of literature. The first impetus was given by Sir Sayyid himself through the medium of his periodical *Tahzību'l Akhlāq* the primary object of which, as its name implies, was the refinement or correction of manners, and in which he strove to remove the prejudices among Moslems regarding the seclusion and education of women and similar matters. The secondary object was to create a new literary taste. Up to Sir Sayyid's day all writers of Urdu prose or poetry had blindly followed Persian models without regard to the technical difficulties involved in the change of medium and without any attempt to escape from the rigid formalism which had crystallized six hundred years ago and which in the case of poetry prescribed the forms and metres which alone might be employed, limited the subjects, and discouraged the use of any allusions, metaphors or similes other than those which had already been stale for centuries. The two main forms in which poetry was cast were the ode and the eulogy. Both abounded in exaggeration and hyperbole. Prose was little better off, for here again form took precedence over meaning and it might require ten or fifteen lines of turgid rhodomontade to acquaint the reader with the fact that some king had marched his army three miles on a certain fine morning. The sterility, the absolutely deadening effect of such a literature is only too apparent. So long as artificial form, insincerity and circumlocution supplied the major part of the equipment of an author it was impossible for Sir Sayyid to call in literature to aid him in his main project, which was the adequate education of his co-religionists. But the common-sense example set by him in his magazine soon found imitators, and by degrees a band of writers came into being who have between them freed the language from the shackles which bound it and produced what they have termed the *nechari* or natural style. The ode and the eulogy with their conventional limited subjects and technique have practically disappeared and have been replaced by more suitable forms of verse which permit the poet all the freedom he may wish in form and in theme. The same has occurred in Urdu prose, which is now as catholic in its style and subject matter as that of any other civilized language of to-day, though it has still much leeway to make up as regards realism. Their new liberty was employed by Sir Sayyid's literary henchmen in producing works written with the set purpose of exhorting, stirring up and educating the Musalmans of India to the realities of the day and of expounding to them the changes which modern Islam must accept as the outcome of logical evolution from early Islam. Some, like Muhammad Shiblī Nu'mānī, became historians of the glorious past, others like Hāfiz Nazīr Ahmad Khān wrote novels or tales each with its own moral. The great poets of this epoch, Muhammad Husayn Azād and Sayyid Altāf Husayn Hālī, wrote many poems with the object of stirring up the Musalmans to a recognition of their evil plight for which they themselves were responsible and from which they must themselves discover and follow the way of escape. In his famous sextet " The Flow and Ebb of Islam," which no friend of the Indian Moslem can read unmoved, Hālī makes it clear to his brethren that the old attitude of fatalism must be abandoned, that fatalism which was the natural outcome of a religion whose very name implies surrender to the will of God, a God whose might, majesty, dominion and power are so continually stressed in the Koran. They must give up, says Hālī, the idea that Islam is immutable and must turn with ardour and enthusiasm towards the new learning and the new standpoint of the West, and assimilate from it all that is good. Mr. Abdu'llatīf quotes a passage from Sir Sayyid's *Tahzību'l Akhlāq* which is worth repeating here, since it explains the position which Sir Sayyid himself held regarding the

alleged immutability of Islam. Sir Sayyid wrote :—
" Religious learning among us is spoiled to a degree. The commands of God which that innocent, simple-minded, truthful and sweet-natured Prophet had communicated to the ignorant and illiterate dwellers of the desert in such a simple, clear and sincere manner have been so much distorted by such unwarranted importations into them of empty distinctions and subtleties, metaphysical propositions and arguments of logic, that their original simplicity has ceased to make its appeal, with the result that the Moslems have been obliged to neglect the real commands contained in the Koran and the authentic sayings, and to follow those invented by X, Y and Z."

Critics are inclined to hold that the present-day writers have receded from Sir Sayyid's position and no longer stress the need for acquiring Western learning and Western culture, but rather postulate the adequacy of the Koran as the sole foundation on which to build up the modern conception of Islam. Be that as it may, Sir Sayyid's work stands. If his aims have not yet been fully achieved, the way at least has been shown and much progress made. The praise bestowed on Sir Sayyid Ahmad Khān by all writers who have studied his life was fully earned. There is no good biography of Sir Sayyid in English. The right perspective can now be obtained and the time seems ripe for a proper account of his life, his aims and objects, and the extent to which they have been achieved.

I have mentioned the somewhat reactionary movements which started soon after the general spread of British rule and which in the main advocated a return to the fundamentals of the Faith as revealed by God in the Koran. In various parts of the country organizations still exist some of which date from that time while others appear to be more modern in origin and to have a wider if similar basis. The best known of these is the Ahl-i-Hadīth which accepts the Traditions as well as the Koran but rejects all subsequent interpretations which have crystallized into the Sunna, and from which the ordinary Sunni may not deviate. The Ahl-i-Hadīth appears to have a well-developed organization and to carry out a vigorous propaganda through its own schools, preachers and newspapers. One of the chief objects of the movement is to purge Indian Islam of the polytheistic and animistic practices which in greater or less extent are found almost universally among Indian Moslems. Like puritans in most other religions the Ahl-i-Hadīth are inclined to be narrow and bigoted and for this reason Kraemer holds their movement to be sterile and without a future. Another group call themselves Ahl-i-Qur'ān, a name which sufficiently discloses their position as fundamentalists. The group seems to have no corporate existence but the movement has left its mark through its suggestion of a particular line of thought, which is popular among the modernists, who rarely identify themselves with any particular group, but are inclined to stress the value of the Koran itself and, by neglecting or abrogating parts of the Sunna and indeed also of the Koran, to endeavour to bridge the gulf between the rigid formal practices of the uneducated and the enquiring, receptive and constructive thought of the cultured leaders of the present day.

This is really the crux of the matter. The new wine and the old bottles. Sir Sayyid's views have already been quoted. A later view is that of the Right Honourable Sayyid Amir Ali given in his *Spirit of Islam* published in 1891. The book is well known and has been subjected to considerable criticism. It is in the first place a defence of Islam and a rebuttal of the erroneous ideas alleged to be held by non-Moslems concerning that religion, which it then goes on to rationalize. I will quote without comment. Mr. Amir Ali says that enlightenment must precede reform and the mind must escape from bondage. Formalism that no longer appeals must be abandoned and we must judge by the use of reason and by our sense of what is right and fit at a particular time. Islam assimilates and its spirit will persist while its form may alter. If the Imams were free to use their judgment and boldly discard 500,000 and retain only 8,000 of the Traditions we must reserve to ourselves a similar liberty of action. Why should one consider that with the last recension of the Traditions the whole of Islam should become as though cast in an immutable mould. The culture and civilization of the Persians had been of great value to the Arab founders of Islam. Close contact with the civilization of the West, says Amir Ali, will be of similar benefit to modern-day Islam. Another writer of the same way of thought is Maulavi Chirāgh Ali. More recently there is Shaykh Khudā Bakhsh of Calcutta who in fact continues his theme at the present day.[1] Not long ago, writing in the same rationalist strain as Sayyid Amir Ali, he said :

"Islam must be on the defensive against the West. We must use the weapons forged in the West. Everywhere we see Western education, Western methods, Western ways of agitation, Western social customs and the Western call for freedom and self-determination. But this wave of westernism has not weakened Islam but drawn us closer to it. Alzurkani said 200 years ago ' Decisions may be made in the measure of new circumstances.' Such is the true spirit of Islam. Universalism is its key ; the unity of God its battlecry ; the brotherhood of man its cardinal tenet ; a will to conquer its aspiration. The rest is the creation of theology and not essential to Islam."

There are many other writers and publicists among the cultured Moslems of modern India who unite in presenting to the world a picture of early Islam very different from that conveyed by Moslem writers and

[1] He has died since the above was written.

historians in the past. This picture conveys to the non-Moslem an impression of Islam which he has never received before, one with more love and kindness and wide humanity in it than he has previously been able to visualize. From the point of view of pure criticism this presentation of their case must be styled an apologetic and should be subjected to scrutiny, but those who are not prepared to enter into the field of criticism will accept it gladly as a contribution to the general fund of humanitarian thought in the world we live in. The average Englishman, either from disinclination or from diffidence or, if a Government official in India, through the requirements of his official position, does not wish as a rule to probe deeply into the religion of other races, and accordingly while the outward forms and requirements of Islam are tolerably well known there are not many Englishmen other than missionaries and educationalists who are acquainted with the nature of the new thoughts which are occupying the minds of educated Indian Moslems and to which from time to time they give expression in their writings. It seems to be of more value to the general happiness of all concerned that we should accept this apologetic gladly at its face value. If we must criticize let us at the most put down this change in presentation of their case to the softening influence produced by contact with an allied faith.

At the present time the most profound thinker

WHITHER ISLAM?

among Indian Musalmans is the poet philosopher Sir Muhammad Iqbal of Lahore. After making his name as an Urdu poet he wrote two poems of great merit in Persian, the *Asrār-i-Khudi* and the *Asrār-i-Bekhudi*, and he has recently published in volume form six essays on Islam which he delivered last year to the students of different Universities in India. Also last year when President of the All-India Moslem League he delivered a most interesting address on his conception of what Islam in India should be. For my present purpose it is of more interest to examine Iqbal's beliefs regarding the evolution of Islam and its future in India than to attempt to fathom the depths of his philosopy as revealed in the first five essays of his new book. What strikes one first in Iqbal is the strength and the fervour of his love for Islam as an ideal which if fully realized should suffice for Man's every want in this world and the next. His wide reading and his poetic temperament have created in his mind so attractive and so inspiring a picture of the simplicity, the force and the appeal of early Islam that his main preoccupation centres round a return to that simple creed in order to regain what he believes Islam to have lost. In the first of his essays he stresses the stagnation of religious thought in Islam for the past five hundred years. He is uneasy at finding that whereas at one time European thought received its inspiration from Islam the converse now holds good, and he even goes so far as to say that the most remarkable phenomenon of Moslem history is the enormous rapidity with which the world of Islam is spiritually moving towards the West. He fears that Islam may be content with the dazzling exterior of European culture and fail to receive its inner message. The extension of his power over Nature has given Man a new faith and it has logically followed that the younger generation of Islam now demands a fresh orientation of its belief. At the same time Iqbal is apprehensive of the danger to Islam of an extension of Soviet atheism across the ancient Moslem countries of Central Asia. On both these grounds there is a desperate need to take stock of the situation and after a restatement of values to make a fresh start.

In a conversation with the writer, Iqbal ascribed the present failure of Islam to its surprising spread in the first century of its existence. The fundamental idea had been to bring men together into a great brotherhood; hence institutions such as congregational prayer, to be carried out under rigidly prescribed forms and directed towards one universally sacred spot, to which also was to be made the annual pilgrimage; hence also the absence of a priesthood and its assumption of exclusiveness and authority, also indeed the absence of all class barriers. This great conception was thwarted by the unexpected political successes of the Arabs and by the resultant imperialistic

WHITHER ISLAM?

mould from which Islam took its shape and which also impressed itself upon the *Sharī'at*, to which it imparted an immutability that was never intended by the founder of the faith. The Mu'tazilite or rationalist movement in the time of the Abbasides drove the conservatives of that period to take refuge behind a completely rigid religious and social code. The more independent of the thinkers rebelled against this worship of form (*zāhir*) and adopted the Sufiistic cult of the hidden reality (*bātin*), and the general run of Moslems found themselves committed to follow intellectual mediocrities who forbade any deviation from the formalism of the recognized schools of jurisprudence. For centuries Islam remained as though in a chrysalis state until the rise of the Wahhabis in the eighteenth century led the way for other reformers with wider and more receptive ideas. And so we arrive at present-day efforts at reform which, says Iqbal, in his sixth lecture, are all of the nature of *ijtihād*. The doctrine of *ijtihād* has been discussed by every writer on Islam. The word implies " personal exertion " on the part of some authority who uses his own judgment in coming to a decision in a religious matter in place of accepting former precedent. The common view is that the permissive employment of this discretion ceased in the fourth century after the Hijra, since when *taqlīd* or conformance with established precedent has been compulsory, but the modernists seek to " reopen the door " of *ijtihād* and we have Iqbal asserting in these lectures that the decision of the Turks to abolish the Caliphate was a perfectly sound exercise of their right to do so. Now we come to Iqbal's remedy for present ills. The great danger that he sees for Islam lies in the growth of the spirit of nationalism of which there is so much evidence in most Islamic countries. The Persians, whose very schism was nationalistic, have long taken pride in their pre-Islamic history, but a similar race consciousness is now well developed in Turkey and Egypt, whose peoples have begun to glory in their ancient pagan history with its Khaqans and its Pharaohs. Even Zaghlul Pasha, the late democratic leader of the Egyptians, is to be buried in a common Valhalla with a couple of score of mummied Pharaohs. Alone in India, with the exception of a small party which under the lead of Dr. Ansari has thrown in its lot with the Hindu Swarājists, do we find the Moslems refusing to draw any patriotic or cultural inspiration from the ancient history of the land to which in most cases they owe their origin. Just as until recently they were the most interested of the Moslem communities in Pan-Islamism, so it would seem that with the collapse of that policy they are now of all Islamic peoples the most interested in the creation of a kind of Moslem internationalism. It is in this last-named system that Iqbal sees the only way of salvation for Islam. His final dictum on this point is that

WHITHER ISLAM?

" Islam is neither Nationalism nor Imperialism but a League of Nations, which recognises artificial boundaries and racial distinctions for facility of reference only and not for restricting the social horizon of its members."

I may say in parenthesis that it is interesting to be told this by an Oriental at a time when so many Europeans feel the need of immediate recourse to some degree of international control of armaments, finance and commerce in order, so they believe, to keep Europe, and in fact the whole modern world, from a catastrophic crash.

What Iqbal's concrete political proposals are will be given presently.

We have seen that education was regarded by Sir Sayyid Amad Khān as the chief instrument for the rescue and the advancement of his people, but education of a new type which was to keep the Moslem a good Moslem, in fact a better Moslem than before. He was to shake off the obsolete bonds created by jurists and follow a simpler faith, at the same time he was to profit by all that was good in the new learning and thereby keep abreast of others in the pursuit of all rightful forms of temporal happiness. All the leaders of the community since Sir Sayyid's time have been in agreement on the main principle that education is the prime necessity for all, so also the Moslems of all classes and kinds with whom I have ever myself personally come into contact, and of these latter none more sincerely and even passionately than the ordinary peasants and yeomen on the land. These last named are very largely illiterate but have a very definite feeling that their illiteracy has cost them dear and that their sons at least must get some learning so that they may hold their own in the battle of life. What is the present state of education? The higher institutions have already received a brief notice. They combine religious secular and cultural learning. Let us consider now the secular aspect.

The latest account of education in India is to be found in the Hartog Committee's report. This committee was formed to enquire into the standard of education in British India mainly with the object of supplying data on which to justify a widening of the franchise in the new India that is being planned. The census figures relating to 1921 show 9.3 per cent. of Moslem males and 9 per cent. of Molsem females of all India to be literate, but the Hartog report states that there has been a great advance in Moslem education during the past fifteen years. A curious feature is that the enrolment of Moslem children in primary schools is ahead of that of other communities and this is especially so where Moslems form a minority of the population. This would appear to bear out in one minute respect the contention previously alluded to that isolation acts as a stimulus to the Indian Moslem, but there, at enrolment, the advantage stops. At each higher rung of the educational ladder more and more of the Moslem pupils drop out, the tendency being more marked among the girls than among the boys. A cause of this rapid wastage is the general poverty of the Moslems who consist largely of cultivators and petty traders. This poverty negatives much of the constant effort of the Government to find a remedy for the backward state of the community. A further difficulty is the prevalence in several provinces, with the notable exception of the Punjab, of what the report terms "special" institutions, in which the courses differ considerably from those in ordinary schools and include teaching in Islamic religion and culture. It is held by the Committee that the continuance of these schools on a large scale is prejudicial to the interests of Moslems and the report says:

"The time is ripe and more than ripe for a determined effort to devise practical plans to transfer the pupils to ordinary schools and colleges and to provide them there with opportunities for religious instruction and observance."

This recommendation met with the strong disapproval of a Hindu member of the Committee, and I am unaware what action has been taken on it. I may repeat, however, that the present-day leaders of the Moslem community recognize as clearly as ever Sir Sayyid Ahmad Khān did that the salvation of the

INDIA

Moslems lies in education, and it can be assumed with certainty that they will make education the chief medium for the attainment of their general aims. Certain also it is that the community will not come into its own until the disparity in educational standards between the sexes is lessened and Moslem women can take a greater share in moulding the thought and guiding the activities of their men. The aims of Sir Sayyid and his lieutenants have made less progress in this particular than was hoped, and very much remains to be done. The desire on the part of parents to get their girls educated is increasing but is hampered by social customs. Where these can be put aside progress will be more rapid. I have had a personal experience which will serve in a small way to illustrate this contention. In the Andamans there is a small, young but completely self-contained colony of Mappillas. Removed from the trammels of their home environment in Malabar they already show interesting signs of progress, the chief being their desire to educate their girls. In each of their village schools may now be seen all the boys and girls of school-going age studying together and even joining in the same physical training classes, to the evident satisfaction of their fathers. The same thing may be expected on a larger scale elsewhere.

The special schools or Maktabs mentioned above are found mainly where there is a fairly homogeneous

Moslem population or where religious zeal runs high. Eastern Bengal abounds in them, also the N.W. Frontier and the Mappilla tracts of Malabar. The teachers for these schools are obtained locally from religious training schools, termed Madrasahs, but in Hindustan they are often trained at the famous Dāru'l'ulūm at Deoband in Saharanpur. This is the centre of the orthodox Sunni 'Ulamā of India. The 'Ulamā have also their organization at Delhi, the Jam'īatu'l'ulamā, to which difficult matters are referred which affect religious observances or the attitude to be adopted by the faithful in some particular question, often a political one. This body has acquired considerable influence especially among those Moslems who know little English, and so long as its pronouncements are the outcome of reason, common sense and toleration it must continue to be of value to the community. There is no suggestion anywhere that the 'Ulamā are as yet abandoning their strict and rigid outlook and the only visible effect of modernism has been to produce the Jam'īatu'l'ulamā, which has brought some sort of discipline and cohesion into what had been a quite amorphous body of theologians. It remains to be seen whether their unification will continue to preserve their orthodox conservatism or whether someday it may assist a general movement forward.

The question of woman, her status and rights, her

education and emancipation, occupies much place in the thought and writings of Moslem leaders in India. Here as in other countries the publicists are busily engaged in defending Islamic practice and even carry the war into the Western camp by declaring with emphasis that woman's position has been higher, freer, more secure in Islam than in Christianity. Once more I shall not examine their arguments or the textual foundations on which they have built them. It is sufficient for the common object of all concerned that there is an improvement in the position of women vis-à-vis men. The pace cannot be so rapid as in a Moslem-ruled country like Turkey where it has been forced from above. Reform will be all the better if it is the general outcome of a self-consciousness originating in the mass of the community. So far there have been some very notable instances of ladies of high position giving up the *pardah* and making a successful entry into the general social, professional and political life of the country, where they have immediately begun to wield much influence, but these instances are few and the innate conservatism of the mass of the community will delay any general extension of the process. Revolt or protest is foreign to the nature of Indian women and so one must rather look for a change of attitude on the part of their men. Education it is that will bring about the change. In the meantime the stupid, vulgar and false picture of European and

WHITHER ISLAM?

American sex-relationships presented every night in cinemas right across the land gives the conservative Moslem the very arguments he requires to support his disapproval of any relaxation of age-old custom.

Indian Moslems have not confined the use of the offensive defensive to the vindication of the Islamic treatment of Woman. By far the most striking and the most sustained development of this method has been carried out for over a quarter of a century by the organizers of the Ahmadiya sect, who have copied the machinery and emulated the vigour of the West in the furtherance of their propaganda. This religious movement through its own dynamic force has attracted wide attention and secured followers all over the world. It is named after its founder Mirzā Ghulām Ahmad of the town of Qādiān in the Punjab. In the year 1889 at the age of 50 the Mirzā announced his mission to the world. Two years later he came forward as *nabi* and *mujaddid*, *mahdi* and Messiah. He announced that Jesus had neither died on the cross nor been removed to Heaven alive, as the Koran states, but that he had recovered after crucifixion, escaped and finally died in Kashmir where the Mirzā had discovered his grave. This alleged natural death of Jesus was held by the Mirzā to substantiate his claim to be the Messiah. At the same time he claimed to be the promised *Mahdi* expected by all Moslems. To substantiate these far-reaching claims he published

INDIA

three books which launched him and his followers into a controversy with orthodox Moslems, with the Arya Samāj body of Hindu reformers, and with the Christians, which persists to this day, and which in the case of the orthodox Moslems led to his excommunication and to the putting to death of his followers when rash enough to venture within reach of the orthodox Moslem ruler of Afghanistan. As *Mahdi* the Mirzā came to preach not the bloody *jihād* that the orthodox believed in but a peaceful one, and while not abating his hostility to Christians he dwelt on the necessity for being loyal to the Government established in India. On that point he laid great stress, to the annoyance of some of the orthodox, who considered their loyalty to the British Government brought under suspicion by contrast. Presently he announced to the Arya Samāj that he was Krishnā, and then that the Messiah, the *Mahdi* and Krishnā were all one. As regards orthodox Islam, the Mirzā appears to have deplored its formalism and its saint worship. At the same time he was in vigorous opposition to the rationalists who were prepared to modify their views on the supernatural extent of Mohammed's inspiration and were anxious to bring some of the social laws and customs of Islam into line with modern ideas.

Basing his claims to the extent that he did upon the Koran, a belief in its infallibility and divine nature was essential to his success. Thus it comes that his

WHITHER ISLAM?

followers have shown special interest in translating the Koran into English and in disparaging previous translations already in existence and even imputing intentional dishonesty to translators like Sale. In social matters the Mirzā was a conservative and a fundamental, refusing to modify any of the practices dealing with women such as *pardah* and polygamy. It is impossible for a non-Ahmadiya to study the Mirzā's published claims and arguments without being struck by their crude and naïve character, and many of his critics have had very hard things to say of him. It may be admitted on the other hand that there must have been a magnetism and a sincerity in the presentation of his alleged revelation for his success to be so considerable as it was. In 1908 Mirzā Ghulam Ahmad died and Hakīm Nuru'ddin, his first disciple, became the first *Khalifatu'l Masīh*. Shortly before Nuru'ddin's death a schism began, owing ostensibly to the participation in a political matter of some of the Lahore disciples led by Khwājā Kamālu'ddin. This came to a head at the election of Mirzā Bashīru'ddin as second Khalifa in 1914, since when there have been two branches with their headquarters at Qādiān and Lahore respectively. There are considerable differences in the beliefs of the two parties, the Lahore one holding that the founder of the sect was little more than a *mujaddid*, a reviver or refresher of Islam. They dislike the dictum of the Qādiānis that orthodox

INDIA

Moslems are *Kāfirs* and prefer to minimize the differences between themselves and the orthodox. What is of more interest to the outside world than the beliefs of either branch and their relations with the orthodox is the vigorous life and the fervent missionizing character of the movement, which displays an aggressiveness and an intolerance unusual among Indian Moslems. Ridicule and scorn are two of the weapons employed in this propaganda, which also quotes freely from the works of eminent European critics of the Christian religion whenever its purpose is served by doing so. The authenticity of the Bible is freely impugned. The person of Jesus Christ in particular is assailed and belittled and the bankruptcy and failure of modern Christianity is continually stressed. Here perhaps it is a case of the boot being on the other leg. There is ample precedent for these attacks to be found in the writings of many Christian authorities on Muhammad and his religion, as collated in books of reference such as Hughes' *Dictionary of Islam*. Even so the Mirzais have acted on Khuda Bakhsh's principle of "using the weapons forged in the West" when they might have been expected to use their undoubted skill and energy in some more original way than a mere *tu quoque*. One of the disappointing features of the Indian's response to Western contacts is his proneness to copy instead of creating something of his own. It is disheartening to think that one of the few Indian inventions has been the sterile hate-engendering non-co-operation movement. But after all the Indian Moslem must at least be absolved from having any share in the creation of that piece of futility. The output of printed matter by the Ahmadiya has been immense and sustained, and from 1892 there have been numerous vernacular periodicals published at Qādiān, also one English paper, the *Review of Religions*. These carry out a vigorous propaganda against Christianity, against the reforming Hindu movement of the Arya Samāj, and against Sikhism. There are well organized schools and two departments, one to organize the Ahmadiya community and the other to direct missionary effort. The Lahore party has very similar activities, but on a much smaller scale. Both have missions abroad and have a sprinkling of converts from Christianity in several countries. I understand the Qādiānis to claim half a million followers all told. The Lahore branch has very many less. It is difficult to prophesy the future of the Ahmadiya movement but it is hard to believe that so rigid a creed can long continue in this age of ours to attract many converts or to retain unchanged the belief of its present followers. Where we find the leaders of orthodox Islam conscious of the vital need for a reconstruction of their beliefs and ready to surrender so much of what has always been regarded as the revealed and unchangeable word of

INDIA

God, which has moreover the hallowing associations of thirteen centuries of belief to strengthen it, we are bound to ask whether the complex latter-day revelations on which the Qādiānis rely and which demands so robust a faith can possibly hold its own in these days of half-belief, when the educated are so often either sceptics or rationalists. The Lahore branch has already found itself unable to accept Ghulām Ahmad's claims in full and it would seem likely that one of these days a restatement of belief will also be necessary for the main branch at Qādiān.

The general question of the Caliphate and, since the suppression of that office by the Angora Assembly, the subsidiary question of a general Islamic congress, cannot be discussed at length in this chapter, but it is important to note what the position of Indian Moslems has been and now is regarding both these matters. So long as the Mughal ruled at Delhi or even existed as a pensioner in the old royal palace the question of the Caliphate had little importance. The Moslems could point to their own Moslem ruler and affect at least to find him sufficient for their needs, but the final suppression of the Mughal dynasty in 1857 made the orthodox Sunnis who form the majority reconsider their position. From that date they have regarded the Sultan of Turkey as Caliph. Their allegiance has been primarily and mainly religious, but the loss of

WHITHER ISLAM?

their own temporal head has brought them back to a consideration of Islam as the Church-State of which every Moslem is really a citizen and in which all the citizens are brethren. With this feeling in their hearts the Indian Sunnis have retained a strong sentimental regard for the Sultan without surrendering their loyalty for the *de facto* rulers of India, the British, and under the influence of this natural emotion they have taken a keen partisan interest in all the numerous wars between Turkey and various Christian powers for the last sixty years. This interest has taken practical shape on occasions through the collection of funds or the equipping of Red Crescent hospitals. The construction of the Syria-Hijāz railway also was materially assisted by money subscribed by Indian sympathizers. Then came the great war, with Turkey on the opposite side to Great Britain. The Sultan as Caliph declared a *jihād*, but outside the homelands of the Turkish empire there was little or no response. The Indian Moslems, though sick at heart, remained loyal to their rulers, and the Moslem troops, with the exception of certain frontier and transfrontier Sunnis and a Shi'a regiment in which the scruples of the men were entirely religious and quite unconnected with the Sunni Caliphate, fought manfully against the Turks. Some Moslem districts such as Rawalpindi, Attock, Shahpur and Jhelum sent almost every able-bodied man of fighting age, and many youths below it, to the war and covered themselves with glory. Behind them, left in India, were many men of peace who were deeply exercised as to the fate of Turkey were she to be badly defeated. With them were others of less simplicity of mind and less honesty of purpose, who found the opportunity suitable for the starting of an agitation on a large scale and the collection of funds also on a large scale. The agitation continued and out of it arose two bodies, the Khuddām-i-Kaʻba (servants of the Mecca Shrine) and the Central Khilāfat Committee. The former of these was chiefly concerned with defending by propaganda the integrity and sanctity of the whole Arabian peninsula and especially the Hijāz, while the latter, also mainly through propaganda, championed the rights of the Sultan of Turkey and his country and strove to mitigate the penalties that the peace terms would impose upon the conquered. The climax of the agitation was reached in 1920 when in the North of India feeling against the Government ran very high. Agitators sufficiently well educated to know the probable results of their advice actually preached the doctrine that India was *Dāru'lharb* and told their hearers that as they could not fight the Kāfir Government they must carry out the alternative principle of *Hijrat*, or flight from an infidel land. It is impossible to understand the callous levity of those who gave this counsel. They must have known that

WHITHER ISLAM?

Afghanistan, which under a Moslem ruler was *Dāru'l Islam* and which they accordingly recommended as an asylum, could not support its own population, but many thousands of simple-minded folk did as they were told. They sold their land, their houses, all their possessions for whatever cash they could obtain and in the great heats of early summer marched up into Afghanistan. There they proved a source of the greatest embarrassment to King Amanullah and his administration, who could offer little in the way of land or employment and nothing in the way of maintenance. After great sufferings and privations and losses through death the disillusioned *Muhājirīn* trickled back into India, where the Government which the agitators had maligned assisted them to regain their recklessly discarded possession. It is to the credit of those to whom they had sold their property that it was restored in almost every case for the price at which it had been sold. A small party of irreconcilables remained in Afghanistan, and little more is known about them. The next folly committed by the Khilāfatists was the stirring up of the fanatical Mappillas of Malabar into violent rebellion in 1921. Here again the instigators must have known what dangerous material they were working on and how illusory were the hopes they held out to these unfortunate dupes. The Mappillas, who number rather over a million souls, are mainly the descendants of converts from

INDIA

Hinduism or if resident on the Coast have some Arab blood in their veins. They are extremely zealous followers of the Shāfiīte school. For the most part they are tenants at will of Hindu landlords and the insecurity of tenure and the consequent economic weakness which they suffer from, added to their fanaticism, has for long years past made them liable to sudden violent uprisings. Such was the material on which the agitators worked. The Mappillas were suddenly carried off their feet. They rose, appointed themselves a King and for a few days directed their attacks against British officials and planters. Then they turned their attention to their Hindu oppressors, many of whom they slaughtered and many they forcibly converted. Loot and arson completed the tale of their excesses. For a year these Mappilla bands continued to resist the considerable bodies of troops that were sent to subdue them. Their end was much worse than that of the *Muhājirīn*, for some thousands were slain and between five or ten thousand were given long sentences of transportation. Of the latter about 1,400 were sent to the Andamans and half as many volunteered to go there subsequently. It is interesting to note that several hundreds of these transported prisoners were joined by their wives and families in Port Blair where many are now happily settled as free men on the land, which they hold directly under Government on terms of complete security. This little homogeneous colony across the sea appears to have shaken off the old fanaticism and lives at peace with all those around it. One of the preachers who had stirred the Mappillas into rebellion paid a visit to the Islands four years afterwards. The Mappillas protested vehemently on seeing him, demanding why he had been allowed to come and trouble them a second time. The next feature of the Khilāfat agitation was the spurious alliance between the Moslem Khilāfatists and the Hindu Swaraj party. For months the bazars rang with shouts of *Hindu Moslem Ki Jai* (Victory to Hindu Moslem Unity). The union was as incomplete as it was unnatural, the only bond being a common opposition to the established Government. The end came suddenly with the election of the second Legislative Assembly under the Montagu reforms, and the inter-communal rivalry and ill feeling which has persisted ever since. In 1924 the National Government at Angora, which two years previously had deprived the Caliph of his temporal power as Sultan, abruptly abolished the Caliphate itself. In any country but India, the land of *Maya*, illusion, in which we may include self-deception, this would have given the Khilāfat Committee its death blow. But not so in India. The Committee continued to function, but announced in 1925 that it had turned its attention to the communal welfare of the Indian Moslems. Its external policy is limited at present to an interest in the Islamic congresses which assemble from time to time and break up without any tangible results.

I have described at some length the left wing activities over the question of the Khilāfat. What are the feelings of the average sober-minded Indian Musalman? Without a doubt his conservative pride has been wounded by the abrupt decree of the Turks who for so many decades have been held up to him as the champions of Islam, but he has heard that the Caliphate has been suppressed before and he patiently hopes that it will be revived. The publicists find the abolition of the Caliphate to be the logical removal of an anachronism. Mr. Khudā Bakhsh writes :

"The abolition of the Khilāfat is the most momentous event of modern times. Far reaching are its consequences for good. It is the final fruition of purely Islamic ideas long struggling into supremacy. It ends a fiction and ushers in modern as opposed to mediæval ideas ; it lays open the path for the development of nationalism and removes the embargo on liberalism. It will fashion for Islam a new sense of unity founded on truth, upon cultural traditions and materialized interests."

Sir Muhammad Iqbal finds the abolition to be a perfectly sound exercise of the right of *ijtihād* on the part of the Turkish Government though he certainly will not be found to agree that it will promote that nationalism which is his bugbear.

WHITHER ISLAM?

A fresh if mild interest has been given to the whole matter by the recent marriage of the Nizam's heir apparent to a daughter of the Ex-Caliph Abdul Mejīd. Several interesting complications might conceivably arise from this union but current opinion among well-informed Indians rejects them all. In the meantime attention is focussed on the Islamic congresses of which the two most notable were held in Cairo and Mecca in 1926. At both of these Indian representatives were present but several important countries were not represented and there was a general air of inconsequence about the proceedings. Another similarly unauthoritative congress is to meet in early December of this year at Jerusalem. The truth is that home problems have become too pressing for the Moslems of any country to pay much attention to external affairs other than the Mecca Pilgrimage. India continues to furnish a very large proportion of the annual number of pilgrims to the Hijāz for whose comfort the Indian Government takes elaborate precautions. For all Indian Moslems and especially for those in greater isolation the pilgrimage remains a link of the greatest value with the home of their religion and with their brethren from other lands.

The Hijrat movement and the Mappilla rebellion are two examples of the readiness of the Indian Moslems to succumb to agitation without pausing to consider the trustworthiness of the agitator. It is sufficient for them to be told that the question is a religious one and that their religion is in danger for them to flock together and start mass action the ultimate result of which is seldom to their advantage. Another instance of this propensity was the Cawnpore mosque incident during Lord Hardinge's Viceroyalty, when the whole of Moslem India was convulsed because the local municipality proposed to remove a small corner of a mosque enclosure, below the "shoe-line" and thus possessing no great sanctity, in order to improve the alignment of a road. During the course of the agitation there were clashes between the people and the authorities which resulted in loss of life, and a personal settlement by the Viceroy himself was required to appease the excitement which had been created. On the other hand the resolute demolition of an unauthorized mosque in 1922 by the Lahore municipality backed up by the magistrates and an adequate display of troops and carried out summarily before any agitation was set on foot scarcely received a mention in the local Press though it was common knowledge that outcaste sweepers had been employed to demolish the very mihrāb of the building. There being nothing left to agitate about, the Press and the agitators for once in a way took a sensible line and ignored the whole matter.

Another instance of the ease with which the Moslem community may be mobilized by agitators is to be seen in the dangerous "Red Shirt" movement in the

Frontier Province which in a very short space of time in the spring of 1931 brought in the powerful trans-frontier tribe of the Afridis against the Government, put the province in a state of war, delivered its capital for several days to mob rule and became a grave menace to the stability of the whole country. The motives of the agitators on this occasion had little to do with the rights or grievances of Moslems; the point is that the community was capable of being brought into cohesive action as a community at the shortest notice. The movement still persists as a potential source of loss of life and property for its ignorant followers. Lastly there was the agitation among Punjab Moslems in the summer and autumn of 1931 against the Hindu ruler of Kashmir and the Brahmin oligarchy of that State, seventy-seven per cent. of the inhabitants of which are Moslem. Here again left-wing agitators styling themselves *Ahrār*, or " The Free," relying on a considerable substratum of truth, were able to stir up the greater part of the Molsem community of the Punjab into active demonstration against the State authorities, who were finally obliged to take the unpalatable step of demanding the assistance of British troops (as distinct from Indian) for the purpose of restoring order in the State and preventing an outbreak of internal rebellion complicated by the active sympathy of the Moslems of British India. It is apparent from the instances given here that like the Sikhs, who form

INDIA

another congregational and anti-caste community, the Moslems have an innate capacity for mass action and are frequently compromised by agitators and led into courses which more often than not gravely injure their interests. They are therefore in constant need of wise and sane leadership. The awakening caused by the reforms has brought more leaders into the field but the supply is still far from adequate.

There now remains for review the more definitely political aspect of modern Indian Islam. We have seen how, ever since the Musalmans of India lost their political power, they have been on the defensive. The first instinct of their reforms was to withdraw into themselves and to fall back on a rigid enforcement of the simple creed of early Islam to the corruption of which they perhaps ascribed their decay and tribulation. Later came the constructive programme of Sir Sayyid Ahmad Khān and his lieutenants and the growing inclination towards rationalism. But still the Musalmans felt the necessity of remaining on the organized defensive. The names and the declared objects of some of their chief societies such as the *Anjuman-i-Himāyat-i-Islām* affords clear proof of their tendency, which even the obvious good will of the Government did not obliterate. The Indian Congress which was started in 1885 failed entirely at first to secure any support from the Moslems and has only for very short periods and in very special circumstances, e.g. the year 1916, had more than a very few Moslem members at one time in its ranks. As a counterblast to the Congress the Moslems in 1892 founded a Defence Association as a vehicle for presenting their grievances to Government in a way that was expressly to avoid anything in the nature of agitation. A further step was taken by the founding in 1906 of the All-India Moslem League, as the Defence Association was felt to be inadequate in face of the growing power of the Indian Congress. Then in 1909 came the first instalment of political concession by the British known as the Morley-Minto reforms, to be followed after the war by the Montagu-Chelmsford reforms. With the formation in 1921 of the first enlarged Government under these latter reforms, with certain portfolios entrusted for the first time to Hindu and Moslem Ministers chosen from elected members of the new Councils, we enter on the intensified communal rivalry between the two communities which has now lasted for ten years and to which under the existing artificial conditions enforced by the presence of British troops in India no one can see any possible end. Forgotten now is the Pan-Islamism in which Indian Moslems showed so much interest before the war. That movement indeed is dead, but harder still, it is unwept. Events in the Hijāz, in Egypt, Palestine, Syria or Turkey appeal now but little to the Indian Moslem's heart and still less to his pocket. All the political consciousness that he possesses is mobilized for service on the Hindu front. Once more defence is the rallying cry, defence of the community, defence of Islam confronted or rather surrounded by a pagan adversary superior in numbers, in education, in wealth, and rendered less dangerous than he might be only through his lack of the cohesion and comradeship that holds the Moslem ranks together. The antagonism between Hindu and Moslem is nothing new. It has always been there and while the two religious and the two social codes retain their present appeal that antagonism cannot be banished. It may be that education or a closer approach to democratic ideals may help the communities to return presently to the condition of mutual tolerance that existed before the reforms sowed the seeds of discord. That is the most that can be said. The word antagonism hardly suffices. It is more antipathy, an antipathy felt by each community and arising out of basic differences which cannot be reconciled. Kraemer's analysis of these differences is most interesting and parts of it may be quoted here. He says:

" Hinduism is a wide, pervasive and elusive mass of mystical religion, intellectually indefinable and allowing all possible definitions through the range of unqualified and intransigent monism, emotional theism, exuberant polytheism and symbolism and frank superstition. The only things in which it is rigid and ' touchy ' are religiously sanctioned institutions and the veneration of the cow. Islam is a rather narrow and rigid theism, distinguished by a jealous defiance of all competitors of God's unique and sovereign majesty and a genuine feeling of the fundamental difference between God, the omnipotent Creator, and His creatures. Doctrinally, Hinduism is all-inclusive, Islam, on the contrary, on the doctrinal side, is all-exclusive. Hinduism has theoretically no difficulty whatever in Hinduizing every new idea or justifying it in the all-embracing comprehensiveness of its spirit. Islam, with its precise and clear religious law, an outgrowth of the mediæval spirit, is coming constantly and immediately to grips with the modern world.

" To Islam the world is God's creation, man is his *'abd* (servant) destined to bear the vicissitudes of life, ordained to do his duty, responsible for his deeds and expecting God's reward. His attitude has a stamp of simple, unbroken manliness. To the Hindu the world is unreal or only partly real, a factor in the process of transmigration and *karma*, just as man himself. Life is enveloped in a spirit of soft and feminine mildness.

"Their historical background is entirely different, and in this case, the Moslems being the conquerors of the country, largely conflicting. The Moslems have no national history in the modern sense of the word. If they have it, it is to them of secondary importance. Their real history is supranational. In history the Hindus revere the memory of Prthi Raj, Partap, Shivaji and Beragi Bir, who fought for the honour and freedom of this land (against the Moslems), while the Muhammadans look upon the invaders of India, like Muhammad ibn Qasim, and rulers like Aurangzeb as their national heroes."

The same antagonism is seen in their linguistic preferences and where both speak what is the same language, Hindustani, the Moslem gives it a completely Persianized form while the Hindu employs Sanscritic words and his own Nagri characters. Their social lives are lived entirely apart and except in rare cases among Europeanized Indians there can be no eating together, much less any form of family relationship.

For brief periods during and after the Great War the Hindu Swarājist leaders succeeded in effecting an outward rapprochement to which the Khilāfatist leaders contributed more than any other Moslem representatives, but the alliance was unnatural and vanished with the prospects of the patronage to be received from rival Ministers under the reformed Councils Scheme. The ancient smouldering fires began to glow in 1922 and burst into flame in 1923. From 1923 onwards there have been repeated clashes between the two communities. In almost every large Indian city there has been grave rioting on one or more occasions and the total number of killed and wounded on both sides has run into five figures. These outbursts have all been unorganized and fortuitous and have been the more difficult to prevent or to cure. Alongside there has been a bitter Press campaign and lastly there are organized movements on both sides devoted to internal reform and to aggressive proselitizing efforts. The Hindus in 1923 began the *Shuddi* movement to win back Hindus half converted to Islam into the fold. The response from the Moslem side was the *tabligh* movement with the object of confirming the same imperfectly converted Moslems in their faith. Other rival efforts are those of *Sangethan* by the Hindus and *tanzim* by the Musalmans, both being directed to the better organisation and instruction of the less stalwart followers of the two religions. The Khilāfat Committee, once so friendly with the Swarājists, is now the chief developer of *tanzim*. All attempts at composition of the differences of the two communities have so far been fruitless. The Moslems demand certain safeguards in the new constitution about to be drawn up; the Hindus deny their necessity and promise fair treatment. The chances of agreement are remote, nor is it easy for those who understand the innate incompatibility of the two communities to believe that a paper agreement can be carried into practice. No one can see the way out of the impasse save through the intervention of Parliament which the Prime Minister has now promised. For the present it is of importance to us to observe how the crisis has brought into one camp, with a very few exceptions, all the Moslems of note. They are all impressed with the gravity of the issue and are determined to defend their ideals and their rights. They have attended both London sessions of the Round Table Conference where they have presented a united front very different to the divided counsels of their opponents. Although the communal question has not yet been decided the British Government, guided by the deliberations of the Conference, has declared its intention of satisfying part of the Moslem demand immediately. Sind is to be made a separate province and the North-West Frontier province is to be raised to the rank of a Governor province. This is an instalment in response to the demand put forward by Sir Muhammad Iqbal at the All-India Moslem League in 1930, to which reference has already been made. In the course of that address Iqbal stated that he dreads the destructive effect upon Islam of a nationalism divorced from religion and insisted that as the units of Indian Society are not territorial as in European countries and as they have no code of behaviour which is determined by a common race-consciousness a communal system alone will form a basis for the creation of a harmonious whole. A Moslem India within India can alone preserve the underlying principle of Islam as a universal polity. The better to secure this object he would centralise the life of Islam in a specified territory. He even names the parts of India he would thus set aside. They are the Punjab, the North-West Frontier province, Sind and Baluchistan. He claims that the creation of this

Moslem block would not only be in the best interests of India but would give Islam an opportunity to rid itself of the stamp that Arabian imperialism was forced to give it and to bring its law, education and culture into closer contact with its own original spirit and with the spirit of modern times. Here at least is a clear picture, but ideals are seldom fully attained. At least the leaders know their minds. Can they carry the masses with them? Yes, provided that the masses take more generally to education. It is difficult to avoid the conclusion that a religion so fundamentally simple in its creed and so free from dogma as Islam will escape from the general rationalization which is modifying other religions the whole world over. There is however one great obstacle, the illiteracy of the great mass of the people and the waning of the power of formal religion over them. Here as elsewhere, there may be a race between the rationalists and a kind of general dull unbelief. If this is to be so then the need for education becomes as pressing on religious and ethical grounds as it undoubtedly is on grounds of economics, hygiene and general welfare. Above all there remains the need for continued good leadership. We can agree with the closing words of Iqbal's presidential address where he quotes the Koran (5.104) " Hold fast to yourself; no one who erreth can hurt you, provided you are well-guided."

INDONESIA
By Professor C. C. Berg

CHAPTER V

INDONESIA

By PROFESSOR C. C. BERG

Introduction

1. General Survey. 2. Different Types of Civilization in the Malay Archipelago. 3. Paganism. 4. Hinduism before the spread of Islam. 5. Lasting influence of Hinduism in Java. 6. Its influence elsewhere.

1. As far as London is from the Persian Gulf or from the African Gold Coast, so far is the distance from the north-west point of Sumatra to the frontier of Australian New Guinea. The Dutch part of the Malay Archipelago extends between longitude 95 degrees and 141 degrees east, joining in the western part the great commercial route which connects India via Singapore with China and Japan, and losing itself in the east in the immensity of Oceania. Here lie the isles which were known already to the ancients as being fabulously rich in gold and spices. For years and years they have had an open door for the Chinese merchant, who, however, has limited himself to carrying on trade throughout the centuries. Western influence entered through the Straits of Malacca, and found its way around the

north through the Philippine Islands as well as through the Java Sea in the south to the Moluccas, the Spice Isles. The stations on the southern route, especially the east coast of Sumatra and the north coast of Java, have become more prominent in the course of time than the Moluccas themselves, and whilst elsewhere the impenetrability of the tropical forests has opposed human penetration up till now, here the exceedingly fertile soil invited Chinese of every type, Hindus and Tamils, Arabs and Armenians, Europeans and Japanese to permanent settlement. The circumstances led there from colonization to a colonial relation to the mother-country in the modern sense of the word. The Malay Archipelago has been colonization territory in the old-fashioned way during the 1,500 years that we can survey its history, and in general has prospered by it. Social problems here are of recent date, to wit, since changes were brought about in the relation to the mother-country, which have given the idea of "colonial territory" an entirely different meaning, changes whose beneficial influence may as yet be called of problematic value.

Right across the island world slings, capricious and indefinable, the frontier of the *Dār al-Islām*. Whilst in the east the Moslem territory is, so to speak, being daily extended by silent, unknown, unpaid, and not officially appointed propagandists, the Muhammadans are fighting in the western part an unequal battle of life and death against European influence on nearly every field of life. It is for this reason that Indonesia displays, as against other parts of the Moslem world, some aspects typical of a border country, whereas, on the other hand, it has various features in common with other countries, and especially with India. In order to be able to conceive and to judge of the significance of the various modern movements in Indonesia and its relation to Islam, as far as such may be possible, we shall have to start by accounting for the nature and the strength of the factors which have defined or at least have affected its development up to the present day.

When studying the Malay Archipelago, it immediately strikes one that it has always been receptive of foreign civilizations. All possible influences have been digested in one way or another. Indonesia has, for its part, seldom been more to foreign peoples than a plantation and a store from the economic point of view, and a marvel for lovers of science and art. It has no more conscious influence on the adventures and the future of the Moslem community than—to exaggerate a little—anyone has by paying his contribution to a society which he does not help to manage, or than a tax-payer has on the government of his country.

That Java will come very prominently into the foreground in the following pages, as if the " Indonesia " of the title of this chapter were a mere mistake for "Java," can be explained by Java's disproportionately great importance in the Malay Archipelago. Even in these days, when countries like Sumatra and Borneo are developing particularly rapidly from the economic point of view, forty-two of the sixty millions of inhabitants of the Dutch Indies live in Java. And although Java is no longer the centre of Indonesian spiritual life, it is at any rate still playing the main part in it. To this it must be added that the scope of this chapter will not allow us to pay attention to all modern currents. I have endeavoured not to give facts in the first place, but to draw the main lines. It is necessary for the sake of clearness to follow the course of each of these lines from a certain point of view. Moreover, even when the fact is not emphasized, the reader should always bear in mind that in reality these lines are steadily converging and diverging, crossing and diverting each other, so that at first glance the whole gives the impression that there is no design in the confused complex of lines. The danger to which the writer, on the contrary, is exposed, is that he cannot help bringing into relief cross-hatching, and emphasizing perspective, which is almost a falsification of the reality of constantly shifting lines.

2. With all possible appreciation of the present Indonesian struggle for unity, one cannot be blind to the fact that the only real unity in the Malay Archipelago

nowadays still is that of the Dutch power. This power, however, is only the mere superstructure of Indonesian society and demonstrates that unity only to the exterior world. In Indonesia itself several races, many nations, hundreds of different languages and appreciably deviating types of culture are still to be distinguished. Some Indonesian peoples have been in touch with foreign nations for centuries, others have emerged from the prehistoric period only a quarter of a century ago. The various Indonesian nations are, from a scientific point of view, still only very superficially known; this is true, not only of the interior of Borneo, Celebes, New Guinea and the many small islands in the eastern part of the archipelago, but also of Sumatra, Java and Bali. We know something of about thirty languages, only a fraction of the total number. With some peoples the ethnologists have a closer acquaintance; the historians have developed the main points of the history of some others.

The two main currents of culture which possessed a wide influence prior to the arrival of the Europeans, namely Hinduism and Islam, have been intensively studied, but the investigation of the forms which they have assumed among the Indonesian peoples is still in its first stage. The number of those who have worked in this field of scientific research is extremely small. The average European in Indonesia has only a very superficial notion of the civilization of his Indonesian neighbours, with a few favourable exceptions; the kind of Malay language which he learns to speak " in three months," is a very poor manner of expression, with which one can help oneself in the daily contact with servants and workmen, but by which one could hardly express thoughts of a higher' order.

3. The inhabitants of the territories into which Hinduism, Islam or Christianity have not yet entered, are usually called " pagans "; but when using this term one is inclined to recall Goethe's words: "Denn eben wo Begriffe fehlen, da stellt ein Wort zur rechten Zeit sich ein."[1] Paganism in the Malay Archipelago is culturally by far the most important, but the least known to us. It is extremely difficult to say what " paganism " really is. We do not get far with the description " polytheism," as after closer acquaintance it will soon become clear that the idea of " god " has an altogether different meaning than it has with us. Science has supplemented its index-term for paganism, " animism," with the somewhat vaguer term " pre-animism," and has subsequently added to this the still more mystically sounding " dynamism." To these denominations Goethe's words are also applicable. A common opinion regarding the origin and the essence of paganism does not exist at all. The well-known ethnologist, Father Schmidt, is of opinion that each paganism has an original monotheism at its base, but

[1] "Just when ideas give out, a word steps in in the nick of time."

many ethnologists of great repute do not agree with him. According to the latter, a vague idea of powers originates from the instinctive fear of primitive people for the numerous dangers which surround them. In the whole material world in which these forces act, they believe a close internal cohesion to be present. This consciousness of cosmic community prevents a sharp distinction of things according to their nature, so that, for instance, the various forms of life are considered not to differ essentially from one another and the living is not clearly distinguished from the lifeless nor nature from cosmos. The whole world and all its powers and appearances are subdivided into groups according to mutual exterior characteristics, the nature and significance of which often escape our observation. Appearances classified in the same group are deemed to be in close relation to each other, even to be identical, so that an influence exercised on one member affects all correlated members. To this last idea magic owes its origin, and out of magic cultus subsequently develops.

The ideas, the faith and the magic practices of the pagans are not argued, not causally thought out, but rather instinctively (or so to speak, pre-intellectually) developed. The little that we think we know of it depends especially on comparative study of the myths of primitive peoples and on watching their ritual observances, as the pagan is not capable of writing down his sentiments or of expressing them verbally on behalf of the investigator. It will have been made clear by the above that the interpretation of the characteristics of paganism, as well as of Hinduism and Islam, when they developed under pagan influences, requires a very thorough ethnological knowledge. One can only acquire an idea of the meaning, for instance, of the paganism of the Malay Archipelago by the utmost endeavour and stupendous study, a study which is made more difficult by the fact that Indonesian paganism shows considerable local differences, notwithstanding a fundamental uniformity.

4. One of the first outside influences that we find acting in historical times is the force of Hinduism. Hinduism may rather be called the native culture of India than a religion. It includes several religious and philosophic systems, which may be in flagrant opposition to each other. All these systems have in common a recognition—theoretical for the rest—of a Holy Book, the Vedas, the belief in the eternal movement of all being (metempsychosis), and the recognition of the inviolability of the caste system, a social system born from the antagonism between the white Aryan race and the dark Dravidian one and aiming at maintaining for ever the supremacy of the Aryan descendants. Notwithstanding the fact that religious wars have occurred in India, there was in ancient times

a remarkable freedom in dogmatics; theistic, pantheistic and atheistic systems could develop undisturbed within the bounds of Hinduism. If, therefore, it was already impossible to speak of a "faith" propaganda of Hinduism, it was rendered still less possible by the fact that the caste system restricted it automatically to the territories inhabited by Hindus.

One section of the Indians who came into touch with the Indonesians through settling in the Malay Archipelago belonged probably to the lowest caste, whose culture did not differ much from Indonesian paganism. These people did not play an important part in Indonesian cultural history. But such a part has, on the other hand, actually been played by Indians of high caste. They have taken possession of political power in Java, as appears from the course of history, and have formed to a certain extent a society of their own above the native, under the pressure of their caste rules. When we take into consideration the facts that the number of Brahmans who came to the Malay Archipelago probably remained very small, and that the other members of the higher castes certainly did not pertain to the upper ten of Indian society and cannot have been the bearers of high philosophic ideas, but were followers of one of the many popular religions,—when we may apparently further assume that the Indian settlers did not bring their women with them, but married women of their new country,—then we shall not be far from the truth in believing that the descendants of the Hindu settlers in Java also stood with both feet in the native paganism. What they received from their Hindu ancestors were Indian social ideas, Indian religious forms, Indian literature and folklore and finally relations with India, by which the road was for long kept clear for further influences on the Malay Archipelago.

5. As a result of the steady increase in the intermixture of stocks, the influence of the primitive native culture on that of the Hindu-Javanese group has grown regularly in the course of centuries, more especially because relations with India were more difficult to maintain when the Europeans arrived in the East. The strong group tradition, which was still supported by the caste system even when this had lost its right to exist, has, however, not only prevented the Hindu elements in the Hindu-Javanese culture from complete ruin, but it has also made its mark on the whole of Javanese cultural history and in fact does so still. We shall see later on that the Hindu-Javanese past has given the Islam of Java its peculiar character, and is indeed still exercising a certain influence on the Javanese nationalist movement of our days. And as Javanese nationalism is a considerable factor in the Indonesian nationalist movement, and as, on the other hand, Islam in the present conditions has the nationalist movement as its natural ally, these few remarks on

Hindu-Javanism are not entirely superfluous here. We shall later on have to express an opinion of the same kind in another connection.

That Hinduism meanwhile has never been a people's religion in Java even in its Javanized form will have become clear from the foregoing. Details of the Hindu culture have, indeed, become the collective property of the whole Javanese people in the course of time, but this was possible only because it had become acceptable in several respects to the primitive people as a result of its excessive absorption of elements of the indigenous culture.

6. Nowhere in the Archipelago has Hinduism been able to exercise the same steady influence as in Java. It has, indeed, been of a certain importance elsewhere, as for instance in various regions of Sumatra and on the Borneo coasts—not to mention Bali, which occupies an exceptional position in many respects—but it seems that we may assume that the radiation of Javanized Hinduism has played a greater part in such cases than the import of Hinduism from India itself. We shall not enter into the details of this process, and it is enough to state that Hinduism in Sumatra has influenced Islam to a smaller extent than has been the case in Java, and that, therefore, Islam appears there in a much purer form.

WHITHER ISLAM?

INDONESIAN ISLAM

1. Characteristics of Islamic propaganda. 2. Islam introduced from India. 3. Concessions to local customs. 4. Confluence with Hindu-Javanism in Java. 5. Its character in other regions.

1. I do not need to set forth explicitly in this place the typical characteristics of Islam and how enormously it differs from Hinduism. Over against the elusive and vague speculation of Hinduism stand the concrete, almost unimaginative dogma and law of Islam, which are as dry as the soil on which they arose, as Snouck Hurgronje says. Notwithstanding all formalism, there still lives in Islam a warm human piety and submission (*islām*) to God, which do not characterize Hinduism, though they are not wanting there. The caste system, by which Hinduism stands or falls, is foreign to Islam; the latter directs itself rather to everyone and has always found its strength in the enthusiastic affection of the masses. Islam really knows the secret of how to make itself popular. Its confessors are proud of their religion, but do not repel in their proudness. " Al-Islām ya'lā," " Islam is superior," thus a pagan is invited by a Moslem propagandist, " become a Moslem and you also will belong to our superior group ! " How simple is conversion to the faith of the Prophet ! No complicated study is necessary, but only the pronunciation of a simple formula

of belief in the Only One God and His Messenger. No priest regulates or controls the religious life. With the lack of a compulsory, concrete doctrinal authority agrees that remarkably mild and liberal standpoint, that notable proof of the dominating need of unanimity and magnanimity, that difference of opinion in the community is a gift of God.

From this mentality results the tried Muhammadan propaganda method : first exterior mission, to make people Moslem, be it only in name, and, if possible, to bring them under Muhammadan rule ; the penetration of Islam into all fields of life will follow in the long run ; the feeling of solidarity, the feeling of being one with the rest of the Muhammadan world, which has been given to the convert already at his change, will develop and will create the favourable condition of mind for internal conversion. The pilgrimage to Mecca which every Moslem should undertake once in his life, if possible, and which millions of Indonesians have undertaken, even though they could have been dispensed from it by law ; the settling of a great number of Indonesians, or Jāwī, as the Arabs say, in Mecca, the cosmopolitan centre of Muhammadan science, whither their enthusiasm for the pilgrimage has conveyed them ; the unifying influence of the Arabic language and the uniformity of teaching methods in the whole Muhammadan world, all these factors have contributed to the fact that the idea of solidarity in the Moslem world has remained prominent, even after the splitting up of the empire of the Caliphs into different states, contrary to the doctrine of the theocratic unity-state, became an accomplished fact. The bad example of " Christian " Europe, which has for centuries been placing individual advantage above the joint cultural interest, has been followed by the Moslem world only in this century, under quite excusable pressure from beyond its borders.

2. In the Malay Archipelago Islam was propagated first of all by merchants, usually peacefully, sometimes also violently. It was introduced into North Sumatra towards the end of the twelfth century, whence it found its way to Java in the course of the fifteenth century. If it was—and is still—usually willingly accepted in pagan regions because of the reasons previously mentioned, even here, where Hinduism had already exercised its influence, success was met with. Snouck Hurgronje has repeatedly drawn attention to the fact that the Islamization of the Malay Archipelago during the early centuries was carried on exclusively from India, where Islam had not been able, of course, to keep itself free from Hinduistic influences. This mixture of Islam with Hinduistic elements facilitated the rapid spread of the new religion among the Javanese people, familiar as it was with Hinduism from olden times, and so also did

the lack of critical insight into the real differences between Hinduism and Islam. Islam encountered, however, vigorous opposition from the East Javanese court circle, where a Javanized Hinduism was still a strong tradition during the entire fourteenth century and probably also during the fifteenth century, an opposition which was broken only after a long and bloody fight, according to Javanese tradition.

3. It was a favourable circumstance for Islam that soon after its appearance on the coasts of Java the accidents of fortune displaced the centre of gravity of political power in Java to Central Java, where Hinduism, at the cost of a good deal of its resistive power, had during the preceding centuries been merged into the indigenous culture to a much larger extent than was the case in Eastern Java. Nevertheless, the success of Islam here—indeed, especially here—has first of all to be credited to its far-reaching concessions to the old customs. We see Muhammadan names appearing in the titulature of Javanese monarchs, we see them adorning themselves with the names of Kalipat Ullah and Panata Gama, " who regulates religion," we see the pangulu taking his place in Javanese society as Moslem lawyer and judge, but on the other hand we find also all sorts of Hindu-Javanese court habits and court dignitaries, a literature soaked in Hinduism, and the wayang play inseparably connected with literature, dance and

music and many other elements of the ancient culture which properly could not be tolerated by Islam, holding their own almost unweakened. The Moslem monarch of Java has no objection to reckoning the gods and the heroes of the Mahābhārata amongst his ancestors next to Muhammad and to the holy apostles of Javanese Islam, any more than the pangulu deems it blameworthy to adorn himself with the name of yogīçwara, which calls up memories of the ideals of Indian ascetics and magicians, ideals foreign to the spirit of Islam.

4. The place which Islam has taken in the cultural history of Java and the influence which it has exercised on the course of events, are therefore quite different from what we find in India. Whilst there Hinduism and Islam, in spite of the influence in the field of religion and thought which they have exercised upon one another, stand opposite each other in sharply separated camps as a result of social and political differences, and a reconciliation can hardly be expected in the near future, all contrasts are fading in Indonesia. Who is to be called the victor in the battle between the animism of the simple country people and monotheistic Islam ? And did Hindu-Javanism or Islam really triumph in the court circle ? It would not be easy to give a completely satisfactory answer to this question. The process of syncretism, of the growing into one of two really different religious or

philosophic systems under the stress of primitive thought, which Java had already once before experienced, when Shivaism and Buddhism to all outward semblance contended for the mastery, took place again after the introduction of Islam. It was Javanese genius, the "agama Jawa," after all, which, until a short time ago, was the real victor, as an uncritical unity of contraries.

Remarkable examples of this syncretism could be afforded in larger number than space allows me. At present it will be enough to cite a few noteworthy cases. There exists a Javanese book, called Serat Cabolèk, which treats of an ulama (jurist), Amad Mutamakim, who is said to have propagated in Tuban (on the north coast of East Java) in the second quarter of the eighteenth century, a mystic doctrine which deviated materially from orthodox Islam. A certain uneasiness arose about this, and finally the monarch was drawn into the case, as Amad Mutamakim's adversaries feared danger, on account of his action, to country and religion. An emissary of the monarch came and started an enquiry. In order to be able to formulate an opinion regarding the points of view of both parties he enticed them into a dispute on religious matters, and one of the principal objects of discussion on that occasion was . . . the mystic doctrine of a well-known book of Hindu-Javanese literature, the Nawaruchi or Bimasuchi, which contains the story of Bhīma, the second Pāndawa, who once wandered about in search of the water of life for Drona, his teacher, and who found at last, after many adventures, supreme wisdom at the bottom of the sea in the belly of a being resembling a child, but enclosing in itself all the universe, called Nawaruchi or Déwaruchi. And, indeed, ketib (chatīb) Anom Kudus, the champion of orthodoxy, actually appeared to be better acquainted with this Hindu-Javanese wisdom than Amad Mutamakim himself! The dispute, however, awakened the interest of the monarch for the Nawaruchi, and instead of troubling about the interests of Islam, he, the " panata gama," the maintainer of Islam, did all that was in his power to procure a specimen of the pagan book with its officially renounced wisdom, for that was what his interest led him to!

As late as in the second half of the nineteenth century, we find in the court circle exactly the same attitude of mind, notwithstanding the augmented Arab influence. To Ranggawarsita, the last great Javanese court poet and court scholar, his royal master was still, as ever, the descendant of Arjuna as well as of Muhammad, and the ghosts and gods of the ancient Indian tales were still for him a living reality, which was not even shocked, let alone destroyed, by his confession of the Only One God of Islam. Ranggawarsita was nevertheless highly esteemed and greatly in vogue because of his religious teaching. The books with which he has enriched Javanese religious literature show us clearly what we are to understand by that. In Ranggawarsita there was still embodied " ngèlmu," the Javanized science and wisdom, in which Islam and Hinduism go together just as peacefully and cordially as in the term *ngèlmu* itself do the Arab original (*'ilm*) and the Indian form ; and they *could* go so peacefully and intimately together, because their real characteristics remained vague for the uncritical Javanese spirit.

That attempts have been made in Java to reconcile the pagan wayang play with Islam, or that legend lets Yudhisthira, the Pāndawa, die as a Moslem, proves, no doubt, that some circles began to feel the contradiction between the two religions, but also that they completely lacked the critical mind which needs separation, distinguishing and keeping separate. In the pesantrèn's (seminaries), whence originated the Javanese Moslem jurists, we may see a continuation of the old Javanese or Hindu-Javanese mandala's (convents), and neither the life of the santri's (theological students), whose name is a deformation of the Indian çāstrī, " who knows the (Hindu) holy books," nor the social position of these theological schools had been considerably changed in Java by four centuries of Islam.

5. Time has incontestably worked for Islam. In Sumatra and in other regions which have remained

more or less outside the sphere of Javanese influence and where, therefore, the thin stratum of Hinduism has worn off quicker than in Java, small kingdoms arose, where Islam, as the only dominating spiritual power, has penetrated more profoundly and has more or less consciously combated the local complex of habits. Popular Moslem literature found its way to the Malay world via India. Religious books, like the pious tales from the Sunnah and the history of the Prophets, as well as worldly Moslem-coloured tale cycles, like the Alexander-romance and the history of Amīr Hamzah, have made themselves at home in Malay garb. As Hindu influence once radiated from Java, so now Muhammadan cultural influence spread from a few centres at the Strait of Malacca, borne by the Malay language. Malay became the official language of the Muhammadan states in the western part of the Malay Archipelago, like Achèh and Menangkabau in Sumatra and Djohor in Malacca, and it succeeded in becoming the *lingua franca* of Indonesia on account of its simple construction and owing to the aid of the Europeans. The Malay-speaking countries, however, have never acquired a predominating political position, for Sumatra and Malacca not only lacked the homogeneity which had contributed to Java's greatness, but the possibility of it also disappeared when Java became the most prominent settlement of the Dutch.

INDONESIA

MODERNIZING INFLUENCES

1. Cultural reorientation as a result of European trade and navigation. 2. The rôle of Mecca and Hadhramaut; Pan-Islamism. 3. The Rise of Egyptian Modernism. 4. Neo-Wahhābism. 5. The influence of the Manār. 6. Modernism on the west coast of Sumatra.

1. The Europeans appeared in Indonesian waters at the beginning of the sixteenth century. One result of the regular shipping traffic to the East, which arose fairly soon, was that direct contact between the Malay Archipelago and Arabia was now established, whereas, together with the Indian competitor of the Europeans as far as commerce was concerned, the Indian cultural influence on Indonesia was also eliminated to a large extent or at least deprived of its significance. Steam-navigation and the opening of the Suez Canal facilitated the intercourse of the two peoples and accelerated the process of cultural reorientation of Indonesia to a large extent.

2. Thus external circumstances brought it about that Arabia began to take the place which India had taken hitherto, which meant a better chance for orthodoxy. In Mecca a Jāwī colony of students of sacred science began to develop, and those who left Mecca fully trained became foci of orthodox influence in their own country. A new kind of Malay literature arose, the so-called kitāb-literature. All sorts of Arabic dogmatic, juridical and orthodox mystic

essays were translated into Malay, and reached, in spite of the peculiar technical style of this Malay, an ever growing public, first in Sumatra, later on also in Java, where we see the pesantrèn's gradually growing more orthodox under the influence of this new Moslem literature.

If this influence, which must not be underestimated, reached the people especially via the learned men, the masses came under the immediate influence of the rigidly orthodox Arabs of Hadhramaut, who in the nineteenth century started to swarm out of their barren country to Indonesia, where not only the better quality of the soil, but also the inhabitants' respect for them, offered them much better conditions of life than their own country had done or even India was in a position to do. Being merchants they succeeded in getting into close touch with the population, and other bonds were contracted by marriage. From the pakojan's, the quarters of the Koja's (Khoja's), as the Hadhramites are called in Java, a great influence was exercised upon the neighbouring population, an influence which might have been of still greater importance, if the Dutch authorities had not put hindrances in the way of the Hadhramites' immigration and liberty of movement.

Of course the duped Hadhramites were not at all grateful towards the Dutch colonial government for its opposition, and it is probable also that the contrast in the field of economics was identified with the principal contrast in the field of religion. For this reason these Hadhramites' complaints gained a wider echo in the Moslem world than could have been imagined under other circumstances. Other grievances too, however, awakened the antipathy of the Moslems towards the Dutch. In Mecca, where Indonesian Moslems met, the fact was, of course, amply discussed that the Indonesian Muhammadans were repeatedly vexed by colonial authorities in performing their religious duties, the more so as the attempts to restrain the Indonesians from the Hajj meant so many assaults on the purses of the Meccans, who live to a large extent on the expenditure of the Jāwī. Add to this that in the latter part of the nineteenth century and in the beginning of this century a war was waged for many years against the ardent Muhammadan Achèhnese, a holy war (prang sabil) to the Indonesians, and secondly that the Indonesian Muhammadans repeatedly saw looming before them the spectre of compulsory Christianization, when too zealous mission friends publicly denied the Muhammadan character of the Sumatrans and the Javanese, and we can understand that the opinion prevailed in Mecca that Holland was one of the most intolerant and hostile of European powers towards Islam. It was quite natural that under these circumstances the Hajj and the sojourn in Mecca in their turn stimulated many

Indonesians to feelings of hostility and opposition to Holland and the Dutch authorities in their country, which seemed, for the rest, to be in agreement with the opinions regarding Holy War which had existed in the Moslem community from the very beginning.

Since the Indonesians were still less able than any other Muhammadan people to think of making active war, considering the defective military organization of the Moslem world, their reaction could not but confine itself to participation in the Pan-Islamic movement, so far as this was possible in their distant country, and to financial support of its undertakings. It is known that in the beginning of this century the consuls of the Turkish sultanate occasionally tried to exploit the existing Pan-Islamic tendency in the interest of their lord and their country : for the Sultan in his quality of Caliph they required the recognition of his sovereignty over all Muhammadans. Lack of data makes it almost impossible to define how deep this Pan-Islamic current went in Indonesia, but it played its part in preparing the soil for later Muhammadan movements.

In our day the fact that the native newspapers keep a broad circle of readers informed of recent events in the world of Islam sometimes proves to be of considerable importance in fanning into flame smouldering Pan-Islamic sentiments. During last year (1931), for example, there were rumours concerning the ill-usage which the Moslems in Tripolitania were said to be suffering from the Italian authorities. The Moslems of the Malay Archipelago reacted to these rumours by writing bitter articles in their papers, by holding indignation-meetings and by planning a boycott of Italian wares, to such an extent that the government of the Dutch Indies had to insist on moderation. It was only a few months ago (Dec., 1931) that the Italian government published an absolute denial of the rumours current in Indonesia, in the form of a statement emanating from a Moslem authority in Tripolitania and asserting the excellent relations between Italy and the local Moslems. So the Moslems of Indonesia do not always seem to be guided by realities in expressing their Pan-Islamic sympathies!

3. Whilst European influence, especially in the course of the nineteenth century, thus contributed, though indirectly and unintentionally, to strengthen the ties of Indonesian Islam with the rest of the Moslem world and consequently helped to procure for orthodoxy in the Malay Archipelago a more intensive influence at the expense of local peculiarities, elsewhere there began to prevail a European influence, just as unintentional, but with respect to Islam destructive in its essence and in its consequences. The vast expansion of Europe on nearly every side crossed in the nineteenth century the frontier of the Moslem

world and brought into it an intensive commotion in place of the relative quiescence of the preceding centuries. The self-sufficient Moslem saw himself overwhelmed by the unbeliever and compelled to become a pupil of Western methods, if he did not wish to be overrun. Young Indians, North Africans, Egyptians and Syrians began to visit European universities, where rationalism was celebrating its greatest triumphs. If the native cultural traditions of the different Moslem groups and the humiliating circumstances which had led to their study in Europe were the first impediment to an easy internal association of Moslems with European culture, the strong dissociative currents present in that culture itself were another handicap. The enormous power which the Europe of the nineteenth century developed may have been able to force respect; but it was not able to arouse sympathy and affection. Association, however desirable it may be of itself, can only be realized on a basis of mutual understanding, and understanding of the rights and wants and grievances of its Moslem subjects could hardly be expected from the Europe of those days, which still firmly believed in its own superiority in every respect and still had to learn from the course of events that the spiritual basis of its power and superiority was, as a result of internal discord, somewhat precarious. It would have been surprising if the spirit of opposition against the prevailing cultural system of Europe, which grew more and more powerful in Europe in the second half of the nineteenth century, had not worked in the hearts of the Moslem strangers too. The existing relation between their countries and Europe caused their opposition to take a political colour in the first place, but it goes without saying that a political antithesis would poison any comprehensive cultural association of real value at the outset.

So many European-bred Orientals returned to their country, saturated with the products of European civilization, of good as well as of bad quality, and not always able to digest them ; impressed by Europe's power and fast advancement, but generally having no more comprehension of the internal strength or weakness of its basis than the average European himself ; having profited by European instruction and the results of European scientific work, but with no private affection for Europe and no inclination to recognize Europe's supremacy in politics and economics as a natural right. In several Moslem countries youth began to aspire to national independence, but being too weak to bring about anything of importance themselves, they had to take refuge in contact with the people whence they sprang. National or political solidarity supposed, however, solidarity in the field of religion ; they too, whose religious basis had been weakened or even destroyed by rationalism, were made conscious of the fact that propaganda for rationalistic principles would render it absolutely impossible to co-operate with people more or less devoted to orthodox Islam. The powerful support of their fellow-countrymen, who could easily be exploited to serve their political aims, will have adequately balanced for many of them the spiritual sacrifice of concealing their own opinions, and the maintenance of a would-be Islam, which is said to be sometimes called " nifāq " in Egypt, was the easier, as they tended to consider religion as a quantitê négligeable in comparison with their nationalist ideals.

This is one side of the question, and we have to turn our attention to the other side too. In his American lectures on *Mohammedanism*, Snouck Hurgronje explains how important changes in the general cultural conditions of a people necessarily result in a religious renewal. In accordance with this thesis is the fact that at the very time of the penetration of European influence we can discover new religious movements in different Moslem countries. We need not puzzle over the question in which country modern currents in the field of religion first appeared nor about the details of each process of development. Goldziher may be right, when he ascribes the first impetus towards modernism to India, but there seems to be no reason to assume that India has exercised a special influence on the general course of events, as causes and circumstances were pretty much the same everywhere.

INDONESIA

Though the influence of India upon the development of modern ideas amongst the Moslems of the Malay Archipelago can certainly not be excluded and even may have been of considerable importance, I prefer to leave this influence out of account here, because modern Islam in India is, as a result of its relations with modernizing Hinduism, much more complicated than elsewhere, and the subject of the connections between modern Islam in India and Indonesian modernism does not yet seem to have been dealt with sufficiently. The modern development of Egypt and its relations with Indonesia, on the other hand, have been treated by some eminent scholars. That in the next few remarks, in the meanwhile, only some of the main lines of the development of Muhammadan modernism in Egypt and of its influence upon Indonesia will be touched on, and that the possibility of the active influence of numerous individual differences in the process of transformation is *a priori* admitted, hardly needs to be emphasized.

4. In Egypt the rising generation found a suitable point of connection between the old Islam and modern opinions by accepting a certain standpoint in the *ijtihād* question which had already been dealt with in previous centuries, in the days of the Muʻtazilite heresy, of Ibn Taimīyah and of the Wahhābites. This point of view, though definitely rejected by the majority of the Moslem community, found, in the

second half of the nineteenth century, in the very days of the penetration of European influence, an ardent and very able champion in the person of the Egyptian Muftī Shaikh Muhammad 'Abduh, one of the most authoritative modern Moslem theologians (d. 1905). He and his partisans, whose group has become known as the Salafīyah, realized that the rationalism of the European-formed youth required a new adjustment on the part of the jurists and the theologians. Patronized by high officials, he finally succeeded in finding a certain recognition of his combination of puritanism and modernism, notwithstanding the opposition of the orthodox circle of al-Azhar. The basis on which the Salafīyah group saw a possibility of uniting those who had objections to the so-called excesses of Moslem doctrine, but for the rest integrally accepted it, with the rationalistic modernists, for whom Islam was only attractive as long as it did not thwart the realization of modern aspirations or even promoted them, was that mujtahids in all times can adapt Islam to existing needs in order to keep it in the rank of a leading religion. It was the periodical *al-Manār* (" The Lighthouse ") in the first place which in Egypt threw the light of this new thought over a larger public.

5. The *Manār* of Cairo did not shine, however, for Egyptians alone. It illuminated the Arabs at home and abroad, the Moslems of the Malay Archipelago who

studied at al-Azhar University or in Mecca, and the solitary Indonesian who had kept up his old relations with the heart of the Moslem world after having returned to his border country of the Dār al-Islām. And all these people now saw Islam in a new light : it is no longer an example of rigidity, lifelessness and awkwardness for them ; it is still the select one amongst religions, the bearer of ideals for all time and of new ideals for every time ; it is, eternally youthful, the standard-bearer of all progress, ardent and nevertheless forbearing. Those who had caught up and preserved the light of the *Manār* in Egypt, became lesser " manārs " for their environments, once back in Indonesia.

That the new thought has germinated in Indonesian soil is apparent from the fact that Egyptian teachers have been engaged in several places, in order to educate the youth in the fresh spirit and in the new ideals. To many others, of course, the new light seemed sharp and false. Opposition towards the new thought was not lacking. The course of this struggle between old and young, the nature and the number of the points of dispute, have been defined by all sorts of factors, differing for different places. It is practically impossible to describe this modernism of the Malay Archipelago in all its features, so long as only a few local manifestations of modernism have been studied and where the sources are almost inaccessible.

WHITHER ISLAM?

Generally speaking one can say that it seems to be much less important than Indian or Egyptian modernism, as a consequence of the fact that the causes out of which modernism developed over there only began to work in Indonesia at the time of its spread. The first appearance of Moslem modernism in Sumatra and Java was premature in a way, and therefore lost itself in trifles, instead of consistently following the main line of development. In the course of the last twenty years, however, the influence of European education has materially changed the general cultural condition of Indonesia, and as a result Moslem modernism is " modernizing " nowadays and growing less naïve.

6. It appears from B. Schrieke's important study on the modernism of the west coast of Sumatra that all emancipation ideals were represented there in the first decades of this century, both in the field of politics and in the social sphere, whereas in the sphere of religion the contest against what were considered to be abuses (*bidʿa sharʿīya*) which had crept in in course of time, went side by side with the defence of new forms (*bidʿa lughawīya*) required by the spirit of the age, as, for instance, reforms of the education system, use of the Latin characters, use of European clothing, delivery of the Friday sermon in the native dialect, calculation instead of observation of the beginning of Ramadhān, etc., etc. Of more interest than these trifles,

for which a war of paper and disputes was—and still is—carried on between the modernists and the old-fashioned—questions as whether to express the *nīya* loudly or softly, whether ritual purity is necessary or not when touching a copy of the Koran, etc.—are the general characteristics of the modernist movement on the west coast which Schrieke emphasizes ; (1) a Muʻtazilite preference for the application of *ʻaql* (intellect and insight) in place of slavish submission to the old mujtahids and their school, this, however, by no means implying that the modernists have already arrived at the handling of Western scientific critics ; (2) and in consequence : rejection of the opinion that only the *Tuhfa* and the *Nihāya*, the two Shafiʻite law-books par excellence in Indonesia, should be the reliable guide, when determining one's attitude towards miscellaneous, particularly actual questions, to the exclusion of the older law-books ; further a more liberal application of *taqlīd*, i.e. adopting in some detail the doctrine of another school ; (3) limitation of the validity of *ijmāʻ* to the *ijmāʻ* of the mujtahids of a certain period and then only in so far as they are not in opposition to Koran and Sunnah.

This Manār modernism which has been propagated in various Malay periodicals during the past twenty years, has created an enormous stir in the Padang Lowlands, and to a lesser extent also in the Highlands. The struggle with the old-fashioned orthodox, which has often taken sharp forms over here, as a result of the people's particular affection for the old customs—it may be remembered that the Menangkabau territory is one of the few matriarchal territories of the world—has materially restricted the activities of the younger school. It has, besides this, been troubled by the fact that political movements have stepped into the foreground, apart from Islam. To these we shall now have to devote our attention.

ORIGIN AND GROWTH OF NATIONALISM

1. Javanese nationalism a result of the disturbance of social organization by the Dutch. 2. The aims of the nobility. 3. Ratu-adil eschatology. 4. Influence of the forced cultivation system. 5. Ethical colonial policy and transformation of native society. 6. Recent development. 7. Peculiarities of Javanese nationalism. 8. Javanese nationalism of the same type as former syncretism. 9. The part played by the Sarèkat Islam. 10. Mohammadiyah and Ahmadiyah movements.

1. It will be recalled that we characterized the old Javanese society as " colonial " in the old sense of the word. The position of the Dutch in Indonesia during the government of the " Associated East India Company " (abbreviated V.O.C. in Dutch) can be compared in many respects to the position of the nobility in the old society; they formed a new superstratum, so that the already dualistic society became

a tripartite one. For the benefit of their commerce they killed the competitive trade and shipping of the Javanese nobility which they met on their arrival in the Malay Archipelago, but for the rest they left society as they had found it, pressing it, however, to some achievements for the sake of their commerce. In this way they indirectly gave the deciding impetus to the transformation of Javanese society which began to display itself from that time. The government of the V.O.C. has, as a matter of fact, never assumed the character of a moral authority, nor has it ever claimed such ; it has aimed solely at being an apparatus for the control of the output and of the transport of the products. It could never, therefore, have taken the place of the old nobility, nor could it have absorbed the nobility, this being already bound to the population by many ties at that time, though still maintaining a distinct position socially. The fact that the Dutch married Javanese women, who, considering the antagonism between the Dutch and the nobility, could by no means belong to the nobility caste, made it still less possible to reach a harmonious solution of the growing contrast, a solution, such as the Philippine Islands exhibit. Whilst the appearance of the V.O.C. made no change in the situation of the peasantry for the moment, the nobility found itself in an exceedingly difficult position ; deprived of its governing authority, it became more and more the intermediary between the V.O.C. and the mass of the population, in political as well as economic matters, having as the only possible prospect a future amalgamation with the rest of the Javanese people.

This degradation was insupportable for the proud imperious caste, which considered itself in civilization far superior to the foreign ruler. It is quite understandable, therefore, that Javanese history tells of violent explosions, which, however, demonstrated more and more the impotence of the nobility. The last big opposition movement was that of Dipanegara, the central figure in the Java war from 1825 to 1830. It is assumed too easily since those days that the attitude of the nobility towards the Dutch has improved or has even totally changed, and the noblemen, who still play a prominent part in the administration of the country, are often called " loyal subjects " on the Dutch side. Only the Javanese nobles themselves, who in the meanwhile know that silence is golden, would be able to state the truth of this assertion. History, however, teaches us that we should not nurse too great an illusion regarding the significance of that silence ; loyalty towards the more powerful ruler yields an advantage not to be under-estimated as well as future possibilities, especially where a new danger to the position of the nobility threatens from the side of the people's movement.

It has been a serious mistake of the Dutch—and not

of the Dutch only—that they did not endeavour to create, if need be with the sacrifice of part of the profits, friendly relations with the populations of the colonies, when it was still possible. One may call this mistake quite natural, considering the circumstances of time and place, one may prove its pardonability with sound arguments, one may feel oneself convinced that many merits of the colonial government have neutralized the mistake later on or have perhaps even created a positive surplus on the credit side, and may stimulate others now to pass the sponge of oblivion over the slate of history; at the same time the mistake has become a fact of importance in the history of the development of anti-European sentiments and can no longer be eliminated or cancelled by denial or concealment, especially when we have handed over to the opponents of the colonial government the weapon of European scientific knowledge of history.

2. What did the enemies of the V.O.C. expect to gain? In material matters probably only their own glory and might. But in the general sense their eyes have presumably been fixed on the ideal of restoring the conditions which existed prior to the arrival of the Dutch, i.e. the restoration of the political and economic power of the monarchs and the nobility. Of course, this could not be a people's ideal; it was merely the ideal of those who had an interest in government. This opposition to the V.O.C. in the first centuries,

therefore, is perhaps not yet to be called a nationalist movement, as the mass of the people not only stood aside from it, but was not even interested in it. I emphasize the word "perhaps," because we do not hesitate in other cases to call a movement "nationalist" without accounting in detail for the proportion, as to quantity and standing, of the activists to the mass of the people.

3. The less the recovery of the old condition of Java could be realized, the more this recovery became an ideology. Out of the aversion from the present and the longing for the past, Messianic expectations are born. So the eschatological ideas which already existed changed to suit the new situation. Some day the *ratu adil* would come, the "righteous monarch" who would put an end to the reign of the foreigners. A new eschatological literature arose, books with forecasts concerning Java's revival, ascribed to a legendary king of Kadiri, Jayabaya, and announcing the end by violence of the Dutch rule. So Dipanegara, the hero of the Java war, for example, constituted himself a "ratu adil" and adopted the mysterious title which is attributed to the expected Messiah, Eruchakra. Dipanegara was neither the first nor the last "ratu adil." The Javanese annals relate of Eruchakras before him and the Dutch colonial reports of others after him. As a result of the growth and consolidation of the Dutch power during the nineteenth century, the

later " ratu's adil " were less dangerous for the colonial government than Dipanegara had been, but at the same time more numerous. Born out of opposition, the ratu-adil belief stimulated new opposition and so rendered itself everlasting. Circumstances to which we shall return later on led to a popularizing of the ratu-adil belief; without losing its local colour, moreover, it could easily be identified with the general Muhammadan Mahdi-expectations, which found their way to the masses at the time of the spread of Islam. Even nowadays it exercises an influence; that the Dutch rule would come to an end in 1930 was the conviction of many a Javanese, based on such ratu-adil belief, which seems to have played a part of some importance in the revolutionary action of the Partai Nasional Indonesia, brought to an end by the intervention of the police in 1929.

4. It is beyond any doubt that the Javanese nobility did not gain in esteem in their new social intermediary function. A part of their prestige in the eyes of the peasantry was necessarily lost together with their power and esteem in the eyes of foreigners. This process was considerably accelerated when, on the coming into force, shortly after the end of the Java war, of the so-called culture-system, a forced cultivation system, the European government started to interfere with the production of certain tropical plants for the world market. This forced cultivation system,

practically a draining system on behalf of the Dutch treasury, which in its intensive form was maintained in practice for about 40 years, has had considerable, though indirect, political results. It made the Javanese peasantry feel thoroughly the economic stress of the colonial domination practically for the first time; moreover, in consequence of the fact that the nobility also was shaken in its intermediary position, it revealed more clearly that a community of interests existed between the Javanese nobility and the peasantry. This would, in the long run, lead to the adoption of the nationalist aspirations of the nobility by the mass of the people, whereas, on the other hand, the immense force of the people would be placed at the disposal of the spiritually superior nobility—and later on of the intellectuals, who for the most part are descended from noble families. Finally, the excesses of the system could not help leading to a reaction, on ethical grounds, amongst the Dutch themselves, in the Netherlands as well as in the colonies; the European revolutionary year of 1848 had not passed without leaving its mark!

5. This reaction, somewhat noisily introduced to the general public by the publication, in 1860, of a stirring book of Douwes Dekker, who under the pseudonym of Multatuli in *Max Havelaar* scourged the Dutch merchant's covetousness and the colonial authorities' incompetence, was founded and made

fertile and effective through the more substantial work of men like van Deventer and Snouck Hurgronje. The digestion of their enlightened ideas in the field of colonial politics fortunately coincided with the so-called Asiatic awakening, so that the stress of the iron hand on the Javanese people was relaxed by upheaval from below as well as by weakening above. The psychological effect was, of course, that the Javanese now really understood under what a strain they had lived, and realized the more the pressure of their need for freedom. From that time onwards each new relaxing of the stress has freed new forces of the people and new desires for expansion, which in their turn have prepared new mitigations.

It was with great speed that events now succeeded one another ; a few years after the Japanese victory over the Russians, which was felt as a possible introduction to an Asiatic victory over the white race, followed the opening up of education on a Western basis to large groups of the native youth. About the same time the youth of the upper ten—to whom the European high school and the special schools had been opened, albeit slightly, in the preceding decades—organized (in 1908) the first political union, Budi Utama. The reserve with which this moderate aristocratic union was received in those days gave no inkling that as soon afterwards as 1912 there would be founded the Sarèkat Islam, a people's organization, which before long obtained an enormous number of adherents, even far beyond the borders of Java. The Sarèkat Islam ran in a few years through the various degrees between very moderate and revolutionary, not least on account of the disorganization of the world and the transformation of all values during the years from 1914 to 1918. After some violent collisions with the colonial government it could return to moderation only at the expense of its influence on the people, who left the Sarèkat Islam in order to enrol under the banner of less submissive organizations.

6. With the granting of political rights by the foundation of the National Council (Volksraad) in 1916 (1918), the avalanche-like development could not, of course, be directed into the fairways traced by the Dutch government. Nor can the reorganization, which will become a fact before long and which will abolish the minority of the indigenous element in the colonial parliament, give satisfaction in the long run. The fact that ten years after the organization such a reorganization is necessary, illustrates better than anything else the speed of this development.

I shall not enumerate the various organizations which have played or are still playing a part in the political life of Indonesia during the last ten years. It may suffice to remark that each is still more keenly nationalist than the other and that the anti-Dutch tendency is showing itself more and more freely. The contrast between "sini" and "sana," the people from over-here and from over-there, as brown and white are significantly distinguished, is becoming more and more defined, partly owing to the influence of the press organs on both sides, which hardly differ in passionate partiality. In 1930 the pressure was relaxed for some time. The energetic action of the government against the revolutionary plans of the Partai Nasional Indonesia, which I have mentioned above in connection with the ratu-adil belief, has disorganized the indigenous political movement, and the present economic crisis absorbs attention in such a degree, and, in view of the extent to which the masses are economically dependent on the political and economic authorities in Holland, renders any political, social or economic struggle for power so hopelessly out of perspective, that important modifications or new manifestations along the lines of development pursued during the last decades have very little chance of success in the near future. Nothing, of course, may be predicted regarding alterations beyond the line of this development ; such alterations are naturally always possible in these calamity-laden days.

7. The nationalist movement in Java has been stepping from group movement to people's movement and from an unorganized aspiration to an organized force for more than twenty years. Outside Java,

organized nationalism is in vogue only in some regions which have been exposed also to European influence to a somewhat considerable degree and over a sufficiently long time. I do not wish to assert at all that in the regions where it exists the whole population is concerned in the nationalist movement. Its activity originates in the great centres and only slowly filters through to the illiterate, conservative, and submissive peasantry. The upper ten are beginning to display more reserve in proportion as the movement penetrates more profoundly amongst the people; for the class-war, the natural sequel of the nationalism of these days, here too casts its shadow before it. Like the ruling princes in India to-day, the Javanese aristocrats to-morrow will probably have to consider whether they will support the colonial government or the mass of their own people as the least evil. I am as far from asserting that a hundred per cent. of those who join political or semi-political movements in Indonesia are also politically conscious and have a clear conception of the ideals for which their organization professes to strive. Nor can this be expected, in view of the almost fabulously rapid changes of the twentieth century.

We may, however, see in the rapid growth of the system of political unions a symptom that sentiments long suppressed are now seeking to find expression. The consequence of the political immaturity of the

INDONESIA

masses is, in a still greater degree than is the case in European countries, that the union is primarily a means to demonstrate one's preference for one group over another and to show one's discontent with the existing situation, while the official programme of the group is, in a certain sense, of minor importance. It is not at all necessary that there should be any congruence between the sentiment of the masses and the official aims and programmes of a political union. This is apparent from the not uncommon discrepancy between the attitude of the leaders and that of the members in important and exciting questions, and from the fact that large crowds at one time join this party and at another time that party, whichever happens to be in vogue. I may emphasize that nationalist unions are merely the *form* by which the present Indonesian generation seeks to express its feelings of discontent, and it is by no means necessary to assume that these feelings have systematized into conscious adherence to a particular political doctrine. The apparent success of communism may be explained by the fact that its propagandists were the least scrupulous in promising fulfilment of all possible desires. The cultural influence of Soviet Russia is as yet neither lasting nor strongly marked, and the unnatural alliance of some years ago between internationalist and atheistic communism and native nationalism, which is connected by many ties to Islam and which is just cutting itself loose from the existing indigenous agrarian communism, is certainly not based upon the conviction of the masses.

8. The very fact that in the nationalist movement the concrete goal of an organization is less of a stimulus to participation than the opportunity to express feelings of solidarity and grievance and instinctive opposition to foreign influence in many respects, renders it impossible to keep political, social, religious, Pan-Islamic, apologetic and cultural action absolutely distinct. The degree of development of the masses does not allow of discrimination, and all action must be seen from one point of view, however many aspects it may show the superficial spectator : all action is reaction against and often opposition to the disturbance of the social and cultural harmony of native society. Of special interest for the students of Indonesian Islam is that in many movements also the influence of the old Muhammadan consciousness of solidarity may be perceived. This is most conspicuous in a people's movement such as the Sarèkat Islam, which has at times numbered more than two million members. Its history exhibits the same queer mixture of heterogeneous elements, combined with a total lack of consciousness of this heterogeneity, which is known to us from both phases of Javanese literature. No West European organization could have succeeded in maintaining such a capricious and inconsistent existence for twenty years.

INDONESIA

This character of the nationalist movement presses us to enter into it more explicitly than the general title of this book seems to permit. But it is a fact that its history has been intimately interwoven with the history of the religious movements, in the proper sense of the word, which have come into the foreground during the last twenty years; the considerable influence of the Muhammadan consciousness of solidarity still plays, as it has always done, the important part of a connecting tissue.

9. We cannot deny, indeed, that the Sarèkat Islam always adhered to its Muhammadan origin, notwithstanding its alliances at times with socialism, then with communism, then again with different kinds of nationalism. It gave the impulse to the organization of the All-Islam Congresses which have been held in Java since 1922, and which aim at organizing the Muhammadan Indonesians in a Pan-Islamic bond, after the Indian example; it took a lively interest in the international Islamic congresses which were organized in Cairo and in Mecca, and at one or both of which, I believe, Indonesian deputies were actually present; it tried, though with a considerable over-estimation of its own force, to make its voice heard in the Caliphate question; it founded a " Majlis Ulama," a council of experts in Islamic questions, for Indonesia; it organized, or rather tried to organize, the opposition to the interference of the non-Muhammadan

colonial government in Muhammadan matters, an opposition which reminds us of the Christian parties' opposition to one of the articles (177) of the constitution of the Netherlands Indies, which limits the liberty of Christian missionaries; briefly, it did everything which came within its scope and which it was in its power to do in the interests of Islam, but most of the time did it so awkwardly that the effect has never been great and durable. Its fundamental mistake was that it wished to do everything, in social, religious, political, economic and cultural fields. Starting from the conception that it must be ready to take over its part of the task of government, when an independent Indonesia should arise, it organized in advance, for example, different departments of administration, which, considering the absolute lack of competent leaders, could not be anything more than an empty show.

10. Whilst in the political sphere it was forced to leave the lead to more radical unions, as has been remarked above, it has been completely thrust aside in the field of religion—and here we take up again the thread of the survey which was interrupted at the end of the preceding section—by Mohammadiyah, a socio-religious society founded on modernist principles in Yogyakarta (Central Java) in 1912. In opposition to the Sarèkat Islam, whose task in the field of religion it took over more and more, enjoying at the same time

the benefit of its pace-making, Mohammadiyah did not touch politics, and, as a result, has succeeded in attaining more within its limited sphere of activity. By founding schools, establishing and throwing open public libraries, by selling books and pamphlets, by founding hospitals, poors-houses and orphanages, by creating a Muhammadan information and propaganda service, by managing waqf-funds and by having important Muhammadan documents translated into native dialects, it acquired a good deal of influence and was able to assist materially in the adaptation of Islam to new conditions, while in many respects it cut in before the Christian mission, whose methods it had taken over. The Mohammadiyah movement originated in Central Java and has for the greater part limited itself to Java. Though it has exercised some influence on the modernist movement on the west coast of Sumatra, which we discussed at the end of the preceding section, it did not succeed in bringing about there an amalgamation of the different movements, for the most part directed to identical aims ; moreover, in contrast to its policy in Java, its activities in Sumatra became involved with politics.

In Java as well as in Sumatra, and partly in competition with Mohammadiyah, the Ahmadiyah movement has been making itself felt during the last few years. The writer of the previous chapter has given an account of the birth of this movement in North-west

India in the eighties, whence it spread even into Europe and America. The doctrine of the Ahmadiyah is of a highly ethical character and it directs itself particularly towards the intellectuals. Its followers, who are not afraid of fighting Christian doctrine by the written and spoken word, divided, after its founder's death in 1908, into two different sects, the Qādiān sect, which of the two is the more independent of Islam, and the more orthodox Lahore sect. Both have found Indonesian followers, and Indonesians have even studied the Ahmadiyah doctrine in India itself. The Lahore sect, however, has made the greatest stir in Indonesia, as a missionary of this persuasion has been active in Java for some years. Although distrusted and combated even by the spiritually congenial Mohammadiyah, which resents the competition of the Ahmadiyah, their missionary, Mirza Wali Ahmad Beig, has managed to form a small community; he has, moreover, given Muhammadan religious teaching at a few government colleges. That the leaders of the Sarèkat Islam and members of the Young Islamic Union have entered into friendly relations with Mirza Wali may possibly be regarded as one of the most recent examples of that uncritical sinking of differences to which Indonesian Islam is always inclined.

INDONESIA

INFLUENCE OF WESTERN EDUCATION

1. Former nobility and Moslem education. 2. Desire for Western instruction. 3. Revolutionary influence of Western instruction. 4. The ideal of a United Indonesia.

1. Still more interesting than the changes which have been modifying the features of native society during the past twenty-five years are the spiritual readjustments which are being brought about; more interesting and presumably much more radical in their consequences. Up to the end of last century direct spiritual contact between Europeans and Indonesians remained very limited; it was confined to a few scholars and some other interested men on one side and on the other side a small number of Indonesians, who had through circumstances become estranged from their own culture. The instruction which Indonesians were given by the Dutch colonial government was limited to a small group of future officials and to the practice of the civil service. For the rest the indigenous youth was left to be educated by parents or environment, or to receive a Moslem religious education, or no instruction at all.

The forming of character and moulding into an honourable member of the community was the most important part of a boy's education in the aristocratic milieu in Java. In the young man qualities had to be developed, which later on would distinguish him from the crowd as a "satriya," a nobleman : courage, discretion, self-control and exquisite manners ; in addition, he was expected to be acquainted with ancestral manners and customs and with family traditions, as these are the pillars on which Indonesian society rests. The young woman, on the contrary, did not need to learn much more than how she should duly serve her husband later on. Various Javanese books show us the character of this kind of moral and social education. Moslem religious education, on the other hand, was based on the small needs of the average people for a theoretical knowledge of Islam, whilst it was deeply influenced by the magicism of the primitive world of thought in which the Indonesian Moslems live ; it was *ngèlmu* which played the most important part in this system of education before the influx of orthodoxy from Arabia, and which has been playing a prominent part ever since. *Ngèlmu* is rather a state of perfect wisdom than science in our, or *'ilm* in the Arabic, sense of the word, and it can be acquired not by talent and zeal in the first place, but by the cultivation of the right susceptibility of mind, by submissive obedience to one's teacher and, last but not least, by receiving God's mercy.

2. Although the preference for *ngèlmu* has by no means disappeared even yet, it has had in practice to make way before the need for Western education under the pressure of circumstances. This need has

been awakened in the Indonesians partly involuntarily through their intercourse with Europeans, partly because they have learned to cherish it consciously as a result of nationalist considerations, and partly because it has been stimulated by the Dutch adherents of an ethical colonial policy, who considered the raising of the cultural level of the native population and the spreading of Dutch or generally of Western civilization to be a prominent, if not the most prominent, duty of a colonial government. Neither the Indonesian nor the European advocates of Western education for Indonesians had an easy task in breaking the resistance of those who saw prosperity only in a colonial policy of the old type. The first ten years of the twentieth century, however, brought victory to the principles of those who advocated the ethical policy. Already before the War the first Indonesian graduated as Doctor in Indonesian Philology at Leiden University. To-day, not twenty-five years after the opening of the Western school to a larger circle of natives, about 100,000 children of various Indonesian nationalities are receiving Western elementary instruction, whilst a considerable number are attending high schools and universities in Indonesia and in the Netherlands, or are already actively engaged in some profession after finishing their studies.

3. I can hardly abstain from mentioning the extraordinarily interesting social and sociological problems

which have become urgent after twenty-five years of experiment in European instruction of the Indonesian youth, especially because these problems at any rate indirectly have a bearing upon the position of Islam in these countries. I have, however, to restrict myself to the direct connection.

The historical development of the Netherlands has given Dutch civilization some characteristic peculiarities, amongst which is a general feeling of independence, inclined to turn into dislike of authority and discipline, as well in politics as in the field of religion and of social customs. Besides this, the Dutch educational system is mainly intellectualist and individualist; it lacks, with the exception of the autonomous Christian education, a markedly moral foundation, and the Christian parties do not play a leading part in the colonial higher educational system. Now, when the European school was introduced into Indonesia, numerous Dutch teachers had to be appointed, whose knowledge of the cultural traditions of the people amongst whom they worked was, as a result of the lack of special training, very limited, and the Indonesians, on the other hand, had to visit Dutch universities in order to continue their studies. And so it happens that, at the most susceptible period of their life, views and opinions find a lodgment in the minds and hearts of the prominent part of Indonesian youth, which are derived from Dutch peculiarities and from Dutch culture, and which differ totally from those which had been traditionally held and honoured in Indonesia. The Dutch teachers, upon the whole, while on the one hand they are unable to substitute for the ancient culture and educational system a new spiritual culture and a new educational system of the same internal strength and coherence, of the same suitability and limited efficiency—as a result of the fact that they belong to a people which gave up its own spiritual unity centuries ago—are on the other hand destroying by the dynamic influence of their Western education the belief in and the respect for the old customs, i.e. the basis of the ancient society, the basis also of Islam, which is closely allied to the traditional beliefs. European education is absolutely revolutionary, and the force of the blow which the native cultures are daily receiving is only realized fully, though not always critically, by the older generation of the Indonesians, with natural exceptions on both sides. The younger generation, indeed, has grown up with the new situation, and the European teacher has stayed outside the indigenous culture, so that they do not notice the difference so much.

The changes with respect to the old culture, which are being wrought in the young Indonesian intellectuals through Western instruction and the influence of the Dutch milieu, are analogous to the changes which were wrought, as we have already seen, in the

Egyptian youth half or three quarters of a century ago. The manner in which the Indonesian youth reacts to Western education also follows this analogy; youth is showing itself hostile towards Western mentality in several respects, but at the same time it can no longer do without Western culture and Western methods and seeks to use them to reach its self-appointed goal; it is strongly nationalist, but notwithstanding this it has become parted in many respects from the people's group in which it was born, just on account of its education. On the other hand, the fact that the greater part of the peoples of the Malay Archipelago display a certain degree of unity as a race, and are akin in language and culture, has been forced upon its attention as a result of the intercourse of young people from all Indonesian islands, Javanese, Sundanese, Madurese, Balinese, Ambonese, Menadonese, Achèhnese, Menangkabau, Batak and others, who come into touch with each other at college or university.

4. Thus there is developing amongst the student body a unitary Indonesian nationalism, which in its main characteristics reveals its European origin and the Western orientation of its protagonists. It is, therefore, by no means an accidental circumstance that this Indonesian nationalism has organized itself in the Netherlands. It is one of the aims of this organization, the " Perhimpunan Indonesia," to bring under one roof all the local-coloured nationalist movements,

by virtue of its own strength as well as with the assistance of established organizations in Indonesia. This endeavour is no doubt on its way to success, for, although the Partai Nasional Indonesia, operating in the Malay Archipelago and most closely akin to the Perhimpunan Indonesia, was dissolved after a conflict with the judicial authorities in 1930, the various youth organizations have followed the watch-word of " unity above all " so enthusiastically, that from the first of January, 1931, almost all local youth organizations have been extinguished, amalgamating themselves in the all-inclusive youth organization " Indonesia Muda," " Young Indonesia." In this case too the maxim holds good that the idea which moves youth is master of the future.

OBSTACLES TO THE SUPREMACY OF ISLAM

1. Youth and Islam. 2. Javanese Renaissance. 3. Neutrality of the Perhimpunan Indonesia. 4. The Young Moslems Union. 5. Its internal strength. 6. Christian missions as a factor in modern development.

1. Many of the young intellectuals have an attitude towards Islam quite different to that of the preceding generation. Under the influence of neutral education they have become indifferent with regard to religion generally, and, so far as they come into touch with

Islam, they are often inclined rather to accept the authority of science, which, critical and asocial as it naturally is, has made the Indonesians also aware of the defects of Islam and its frequent pious deceit. Consequently their adherence to some Moslem traditions at sacrificial meals or funerals is not much more than a folklore survival.

2. Still another factor is important for the Javanese younger generation. The old Hindu-Javanese traditions of political and secular culture, which had continued to exist in their circle, have found new support in the results of Western scientific research. The reconstruction of the history of Maja-Pahit has revived for them a past glory, which they are proud of, although they sometimes over-estimate the extent of that glory. Great figures of ancient history, as King Er-Langga, King Ayam-Wuruk, and Gajah-Mada, the chancellor of the empire of Maja-Pahit, who after being almost totally forgotten have been dug out of the dust of history by archæologists and linguists, have become heroic ideals for the young Javanese. It is obvious that a comparison of the glory of the Hindu-Javanese period with that of the Muhammadan period, which is unfavourable to the latter (although this is by no means a consequence of the nature and the relative interior strength and merit of the two systems), could lead only to the glorification of Hinduism at the expense of Islam. There need,

therefore, be no surprise at the fact that Budi Utama, the aristocratic political organization in the very heart of Javanese court culture, Central Java, inscribes on its banner neutrality towards the different religions ; that the Taman-Siswa schools of Ki Ajar Dewantara, which originated in the native principalities and are an attempt, as remarkable as rare, to take education into their own hands again, are teaching the pupils a preference for the old Javanese civilization, i.e. for Hindu-Javanese civilization, to Islam ; finally that theosophy, with its strong influx of Hinduism, has succeeded in acquiring a certain footing in Central Java. As the Central Javanese element is fairly strong amongst university students, these pro-Hindu-Javanese ideas also found their way into the students' societies and into the Pan-Indonesian sentiment which they represent.

3. The propagandists of United Indonesia have to take these currents into consideration, as they have likewise to face the fact that some Indonesian tribes which supply a large number of intellectuals, like the Minahassans, the Ambonese and the Batak, have for the most part been converted to Christianity, whereas the Balinese still confess a naturalized Hinduism and other tribes are pagans. These circumstances themselves, as well as the attitude of mind, which among the intellectuals in Egypt, for instance, led them to maintain a formal attachment to Islam, have in

this case led finally to the intellectuals' declaring themselves religiously neutral, as the president of the Perhimpunan Indonesia recently emphasized strongly at a meeting of Dutch students in Leiden. The young Indonesian unity movement thus officially holds aloof from the Moslem struggle for unity, but as the latter, although only a section of the Pan-Islamic movement, is in effect helping to make the "Jāwī" a unit, the interests of the two parties run parallel to some extent, and this leads to a great degree of mutual sympathy. Besides, the claim of Islam to be the official religion of the new empire of Indonesia, which, it is hoped, will soon be realized, is indeed regarded by many sincere Moslems as impossible of acceptance, because of the internal strife which such a privileged position would create.

4. On the other hand, some difference may already be observed between the younger generation of the Perhimpunan Indonesia in Holland and the latest generation in Indonesia itself. It has been a result of the expanding radius of Western education that the original plan of limiting such instruction to children of the native upper classes could not be maintained. The opening up too of the outlying regions of the Dutch Indies between 1890 and 1910 had the consequence that elementary Western education began to show a more marked democratic tendency, on account of the fact that nowhere in Indonesia are such keen

caste distinctions made as in Java. A greater proportion of the pupils of the high schools is beginning to come from humbler families, where Islam exercises more influence than in the higher classes of society. Although the youths from these families also feel the attractive power of the nationalist Pan-Indonesian movement, they still wish, under the influence of their surroundings, to keep to their parents' religion, albeit in a more modern form. Their ideal is the agreement of Islam and the modern state, as it exists in Egypt. They attempted to introduce this ideal into the various youth organizations which existed before the first of January, 1931 : next to uniformity of language, culture and nation, also uniformity of religion ; and when they failed to have their radical claim accepted by the whole youth organization, and the majority declared in favour of neutrality in the field of religion by founding " Indonesia Muda " on behalf of a more comprehensive Indonesian unity, they refused to co-operate and kept apart in their " Young Moslems Union."

5. Is this desire to stand aside to be interpreted as a proof of inner strength and self-assertion, and comparable with what we observe in the modern religious youth organizations in Europe ? It would be premature, in this early phase of the Union's existence, to draw conclusions from it with regard to possible future developments. The question is, indeed, whether this

strength is not a heritage from the past with its unconditional belief in and affection for Islam, and whether piety does not, perhaps, play a more considerable part in the Young Moslems Union than may be good for its viability. Is there to be found amongst them a deep realization of the superiority of Islam above other religions, a realization based on their own critical insight? Do they know the needs and wants of Islam, and have they a passionate love for Islam, whence comes the urge to make it a living spiritual power in their hearts and to communicate its blissfulness to others, as is the case with many Christians of various persuasions? I believe that an impartial critic, who has a full sympathy with Islam, will be inclined to reply in the negative to this question, though with every reservation which must be made when replying to a question that affects the spiritual life and the inner feelings of a group to which one does not belong oneself. One may arrive at this negative conclusion by observation of their apology for Islam, which is very often narrow-minded and takes the form of attempts to prove that the West is not at all better than the East, and that Christianity is not at all better than Islam. When they judge Christianity by an atheist's caricature, and attribute to the Christian community the whole dossier of mistakes of European imperialism and capitalism which the socialists have seen fit to put together, they are obviously too dependent on their European predecessors in their criticism and lack critical insight of their own. When in their declaration of principles they profess tolerance towards other religions—a tolerance which is, beyond certain rather narrow limits, foreign to the spirit of Islam, as it is foreign to the spirit of Christianity, unless its motive force be love for fellow-creatures—then they are obviously only the pupils of Western Liberalism and do not understand that tolerance becomes a symptom of decadence, as soon as it implants itself in the masses, inclined as they are to indifference. In such cases they show themselves to be running a decade behind Europe, where exaggerated tolerance has brought culture to the edge of the precipice, and where, in several countries, an effort is being made to remedy the fatal consequences of *quot capita, tot sensus* with vigorous, if one-sided, discipline. So long as the self-assertion and the self-criticism of the Young Moslems—apart from some possible exceptions —do not rise above the present level, its inherent value will remain small, and the basis on which the organization has been erected will prove unstable. Only when, perhaps, riper critical insight has forced its way up, either through their own activity or under the advanced influence of European education, will it become clear whether the Young Moslems Union really has the strength to do its share in resisting the tremendous storm which is shaking the foundations of the

Moslem world, and to overcome the spiritual crisis which scourges its community.

6. We have now arrived at the discussion of the last factor in the present process of development: the Christian missions in Indonesia. After gaining a firm foothold in the sixteenth and seventeenth centuries in Ambon and in the Minahassa, they produced very little of outward value in the eighteenth and the first half of the nineteenth century. Since that time, however, they have displayed a great activity and have gained considerable successes in various regions. These regions, however, belong to the least important of the Malay Archipelago. In those parts which are politically and culturally most prominent they have encountered the combined opposition of Islam and nationalism. No one who has given any attention to the struggle between Islam and Christianity in other parts of the world will need to be told that in Indonesia also the Christian missions find Islam a dangerous competitor and opponent, and have succeeded only in acquiring minor gains, against which must be set the losses suffered by Christianity owing to the quicker extension of Islam. That Islam and Pan-Indonesian nationalism, however, once again stand together in opposition to Christianity needs some explanation. The fact is that the Christian missions are frequently regarded as a cultural force inseparably connected with Europe, in this instance with the Netherlands,

and their victory would, it is thought, mean definite political annexation by the country whence they originate.

This widely held opinion, although not altogether true, at least not at the present time, is quite comprehensible. Nation and religion are one for the simple Indonesian peasant, and the possibility of a nation with five or six different religions would seem absolutely absurd to him. Christianity is for him the religion of Holland ; the distinction between Catholic or Protestant, even assuming that he knows these names, means no more to him than a difference in *madhhab* or *tarèkat* (religious congregation), whilst it is true of the Dutch, as of his own people, that amongst them are " red " and " white " (" slackers " and " pious "), and that the majority are, of course, of varying shades of " red." The worldly-wise hajji very likely knows better, but he has been well posted in the cunning plans of the Dutch government, and he knows how to warn his compatriots of the Christian danger, when he returns to Indonesia. For the hundred per cent. nationalist everything that comes out of the West is *a priori* to be rejected and it is with ill-concealed pleasure that he repeatedly points to the difference between the theory of Christianity and the practice of the so-called Christian nations. The moderate nationalists may not, for their own part and in theory, be markedly hostile towards Christianity, yet they are very unlikely to feel much sympathy with it, when conversion to Christianity is considered by many of their fellow-countrymen not only as a forsaking of the ancestral religion, but also as treason to the national cause. We therefore find that an organization with a preponderantly political history such as the Sarèkat Islam—to whose development the popular fear of compulsory Christianization has contributed its share—is at one with unions like Mohammadiyah and the Young Moslems Union where opposition to the activity of Christian missions is concerned, and that the opposition of these latter by no means suffers from the " tolerance " expressed in their declarations of principles.

I need not explain here the error which underlies these conceptions and ideas entertained by the opponents of Christian missions, but one has, in the meantime, to take them into account. Although one may unconditionally believe such authorities on Christian missions, as well as on indigenous manners and customs, opinions and conditions, as Adriani and Kraemer when they say that the influence of the missions is much more intensive than would appear merely from the figures of converts, it must nevertheless be remarked, that where this influence has had outward and visible effects, it has been of as much benefit to their opponents as to the missions themselves. I am thinking here, for instance, of the reaction which their activities have awakened in Mohammadiyah, a reaction which has contributed not a little to the progress of this indigenous union ; I am thinking too of the influence of the mission schools with their many pupils and relatively few converts.

Seen from a liberal point of view, this negative influence of missions, of course, is also a testimony to their success, but it gives Christianity itself a rather indefinite position among the currents which are helping to determine the course of events. It might, perhaps, have been much stronger and might have exercised much more influence, had it not been obliged to combat the opposition of those amongst its nominal supporters who believe in the possibility of combining a positive confession of Christianity with an exhibition of their belief in the superiority of the white race over the natives, and the opposition also of those who try to induce the Dutch government to patronize the missions directly or indirectly, although it has from the very beginning maintained an attitude of strict neutrality in matters of religion, and has maintained, for three centuries, the standpoint that it should occupy itself with manners and customs of the indigenous tribes no more than seemed strictly necessary.

Whether or not the Christian missions in the future will win in their struggle with Islam, as yet their only spiritual opponent of importance, finally depends, humanly speaking, on the stability of a Dutch power in Indonesia of the same character as the present government. The elimination of Dutch control would mean the removal of the biggest obstacle to the missions, the political obstacle, though nobody will dare to say that their success would thereby be secured ; one might say at the most that their chances against Islam in the future are better than in several other countries of the Dār al-Islām, considering the peculiarities of Islam in Indonesia.

Whither Islam?

Destructive forces are, no doubt, at work against Islam all over the world, and their strength ought not to be under-estimated. The theocratic character which Islam has borne since its early days has, for more than twelve centuries, brought it into close connection with supra-national empires, in which it supplied the most important cohesive force. As Snouck Hurgronje demonstrated in his rectorial address in 1922 on " Islam and the Race Problem," it has earned positive merit by its contribution to solving the problem of the mutual understanding of nations, a merit which cannot be denied even by the non-Moslem, the follower of another faith and another conception of life. The imperialistic development of the West—which itself, fairly soon after its great struggle with Islam in the time of the Crusades and in many respects also as a consequence of that struggle, broke with the semi-theocratic state of the middle ages and sought refuge in individualistic nationalism—first brought about a spiritual separation between Europe and the world of Islam, which later on, on account of Europe's need of expansion, had to be eliminated again, and which *could* not be eliminated except by drawing the world of Islam into the sphere of Western influence. European ideas, essentially opposed to the ideas which had prevailed hitherto, have nestled like cells in the centres of the Muhammadan world, have germinated in the leading members of Moslem society and have caused a process of decay, resulting, in the field of politics, in the formation of smaller Europeanizing states; these recognize Islam as a religion, sometimes even as the most important religion, but do not feel at one with it any longer. The Moslem supra-national community is about to split into consciously national groups, and its members will have to show which they will in future prefer: Islam or nationality. For the near future the signs seem to point to the latter. The Caliph, the symbol of Moslem unity, although sometimes an unworthy one, no longer exists. Islam, lacking a hierarchy, lacks also international organs, such as Catholicism has and Protestantism is building up in some spheres. Central management as well as organized deliberation are missing. Such attempts to initiate organized deliberation as have already been made in the last few years will probably continue to fail, in the near future at least, in consequence of the fact that the newly arisen Moslem lay-states have not yet acquired sufficient practical knowledge and experience of European political nationalism to see its dark side.

In the meantime Western education of the modern type, as foreign to the spirit of Islam as it is to the spirit of Christianity, proceeds, though in silence, to lay the seeds of further dissolution.

These are some symptoms of the decay of the Moslem world. At the other end, Europe too is experiencing a spiritual crisis, which is by no means a purely temporary phenomenon, but is indeed in the last resort the inevitable outcome of that force which, since Europe's estrangement from Islam after the Crusades, has dominated its development : exaggerated individualism. This spiritual crisis might possibly lead to the elimination of the greatest of the dangers which are now threatening the Moslem world : the unbridled passion of the West for expansion, imperialistic in the political sphere, capitalistic in the economic sphere and critically individualistic in the cultural sphere. Such a development might possibly result in the long run in a decrease in the rate of decay of Islam. Besides, the expansion of Europe stimulates, on the other hand, the opposition to its activities and methods and to the philosophic point of view which stands at the background of our spiritual crisis, in Europe as well as outside it. A section of the intellectuals in particular, who have best learned to know the spirit of European civilization, are, consciously or unconsciously, shrinking from accepting it and inclined to fight against it. Thence, perhaps, new powers might be born amongst the Oriental peoples, which would check the present decay of Islam or even turn it into new growth, if Europe were to continue along the lines which it is following just now. Who would deny the possibility at least of such a new development, after seeing, for instance, how movements like the Ahmadiyah, with its strong ethical powers and its no doubt deep religious feelings, are able to exercise a certain influence far beyond what has so far been considered to be the frontier of Moslem territory?

It depends largely on the particular view of life which we have chosen for ourselves from amongst the various existing views, what our attitude will be towards Islam and towards its struggle with the problems created by European political, economic and cultural penetration, how we stand with regard to its possible downfall or resurrection, and what value we place upon the phenomena which present themselves to us in the course of our study. An objective appreciation of realities, in the meantime, seems desirable in any case, on whatever *a priori* standpoint one may place oneself, and it is the task of the scientific study of

WHITHER ISLAM?

Islam to render possible and to promote that objective appreciation. It would be outside my task to press my own subjective appreciation, so I shall say no more here than this. It would not be at all unnatural, if the line of separation which to-day divides Christianity and Islam were to become less conspicuous—even without either of the two religions denying its nature —in proportion as a greater number of people catch sight of the wider gulf which separates the two acritical and solidaristic religions with their ideal aim and their orientation to the Great Beyond on the one side, from the critical, individualistic modern areligionism with its motto " wealth, prosperity and worldly advancement " on the other side.

In Indonesia we are observing essentially the same aspects, the same struggle, the same future possibilities as in the rest of the Muhammadan world, in spite of the difference of local circumstances and historical development. Against Islam there are working the modernization of colonial society, the Pan-Indonesian nationalist movement, the intellectualization of youth, to-morrow also, perhaps, the proletarization of the masses which may result from the increasing over-population, in view of the experience acquired in Europe that the rejected ones of this world are not seldom apathetic to religious sentiment. On behalf of Islam there are still working continuously the strong feeling of solidarity of the illiterate Muhammadan community and the reaction against European influence among the intellectuals. The Christian missions are co-operating and thwarting. They are thwarting, in so far as they make it their constant endeavour to reduce the territory of Islam ; they are co-operating, in so far as they represent a powerful moral force, which will be able to harmonize with other moral forces and to strengthen them. Islam's future in Indonesia will be determined by the manner and the rate in which Islam, nationalism, Western education and Christian missions react upon each other in the near future. Both manner and rate will depend to a great extent on the Dutch colonial policy. In the Netherlands, as in the rest of Europe, various forces are at work, which aim at steering it in entirely different directions. But the future conceals the secret of the relative proportion of those forces, and of the influence which they will exercise upon each other, in its womb !

WHITHER ISLAM?

By Professor H. A. R. Gibb

CHAPTER VI

WHITHER ISLAM?

By Professor H. A. R. Gibb

"Is there an 'Islamic World'? In other words, are the principal races professing Islam knit together by a common bond of sentiment, of interest or of ideas in virtue of their religion and peculiar thereto? The question is fundamental; to ask it is to invite a variety of answers."

To this question, at least in the terms thus formulated a few years ago by a writer of long administrative experience in Asia, those who have read the four preceding chapters will have no hesitation in answering "Yes." That in spite of all new tendencies and modern infiltrations from Western Europe, in spite of political disunity and cultural inequality, " a common bond of sentiment, of interest and of ideas " still exists, seems to be a proposition as little open to doubt as that the foundation of the common bond is to be found in the common religious profession and common background of religious culture.

On the other hand, it may be urged—and with a certain plausibility—that the social solidarity of Islam, in so far as it still exists, is mainly a survival from the recent past. The introduction of the new ideas and the new institutions associated with them is still too fresh and sudden to have succeeded in counteracting or destroying entirely the force of old sympathies amongst the majority of the adherents of Islam; but (it may be said) the new ideas are the active generating forces amongst the Moslem peoples, and it is to them that the future will belong, unless some unforeseen factor intervenes to sterilize them, whereas the old religious bond, having outlived its usefulness, will steadily weaken.

The question must therefore be phrased a little differently, in order to get at the real heart of the problem. Are the bonds of unity strong enough, or can they be made strong enough, to maintain the solidarity of Islamic society, to govern the outlook and development of its peoples, and to mark them off as a distinct cultural group? We must take care in the first place not to be misled by narrowing down too closely the terms of the question. The point at issue is not whether the *old* bonds of unity will persist unchanged, whether in the shape of uniformity of doctrine, allegiance to a common religious law, or common acceptance of a single cultural tradition. On the contrary, the outward forms may be radically changed, new organizations may arise in conformity with new views on the nature of government and society, the cultural background of different regions may be expanded and individualized by the resuscitation of ancient traditions or the influence of local factors, different aspects of religious belief may be differently stressed, the whole conception of unity may differ totally from the mediæval conception. All this is secondary. Fundamental is whether in their conceptions, their organizations, their attitude towards new problems, their internal spiritual and material evolution, the Moslem peoples will show a common tendency, will draw from a common stock, and be guided by the sense of a common task and common goal, or whether the pressure of new ideas and new needs will drive them ever further apart, and succeed finally in shattering the fabric of Islamic society.

Let it be said at once that no definite and unequivocal answer can be given to-day, nor, in all probability, for a long time to come. At any moment some new and unobserved factor outside our calculations may intervene to change completely the course of events; indeed, we may regard it as certain that more than one such factor will intervene. The evolution of societies seldom, if ever, follows a straight line, even when they have acquired relative stability after a long period of development in a well-marked direction; how much more likely to occur are sudden derangements and diversions, when the very foundations of a society are shaken and it is groping its way forward to a fresh adjustment of its forces ? An instance on a small scale is before our eyes in the case of Turkey since the establishment of the republic, and while it would be premature to assume that what has happened in Turkey is a premonition of what will happen in all other Moslem countries, we cannot rule out the possibility that they also may be the theatre of equally unforeseen developments. The suggestive paragraphs which Professor Massignon has prefaced to his description of the currents of opinion in North-west Africa should be sufficient to warn even the most confident of observers how unstable the ground is beneath his feet, how treacherous the surface features which he surveys.

Moreover, no society lives wholly unto itself, especially in these days of world-wide movements, when the technical achievements of western civilization have brought all sections of mankind into closer contact than ever before. Just as the impingement of the culture of Western Europe upon the Moslem world has been responsible for the present crisis in Islam, so the future course of its evolution will be affected not only by the further developments of Western European society, but also by the development of other societies. To take an extreme case by way of illustration, it might happen that before Islamic society had readjusted itself sufficiently to meet the crisis, the new communist society of Russia asserted its supremacy in Western

Asia, a revived Hindu society reasserted itself in India, and a Far Eastern society in Indonesia; or alternatively one of these societies might obtain such a cultural preponderance as radically to transform the course of evolution in the Moslem countries. We cannot, of course, deal with such speculations here. All that we can do is to take the Moslem world as it stands; to take stock in the first place of the extent to which western social and political conceptions have actually made themselves felt, and what indications there are of the extension of their influence; then, in the second place, to consider how the Moslem peoples individually and the Islamic world as a whole are reacting to the pressure thus brought to bear upon them; and finally to strike a balance which will indicate the general direction in which Islamic society appears to be moving at present.

The most remarkable feature of the Moslem world in these early decades of the twentieth century is not that it is becoming westernized, but that it desires to be westernized. It would be difficult to point to a single Moslem country which entirely rejects the contributions of the West in each and every field of life and thought. No Moslem leader has arisen, like Gandhi, to call his fellow-countrymen to a war on " Satanic " civilization. On the contrary, in spite of much criticism of the details of western civilization, in spite of rhetorical denunciations of western " materialism," every leader proclaims that the aim of his party is the political and economic organization of their country on western lines. Some may add that due allowance must be made for the differences of background and tradition, but in practice the usage of western countries is accepted as the norm. Even those conservative Moslems who seek for encouragement or example in their own past, and who relate incidents in early Islamic history to show that the principles and qualities sought after to-day are to be found in their own tradition, consciously or unconsciously select those instances which accord with the western point of view, and neglect all that too sharply contrasts with it.

However greatly the degree of westernization may vary from region to region, the writers of the four preceding chapters have shown clearly that it is present in all. For our present purposes it is important to trace the stages in the increasing mobilization of western influences, and to assign them their true place in the framework of Islamic society.

The first stage is the imitation or adaptation of outward forms of occidental life. The thin end of the wedge of westernization has generally been the adoption of western military apparatus and technique, in some countries now more than a century old, with results which have been referred to in the Introduction. This has usually, though not always, been followed by the adoption of western dress, and in some regions has extended to houses, furniture, social habits, manners, forms of speech and many other intimate details of behaviour. The traveller who lands at Alexandria or Port Said, travels in a luxurious train to Cairo, lodges at an hotel in the business quarter or in a modern flat or villa in the residential suburbs, and finds all the common amenities of European city life awaiting him, not excepting cinemas, jazz bands, and electric sky-signs, may well be inclined to admit the claim made by Egypt's Khedive more than fifty years ago, that " Egypt has become a part of Europe." Outside a few such cosmopolitan centres, of course, the conditions of life are more " primitive," and the romantic may seek there for the " oriental colour " that has faded out of the great cities. Yet, however far he goes, he will find it hard to escape the expanding tentacles of outward westernization, whose newest ally, the internal combustion engine, has made it free of the remotest and most inaccessible haunts of mankind. The motor, the aeroplane, and the petrol pump have already taken their place alongside the rifle even in the Arabian desert and in mid-Sahara.

If one asks what all this means in terms of our problem, it would be hard to maintain that the mere adoption of western externals, whether these be represented by an opera-house or by the treasured possession of a nickel spoon and fork by the village shaikh, implies in itself anything more than a desire to emulate the manners and take advantage of the new inventions of the West. It involves, no doubt, a certain recognition of the fact that in these matters the West has gone ahead of the East, but need not go on to indicate an equal degree of respect for western social and political ideas. Still less must we accept it as valid evidence for the assimilation of the spirit behind the western original. The more faithful the copy, it may be, the less the real understanding of the original. Above all, it certainly does not in itself convey the connotation which the old-fashioned Moslem doctors associated with it—the connotation of weakening attachment to the religion of Islam. It is surely significant that even in those Moslem countries which have the longest history of westernization, there is one outward feature which the population has uniformly rejected, professedly on religious grounds—the European hat, and has tenaciously adhered to its own form of headgear. Whatever the limbs might be draped in, the head at least would remain Moslem. Even in Turkey the imposition of the western hat was resented more than any other measure taken by the republican government, and was acquiesced in only by reason of the fear which it inspired ; in Afghanistan, the introduction of hats was the last straw, which cost an over-hasty reformer his throne.

Where, however, the outward assimilation to the

WHITHER ISLAM?

West has gone as far as may be seen in Cairo, something more than simple imitation and adaptation has been at work. The second stage of westernization is the adaptation of western technical processes to oriental life. Here the effect goes deeper, in proportion to the range of interests embraced, and touches most nearly the lives of the great mass of the people. In the first place, the economic changes which it has brought about in each region have already been stressed in several of the foregoing chapters, and it is not necessary to recapitulate the local results here. But, leaving aside for the moment the political and economic reactions of these movements, there remains the important social aspect to which, perhaps, scarcely enough attention has been paid. The growth of industry under European direction and the expansion of the old walled cities into great urban agglomerations (Cairo has over a million inhabitants, Alexandria nearly 600,000, Baghdād and Algiers 250,000, and the cities of Northern India and Java also contain a high percentage of Moslems) has brought into existence an urban population, composed largely of wage-earners, in contrast to the guild craftsmen and artisans of the mediæval towns. At the same time the introduction of machinery and mechanical transport is producing in the Moslem lands the same type of worker which it has already produced in Europe, one who is quick of hand and brain, alert, but restless, excitable, déraciné, and tending to adopt an attitude of indifference to old customs and prescriptions, religious and social. These results—in contrast to the other forces of westernization—are especially marked in North-west Africa, where the tendencies arising from the movement of African workers to France, described by Professor Massignon, have been reinforced by the effects of conscription for the army.

Alongside this urban "proletariat" there is also to be found in many countries, notably Egypt and Java, a rural "proletariat" created by the application of European technical methods to irrigation and agriculture. In Egypt the change from basin irrigation, which yielded one crop a year, to perennial irrigation, which allows of three crops a year, together with the introduction of cotton and other staples, enriched the landowner and depressed the cultivator to the level of the coolie. The social cleavage between landowner (who is frequently an absentee landlord) and peasant, though not to be exaggerated, is thus much greater than it was a century ago. Professor Berg has noted a similar development in Java in the relations between the peasantry and the Javanese aristocracy—a striking instance of similarity of development in two widely separated Moslem countries under pressure of the same factors. Nor, in most oriental countries, is the free or landowning peasant in much better case, since he is chronically entangled in debts owing to the usurious village moneylender.

These classes, which have felt more severely the disruptive effects of western intervention, are peculiarly susceptible in consequence to propagandist activities of all kinds. It is not surprising to find them supplying ready tools to-day to nationalist and communist organizers, to-morrow maybe to preachers of the Holy War ; nevertheless, their rôle is in the strict sense passive, although it is through them, and will continue to be through them, that the active elements seek to achieve their ends.

Much more important, as a factor in westernization, is the growing tendency amongst Moslem employers of labour to apply European industrial methods and economic principles on their own account. Notable examples of recent years are the Banque Misr in Egypt and its affiliated banks in Syria, the establishment of capitalist commercial and industrial societies in India and Java, and the organization of Turkish industries under the Turkish republic. This economic reaction is still, however, only in its infancy, how far it will go cannot yet be seen.

Far-reaching though the economic effects of westernization may be, a more prominent place in the public eye is taken by the application of western technical methods to the organization of government and administration. Not only in territories under direct and indirect European control, where it might be taken for granted, but also, as we have seen, in most of the independent Moslem countries, the departments and methods of administration have gradually been reorganized on European models to such an extent that they may now be said to be completely westernized. It has been pointed out that this was indeed the primary object of the early reformers in Turkey, and where they failed, their successors have been more fortunate not only in bringing their plans to fruition but in carrying them to still more radical lengths. Every Moslem government at the present day, except Afghanistan and Yemen, that most mediæval of survivals, now has its bureaucratic departments of state under responsible Ministers, and not only for justice, foreign affairs, and education, but also for police, irrigation, public works, medical and sanitary services and the like.

Even more significant of the westernizing current in administration is the establishment of municipalities and organs of local government on a representative basis, not only on account of their proved value as training-grounds for state administration, but because they form an entirely new feature in the organization of the Moslem state. It is hardly necessary to insist on the eagerness with which representative institutions have been claimed and introduced, and the gratification which they have supplied to national self-respect.

Parliamentary government is accepted, in the present phase of political evolution, as the outward symbol of full nationhood. The somewhat erratic workings of the representative system in most Moslem countries do not detract from the significance of the principle. The theory of absolutism has been definitely discarded, and its place taken by the theory of national sovereignty. This marks the culminating point in the outward adoption of western models, a point which has been reached only at a very recent date. The early Turkish and Egyptian reformers were by no means democrats; the full appreciation of the representative system had to wait upon political education, and it has taken nearly a hundred years of western infiltration before its appearance as an active factor in Moslem political life.

Yet the very fact that this political system has been so recently transplanted itself suggests that its foundations must be even less stable, and its principles less thoroughly assimilated, than those of the other external features of western organization which have been superimposed on the traditional life of the East. Even allowing for the existence of a small European-educated minority who have grasped its real function, we cannot but regard the constitutional forms of political life in Turkey, Egypt, Persia and elsewhere as still external to their real life—that is to say, as mechanical applications of western methods in the

WHITHER ISLAM?

field of government, exactly on the same footing as the application of machinery to industry and of bureaucratic organization to administration. There are critics who have gone on to assert that the representative system can never be anything more than this, that it is fundamentally alien to " the East " and can never take root there. The historian is indeed bound to admit that the traditions of government in the Islamic world are not of a kind which tends to develop the qualities required for the successful working of democratic institutions, but to deny the possibility of their development under new conditions is to make an irrational leap from history to prophecy. The argument from " racial characteristics," even allowing it to possess any scientific value in this field, can hardly be applied to a society which embraces at least seven totally distinct races.

In any case, the point of immediate importance for us is that, though these are amongst the most striking examples of the impact of Western Europe upon Islam, the future of westernization and the part which it will play in the Moslem world does not depend upon any of these exterior adaptations. The outward forms are subsidiary; here even more than in material things, the more perfect the outward imitation the less is the interior assimilation, since with the more thorough grasp of the spirit and the principles underlying the outward forms there will usually be linked a perception of the adaptations required by local circumstances. Many of the existing western institutions may be swept away, and yet the Moslem world be no less westernized than before, perhaps even more so. If we are to find the real measure of the influence exerted by western culture upon Islam, we must look beneath the surface, and in the first place for ideas and movements based upon a creative assimilation of western thought after intensive inner preparation. All the rest is superficial, and however difficult the task may be, we must make an effort to distinguish from the mass of imported and often shoddy western materials that now clutter the domain of Islam those which really form the first courses of a new cultural edifice.

The main—indeed, if the word is taken in a wide enough sense, the only—sound agent of westernization is education, and it is by the criterion of its education in western thought, principles, and methods that the extent of the westernization of the Moslem world is to be judged. But this education is of many kinds and carried out by many agencies. At bottom, of course, there must be a western education in the narrow sense, at school, technical college, and university; without this, nothing else is possible. We have seen the stages by which education of this kind was introduced into the various regions of the Moslem world, and the influence which it has exerted on the mentality of the secular leaders and some few of the religious leaders of Islam. Yet, if we are to accept the usual statement that ninety-five per cent. of Moslems are illiterate (though for the rising generation this must be a serious underestimate, in view of the rapid extension of elementary education in all Moslem countries—the most recent figures show that over 500,000 children are now attending elementary schools in Egypt), and must further allow that at least half of the literates have enjoyed an education on traditional lines only, the remaining fraction of western-educated men is clearly too small, in spite of their leading position, to account for the general westernizing tendency found in nearly all parts of the Moslem world. On the other hand, with increasing literacy there will, under present conditions, be an increasing impetus towards broadening and deepening the current of westernization, especially in conjunction with the other educative agencies which are impelling the Moslem peoples in the same direction.

Amongst these we may reckon the effects produced by the mere existence of some at least of the outward adaptations of western forms described in the preceding paragraphs. The part played in this respect by the introduction of European industrial methods has already been remarked. Similarly, the fact of administration on western lines is bound to result in the acceptance by the administered of a western standard in administration, and in the demand for it. No modern Moslem government, for instance, can afford to neglect the provision of medical services or the extension of educational facilities. The existence of representative institutions is, in the same way, the first step in the political education of the electorate. Admittedly the institutions themselves form no more than a first step ; they give no guidance as to the means by which to ensure efficient administration or to control political action. For this further development, without which the outward forms must remain mere surface display, it is necessary to rely not only on the provision of elementary and secondary education, but still more on the creation of an instructed public opinion. This is the special province of yet another educational instrument inspired by the West, the Press.

The rapid rise and extension of journalism in the Moslem lands has both a debit and a credit side to its account. On the one hand, it has, without question, succeeded in creating the elements of a political sense amongst the mass of the people, and has been the principal agent in raising the general intellectual level. Journalism in the literate West may sometimes be a narcotic; in the illiterate East it is rather a stimulant. Against these services must be set the occasional abuse of its immense influence, and some inherent weaknesses due to the recency of its growth and its lack of stability. Nevertheless, the printing press is far and away the most revolutionary and influential of all the contributions of Europe to the Moslem world. Already the number of journals issued in all the languages of Islam exceeds one thousand, and the list continues to lengthen. Professor Kampffmeyer has indicated the variety of interests represented in Egyptian journalism, which, especially since the war, holds pride of place in the Moslem literary world, but there are other centres which do not lag far behind Cairo. To keep in touch with this vast mass of ephemeral publication —which is, after all, the truest mirror of current ideas and tendencies—is beyond the powers of anything short of an organized institution. Even the Italian Istituto per l'Oriente, which has the merit of publishing, in the monthly journal *Oriente Moderno,* the most valuable, and indeed indispensable, survey of current Moslem affairs, does not include Central Asian, Indian, and Indonesian journals among its sources.

We can, however, pick out some general characteristics which have a bearing on our problem. The directors of the daily Press generally belong to the most advanced sections of opinion in their respective countries, and the outlook of most of the daily journals is in consequence dominated by western influences. They are the protagonists of constitutional movements and the chief critics of internal administration, as well as of European governments in Islamic lands.

Not only do they help powerfully to mould public opinion in regard to local affairs, but by maintaining an adequate news service, by articles explaining European political and economic movements, and by translations from European journals, they keep their public informed of events and opinions in Europe and their repercussion on the East. In addition they show a lively interest in the affairs of other eastern countries, much more so, in fact, than the European journals, and thus nourish the feelings of sympathy which are evoked by community of aspirations and the facing of common problems. Thus the Press in Moslem lands is an educative force not only nationally, but also internationally, and this tendency is strengthened by the diffusion of the Arabic Press in particular throughout the other Islamic countries. Between the Press of the different countries, however, certain differences may be remarked in the general currents of thought and the strength of religious influences. The Turkish Press, of course, is wholly secularist and nationalist (and dare not be other, so severely is it controlled by the government) ; in contrast to its revolutionary spirit, the Egyptian Press is more evolutionary and shows a healthy variety of opinion, but is generally secularist in its tendencies. That of the Arabic countries in Western Asia is rather less so and strongly pan-Arab, while the Moslem Press in India is still dominated by religious feeling, reflecting the strong tendency to religious particularism still characteristic of Indian political life.

The daily Press is supplemented by a host of weeklies and monthlies, mostly devoted to special interests ranging from Islamic theology and general literature to the theatre and the cinema. These too exercise an influence which frequently radiates beyond their country of origin. The religious reformist journal *al-Manār* has a world-wide circulation and, as Professor Berg's account of its effects in Indonesia has shown, is playing an important part in the readjustment of theological views. About this we shall have more to say later on. The literary journals, which are still the main vehicles of modern literary activity in the Moslem countries, have the same secular character as the daily Press, and exercise a cumulative influence in the revival of literary culture and the formulation of the new intellectual tendencies. The women's movement too has its own journals, some of which are directed by women; there are Boy Scout journals, educational journals issued by the various universities and training colleges, and journals of associations of all kinds.

The net result of all this educational activity has been to secularize, in the measure of its influence and to a large extent unconsciously, the outlook of the Moslem peoples. This, and this almost exclusively, is at the heart of all effective westernization in the

Islamic world, and forms the criterion by which we may estimate the relative strength of modern and of conservative opinion. Islam, as a religion, has lost little of its force, but Islam as the arbiter of social life is being dethroned ; alongside it, or above it, new forces exert an authority which is sometimes in contradiction to its traditions and its social prescriptions, but nevertheless forces its way in their teeth. To put the position in its simplest terms, what has happened is this. Until recently, the ordinary Moslem citizen and cultivator had no political interests or functions, had no literature of easy access except religious literature, had no festivals and no communal life except in connection with religion, saw little or nothing of the outside world except through religious glasses. To him, in consequence, religion meant everything. Now, however, in all the more advanced countries, his interests have expanded and his activities are no longer bounded by religion. He has political questions thrust on his notice ; he reads or has read to him a mass of articles on subjects of all kinds which have nothing to do with religion, and in which the religious point of view may not be discussed at all and the verdict held to lie with some quite different principle ; he finds that in many of his difficulties and disputes it is useless for him to apply to the religious courts, but that he is bound by a civil code which derives its validity from he may not know where, but certainly not from Koran and Tradition. The old religious interests have ceased to furnish his sole, or even his main social link with his fellows; other and secular interests claim his attention. The authority of Islam is thus loosened in his social life, and it is relegated little by little to a narrower range of activities. Much of this has taken place quite unconsciously; only amongst a small percentage of educated men has it been consciously realized, and amongst a still smaller proportion consciously pursued. Nevertheless the process has gone on inexorably, and where it has already gone far enough it is irrevocable. It seems impossible now, especially in view of the increasing demand for education and the increasing adoption of western institutions, to reverse the current and to restore Islam to its old unquestioned monopoly of social and political influence.

If this be accepted then as the criterion of westernization, how far has the world of Islam actually been westernized? It is clear from the preceding chapters that its progress in this direction has been very unequal, and that nearly all stages are represented in the Moslem world of to-day. The governing classes in Turkey, for instance, stand for westernization in its most revolutionary form; in Arabia, on the other hand, it has not yet gained a footing. In North-west Africa the process has little more than begun, and has apparently gone farthest in Tunisia. In Egypt it is proceeding apace, but by gradual and non-violent stages ; 'Iraq and Syria seem to be following in the footsteps of Egypt, Persia in those of Turkey, but with rather more moderation. Afghanistan, after the hectic experiment of ex-King Amanullah, has apparently sunk back, if only for the moment, into mediævalism, while the Central Asian Soviet republics, under pressure from Moscow, have completely disestablished religion. In India the communal question has helped to keep the minds of the Moslems focussed on their religion, but even without this it is doubtful whether the mass of Moslems would yet have adopted a westernized outlook to any extent. Indonesia shows such a variety of cross-currents that any general statement can hardly be made, yet except for a minority it would be rash to assert that westernization has yet struck deep roots. African Islam is still in a relatively primitive stage.

Perhaps the safest conclusion would be that we must distinguish two main strata ; an upper stratum, which includes not only individual leaders but also the most influential centres of Islamic thought, and in which the influence of western ideas is already strongly pronounced ; and a lower stratum, comprising the great bulk of inarticulate Moslem opinion, in which its action is still relatively restricted, though seldom vigorously opposed, except in Arabia itself. Since, however, it is the leaders who count, and more especially the leaders among the younger generation, we may conclude that within a very short time, unless some new factor intervenes to deflect the existing currents into another channel, the greater part of Islam will have definitely adopted a secularist outlook.

But, it may be asked at this point, why has nothing been said about nationalism in the Moslem world? Is not this, in fact, admitted on all hands to be the most striking and unmistakable evidence of westernization? The answer will depend largely on the exact meaning which we attach to the word. If it means what we have come to understand by it to-day, militant economic and political nationalism which, in consecrating its energies to the sectional interests of a single group, forgets the wider interests of the society to which that group belongs, then we can fortunately discern comparatively little nationalism as yet in the Moslem world. It is present to a certain extent in Turkey, and for the moment at least sets the pace in Turkish policy. There was a time after the war when it seemed to be spreading through other Moslem countries as well, but the mood has either passed or died down. Turkey, however, looms so large in the view of most western observers of Islam and has such a tradition of leadership behind it that its action is too often regarded as typical of what either is happening or will happen in other sections of the Moslem world. There is support for this view in the fact that nationalist movements and aspirations undoubtedly exist in these too, but on closer examination it will probably be found that the immediate objects and ideals of these nationalist movements show a widely different spirit from that of the Turkish republicans, a spirit less revolutionary and more humane. It is perhaps impossible as yet to distinguish all the elements which go to make up Islamic nationalism ; as Professor Berg has demontrated in the case of Indonesia, it combines or attracts to itself a variety of activities directed to quite different ends. It is militant in the sense that its primary object is to combat European intervention and to regain freedom from European control, but this militant aspect is reserved for Europe. In pursuit of its aims it sees the most effective means to be the stimulation of a feeling of solidarity amongst all the members of each community, and the historical circumstances sketched in the Introduction have brought it about that its action is directed in the first instance within a regional framework. But only in the first instance ; for in not one of the Moslem countries, with the exception of Turkey and the partial exception of Indonesia, is the community of interests and aims which bind them to one another neglected or forgotten. Even in Egypt, though the immediate local problem, there as elsewhere, is uppermost, it is the frequent boast even in the most " advanced " circles that Egypt is the leader of the Arab or of the Moslem world, and the separatist tendencies are confined, for the most part, to the sphere of government.

The difference between nationalism of the western type, as seen in Turkey, and this modified Islamic nationalism may, of course, have to be explained in the last resort as symptomatic of their respective strength or weakness. A country which feels itself able to maintain its independence by its own efforts and to stand on its own legs is more apt to fall victim to the virulent type of nationalism. Those which feel themselves economically or politically weak will look for support to some outside organization, and in this instance hope to find it in the maintenance of an Islamic solidarity. Whether this explanation is in fact a valid one, and the ideal of Islamic solidarity a disembodied ghost, whose existence is half hoped in as a mass weapon, half disbelieved in as a phantasy, only the future can show. We shall have more to say later on the subject in general ; in the meantime, we must accept it as a limiting element in the current conception of nationalism in most Islamic lands.

We must thus provisionally define Moslem nationalism as the effort to reorganize Islamic society on the basis of self-governing units. It is the outcome, on the one hand, of the introduction of western political conceptions, on the other, of hostility to western political and economic supremacy. It is national, not nationalist, in feeling. There is at present little sign, outside

Turkey and perhaps Persia, that it will go farther along the fatal path of western nationalism; nor can it even be said that national consciousness is as yet a fixed and dominant feature in any Moslem country. It still carries with it an exotic flavour, and racial barriers have ever been so contrary to the whole tendency of Moslem feeling that it is difficult to believe that they will easily be erected now.

Yet there is a section of opinion in some countries which is attracted to racialist ideas. They are again strongest in Turkey, where the Pan-Turkish ideals of pre-war days received a strong impulse during the war and have been responsible for several of the subsequent activities of the republican government. North-west Africa, as Professor Massignon has shown, has its protagonists of Berberization, and the Pan-Arab movement in Western Asia is not entirely free from similar elements. One of the most curious results of westernization has been to foster such tendencies by the disinterment of the ancient civilizations which flourished in the lands now occupied by Moslem peoples. The ghost of Hittite culture exercises a strong fascination on some of the Turkish leaders, and the discoveries in the tomb of Tut-ankh-amen gave a stimulus to the revival of " Pharaonic culture " in some literary circles in Egypt, which has not yet exhausted itself. Like results have been produced, as we have seen, in Indonesia by the recovery of the old

Hindu-Javanese culture, and it may be that Sumerian and Babylonian culture will exercise a similar influence in 'Iraq, as the recovery of the ancient Persian cultures has undoubtedly done in Persia. It is, however, unlikely, to say the least, that in the greater part of the Moslem world such " ghosts " will have an effect upon their peoples comparable with that of the revival of the Hellenic tradition on Greece at the beginning of last century. So far, indeed, they seem to be prized most as a means of gratifying anti-European feeling, though in the future they may possibly form an enriching element in national life.

Now that we have seen the extent to which European educative influences have pervaded the Islamic world and have created a new spirit and a new outlook among some sections of its peoples, it is time to turn to the other side of the medal. What effect has this had upon Islam? In what way has the attitude of Moslems changed towards their traditional religious culture? To what extent do they still value Islam as an element in their national life and in their mutual relations? How far is the thought of Islam adjusting itself to meet the new circumstances? To some of these questions partial answers have already been given, but even at the risk of repetition they must be taken up and dealt with again here as a whole.

WHITHER ISLAM?

In introducing our discussion of westernization the general statement was made that the Moslem world desires to be westernized. At the outset of this part of our investigation another general statement, even more categorical and no less fundamental, must also be made. The Moslem peoples remain deeply attached to the religion of Islam and intensely convinced of its superiority. That here and there individual Moslems, especially of the upper classes, are lukewarm in their faith and neglectful of its observances, or even confess themselves atheists, matters as little as that amongst those who call themselves Moslems there are groups whose religion is little more than a compound of primitive superstitions. The vital forces of Islam, as a creed, as a rule of life, and as an ethical system remain unimpaired. The critical moment which threatened at the end of the nineteenth century has been passed, largely through the instrumentality of Shaikh Muhammad 'Abduh and his disciples. The effect of his lifework, like that of Sir Sayyid Ahmad Khan in India, was to remove the paralyzing inhibitions that were holding back Islam, and to release fresh energies for the task of bringing its teachings and institutions into harmony with the new life of the Moslem countries. The very fact that Islam is no longer a thing to be taken on trust, but, in this age of stress and disintegration of the old social order, a thing to be fought for, is itself a powerful stimulus to a new appreciation of its value. Islam has always been religion-conscious; to-day it is more so than ever.

Although the old uniformity of Islamic society has been broken under the pressure of the new forces and ideas from the West, and although Islam has largely lost its legislative prerogatives in the political field, yet the old ideal of Islamic unity retains its hold on the imagination of the Moslem peoples. So far from weakening, it has during the last century steadily grown stronger and more conscious of itself. On the one hand the reaction to European intervention and economic pressure, on the other the active Pan-Islamic propaganda carried on from Turkey between 1878 and 1910, together with the diffusion of literature from Egypt and other centres, have all contributed to give a new prominence to the common link; while the improved means of communication invented in Europe have helped to make it more of a physical reality than before. As in the case of most Islamic institutions, its existence is apt to elude the observation of those who judge of the strength of a movement by its outward organization. Only those who realize that its essence lies not in outer forms but in the acceptance of an ideal by the will can grasp the true nature of the forces which are active beneath the surface. An apt illustration is afforded by the Ottoman Caliphate, which was regarded by European observers as the keystone of Islamic unity, and its abolition by the

Turkish republic as a fatal blow. In reality, the Ottoman Caliphate was no more than a very imperfect symbol, and even as such by no means universally recognized by Moslems—witness, for instance, the utter failure of the attempt to proclaim a Holy War in 1914. Its abolition created consternation, it is true, in orthodox circles, but in no way weakened what solidarity it stood for between the Moslem peoples. On the contrary, it removed a likely cause of friction and disunion, more especially as the Caliphate stood for an autocratic mediæval conception of unity, with which the new ideals of the Moslem peoples were out of sympathy. Nothing could have been more opportune than the disappearance of this wraith from the Middle Ages just in time to leave the way clear for new conceptions more in harmony with the new situation in the Moslem world.

The social solidarity of the Moslem peoples may, however, be put down, as we have seen, to the survival into a different age of a legacy from the past. But is it then so certain that there is nothing in the old ideal of unity which appeals to the modern western-educated classes and which they are eager to preserve? Surely their interests, if not their personal sympathies, must assure them that there is much, both on the negative or defensive and on the constructive side. Face to face with the formidable superiority of force which Europe, faction-riven as she is, still possesses, the Moslems are conscious of their individual weakness. The separate units which compose the Moslem world are numerically weak—even the strongest of them, the seventy million Musalmans of India, is in fact one of the weakest by reason of its local confrontation with the immense force of Hindu nationalism. The danger of isolation is plain to them all, and not merely the danger in a military sense, but also the menace to the springs of their cultural life. It has already been suggested that the sentiment of unity is a defensive weapon not to be lightly discarded. It gives moral strength to the individual units; moreover, the success of the Indian Moslems in organizing popular sentiment in defence of Turkey has shown them the practical advantage which is to be reaped from the mobilization of sympathetic action. Though this new weapon is admittedly still in a rudimentary stage (which may explain in part the action of the Turkish leaders in turning their backs in their extremity on their Moslem allies and accepting the support of Soviet Russia instead), we shall see that the effort to increase its efficacy is one of the most significant movements in the Moslem world to-day.

Linked up with this effort is the growing realization of another aspect of Moslem unity. While the national movements whose evolution we have already followed up are the fruit of the western conception of the national sovereign state, the Moslem peoples have as yet taken only the first step towards the creation of national units. They have not, like us, grown up in the bosom of national institutions, and are still sufficiently independent of them in the intellectual sense to be able to judge them dispassionately and frame their own ideals and policies accordingly. Their increased experience of Europe and acquaintance with European history has already given them an insight into the fatal results of western nationalism when pushed to its ultimate consequences and exalted to a position above that of its parent society. There is already perceptible in several sections of Moslem society a revulsion against a system which, as Professor Berg has put it, places individual advantage above the joint cultural interest. This reaction against the non-ethical principles of European culture is inevitably leading the Moslem intellectuals to place increased emphasis upon Islamic ethics, and to stress more especially the doctrine of brotherhood which is at the basis of the Moslem social ethic. Thus on ethical grounds the tendency to reassert the social link between the Moslem nations is visibly gaining strength, especially with the growing political influence of the middle class, amongst whom the ethical teachings of Islam have always exercised a stronger influence than amongst the old military aristocracy. The more democratic the future national states are, the more will the Moslem view predominate in their political relations.

Finally, here too the influence of western thought may lead in the same direction. The new tendencies in Europe which, likewise in reaction to the extravagant militant nationalism of recent decades, are moving towards the association of the national states in some larger group and the abandonment of the extreme doctrines of national sovereignty, cannot fail to exercise in due course an analogous influence on Moslem political thought, and to strengthen the hands of those who are striving to draw closer the ties of unity in Islam. It is a further point in their favour that there is no reason to suppose that the economic competition which has sharpened national antagonisms in Europe is likely at any time in the near future to trouble the mutual relations of the Moslem peoples.

One factor may, however, intervene to hinder the full realization of Moslem unity, namely the cultural inequality of the Moslem countries. We have seen that there is already a fairly sharp distinction to be drawn between those countries which have begun to reorganize their governments on western lines and those which are still in principle faithful to the traditional institutions. Even within the former group there are wide differences in the degree to which western institutions have been adopted. These differences are likely to persist, yet they are not a fatal obstacle on the path of unity. After all, the adaptation of the same western ideas to a common substratum must necessarily follow more or less parallel lines. Even between the most " advanced " and the most " backward " countries the common substratum will continue to exist and to provide a common meeting-ground, thereby marking off the Moslem group from the European, Hindu, and Far Eastern groups, while the differences in the adaptation of western institutions are likely to remain, on the whole, matters of detail. The problem has also a religious aspect, however, which will be considered more fully presently.

Meanwhile, to return to the present, the sentiment of unity not only continues to exist, but gives outward signs of its existence in a strikingly uniform way. No incident which touches on the life of the Moslem world passes without eager and interested comment in the Press of half of two continents, and when these incidents assume a graver character, whether in Morocco, Libya, Palestine, India, or Indonesia, resolutions of protest are recorded from all quarters, all alike in tone and even in language. It was not so long ago that the greater part of Islam seemed to be sunk in such lethargy that men deemed it dead ; to-day a relatively trivial incident like the execution of 'Omar al-Mukhtar acts as an electric shock, as the preceding chapters have shown, from Morocco to Java, and generates a current of burning resentment. True, the feeling so generated is but temporary, but the cumulative effect of such shocks (the most recent of which have been referred to by Professor Kampffmeyer) is to make the reaction ever stronger, and to increase the self-consciousness of the Moslem world.

Nor have the old institutions which fostered the growth of unity all lost their force in the modern world. Though legislative unity has gone and national cultures have begun to supplant the former cultural uniformity, though differences of social customs have become more marked and the traditional religious education is confined to a diminishing section of the population, the religious institutions themselves remain. It were a bold assertion that the Koran is any less studied than it used to be, or that its haunting rhythms have lost their power over men's minds. The ritual observances of Islam are still a source of satisfaction and assurance even to those who are themselves careless of their fulfilment. The fraternities or mystic orders are banned in Turkey, and shorn of much of their influence in Egypt and Western Asia, but elsewhere competent observers declare that their ascendancy is increasing. The sense of devotion to the person of Muhammad and the enthusiasm which it evokes amongst all classes may well prove to be one of the most significant features in modern Islam. "They call me an atheist," said recently one of the most prominent exponents of western thought in Egypt, apropos of certain European works on the early history of Islam, " but when I read what L—— writes about Muhammad I am so filled with indignation that I feel myself a stauncher Moslem than any of my critics." If those who deny the vitality of Islam in Turkey or elsewhere were to try a similar test, they might perhaps find cause to revise their opinions. In the more organized sphere of religion, there appears to be no falling off in the provision of *waqfs* or pious foundations, whose revenues are applied to charitable societies, hospitals, libraries, orphanages, and other works of religious and social service.

Most effective, however, of all the religious institutions that nourish the community spirit of Islam is the Pilgrimage to Mecca. No Moslem who has shared the spiritual exaltation of common worship with myriads of his fellow-believers of every race and sect (for at Mecca even the bitterest sectarian animosities are stilled, notwithstanding occasional exhibitions of fanaticism) can ever forget that supreme experience, with its revelation of the inner power and outward expansion of his faith. Each returned pilgrim bears witness to his own circle of the unity which transcends all lesser divisions, and becomes a centre of fresh enthusiasm for the supra-national ideals of Islam. The events of the last two decades have, it is true, brought about a diminution in the number of pilgrims of recent years, but it is as yet too soon to conclude that this temporary decrease is symptomatic of a permanent tendency.

WHITHER ISLAM?

But religious zeal alone, no matter how intense it may be, cannot maintain unity, still less re-create a broken unity in face of powerful disruptive forces. Of this too the Moslem leaders are aware, and while the spirit of unity is yet alive they have begun to take steps to reinforce it by the creation of new institutions which may utilize and supplement the traditional institutions of Islamic society. It was pointed out in the course of the introduction that one of the principal weaknesses of the mediæval system was that it atrophied the faculty for organized action in any but a military sense, but that the influence of western education had given an impetus to the formation of organized bodies for the prosecution of definite aims. The most prominent of these new organizations are, of course, those formed for political ends. It could not be long, however, before the religious interests also began to realize the benefits to be gained from organized action. Since there is no priesthood in orthodox Islam, the class corresponding to the clergy have never been organized in any sort of hierarchy, nor does it seem likely that they ever will be. But of recent decades the ʽulamā or religious authorities have shown a tendency in various lands to form associations for the defence of the heritage of Islam, for the establishment of religious seminaries, and even for the furtherance of missionary efforts amongst non-Moslems and nominal Moslems. In this field the

WHITHER ISLAM?

Moslems of India have again been the pioneers, and India now has its *Nadwat al-'Ulamā*, its association called *'Ulamā al-Hadīth* and numerous other associations which have been described by Colonel Ferrar. The Ahmadīya movement, referred to several times in the preceding chapters, is largely a movement of the same kind; in gradually discarding its original heretical and sectarian features, it has become essentially a Moslem propagandist society, though still looked upon with suspicion by the orthodox *'ulamā*. To it belongs also the credit for the development of a modern Moslem apologetic which, though not yet fully able to handle the western technique of argumentation, is far from negligible, especially in the East and in Africa.

It is only natural that these new religious organizations should be more active in India and Indonesia than in the central Islamic lands. Here the non-Moslem element is numerically small; there Islam is confronted with the missionary activities of Hindu and Christian bodies. The Moslem societies are in effect resuming under altered conditions and in a new form the traditional missionary policy of Islam in face of the old oriental societies, and it is a sign of its vigour in these eastern lands that it should have so rapidly succeeded in adapting its activities to new circumstances. In Africa, on the other hand, there are few signs of any similar organization. The merchant classes to whom the initiative of conversion largely belonged have declined in importance and prestige, and in many regions Islam is stationary, or even regressing; for its advance it depends upon the old brotherhood organizations or the imported Indian missionary societies, who have, however, built up a strong Moslem community in South Africa. The problem of converting the old military Islamizing activities of such peoples as the Fulas into peaceful mission organizations has not yet been solved, and upon its solution seems to depend the future of Islam in negro Africa.

Of greater importance, especially in the central lands, are the more recent Moslem religious associations in which the lay element predominates, since they appeal to much wider circles and lay stress on the ethical rather than the theological teachings of Islam. Professor Kampffmeyer's full analysis of the " Association of Young Moslems " (Y.M.M.A.) makes it superfluous to recapitulate here their methods and aims, since the others, such as the " Association of Islamic Guidance " in the Arabic-speaking zone, and the Indonesian societies described by Professor Berg follow much the same lines. The Pan-Islamic interests of these societies, the international character of many of them and the relations which they maintain with one another, all indicate that they may well play a decisive part in strengthening the sentiment of Moslem solidarity, perhaps even in preparing the way for some more organic union of the Moslem peoples in the future. Already indeed the first steps have been taken in this direction. In all the thirteen and a half centuries of Islamic history up to a few years ago, it would be difficult to point to a single occasion on which representatives from the length and breadth of Islam have met together to consult on problems of common interest and to decide on a common course of action. Yet from about 1900[1] the idea of holding Islamic congresses has gradually forced its way to the front, and since 1926 three Moslem congresses have actually met, two in that year at Cairo and Mecca, the third in December, 1931, at Jerusalem. The objects and issue of each Congress have been widely different, and not less interesting have been the differences in their composition. The Caliphate Congress at Cairo, the main features of which are described by Professor Kampffmeyer, met with a somewhat theoretical object—the determination of the future of the Caliphate. Its personnel was overwhelmingly clerical, and its results (as was only to be expected) negative. The continuing committees which it foreshadowed do not even seem to have been brought into existence. The subject had too little reality and the means of approach were too mediæval for the Islamic world of to-day.[2]

[1] The meeting held at Mecca in 1898 behind closed doors cannot be called a congress.

[2] The full procès-verbaux of the Cairo and Mecca Congresses are translated in the *Revue du Monde Musulman*, vol. lxiv. (Paris, 1926).

WHITHER ISLAM?

The second Congress at Mecca had originally a more limited and tangible object—the determination of the status of the Hijaz and its Sanctuaries. As in the interim, however, the Sultan (now King) 'Abd al-'Azīz ibn Sa'ūd had been proclaimed King of the Hijaz, the delegates found themselves forestalled, and the proceedings of the Congress resolved themselves into a diplomatic duel between the representatives of Najd and the Hijaz, whose object was to secure financial aid as well as moral support and technical assistance for their government, and the foreign delegates, who adopted a somewhat critical, not to say querulous, tone in regard to the religious, administrative, and especially sanitary conditions of the country. In vain did the King intervene with a pointed message, the burden of which was summed up in the sentence : " To leave us to walk by ourselves and to take up an attitude of criticism is unworthy of the ties of Islamic brotherhood which unite us " ; the foreign delegates refused even to allow the letter to be discussed. Ibn Sa'ūd's disappointment at the result is clear from the fact that the Congress which, according to the third article of its Statutes, was to meet annually at Mecca during the Pilgrimage, has remained in abeyance down to the time of writing.

Yet it would be false to conclude that the Mecca Congress was a failure. The range from which its personnel was drawn was wider than that of the Cairo

Congress, not only geographically (in addition to the Najd and Hijaz, Turkey, Afghanistan, the Sudan and Russia were represented at Mecca but not at Cairo ; on the other hand 'Iraq, Poland, North-west Africa, and South Africa were represented at Cairo but not at Mecca), but also by a larger admixture of lay members, though the clergy still predominated. On most of the problems which were discussed, different points of view were found capable of synthesis to form a basis of common action, and even where action was precluded by the presence of other factors it was not a small matter that a common standpoint was reached and that Moslem public opinion could express itself and receive a sort of ratification in a representative assembly. In regard to the first and second of the objects enunciated in the Statutes—the provision of opportunities for mutual contact, and the examination and improvement of the religious, moral, social and economic conditions of the Moslem peoples—it could at least be said that a beginning had been made, and that the congress method, once introduced, would be pursued farther.

There is one question which naturally occurs to the mind of the western reader in regard to these congresses and their delegations. Who is in a position to summon such a congress, who appoints the delegates, and whom do they represent ? There seems, from our point of view, to be a lack of method about them ;

"delegates" come forward to represent countries from which they are political exiles, and in any case few of the members bear any official mandate. The answer is not easy to make clear to those who have not grasped the flexible and voluntary nature of Moslem institutions. Underlying the whole system is, in brief, public opinion. Not everyone may convene a congress, but only those whom public opinion (as guided by its leaders and creators) recognizes to hold a position of natural leadership. The same applies to the "delegates" and members. Each of them is known, the extent of his influence is known, his political position is known. While some members represent nobody but themselves, "unofficial" delegates and even exiles may sometimes represent the public opinion of at least a section of their own countrymen much more truly than official delegates, whose hands and tongues are tied by the restraints imposed upon them by political considerations. This was particularly marked at the Mecca Congress, when the Turkish and other delegations frequently withdrew in order to avoid embarrassments for their governments. Nor are all governments of Moslem countries favourable to the congress idea, and a contributory cause of the suspension of the Mecca Congresses is doubtless the stipulation that each country shall pay an annual subscription of £E.300 per delegate for the privilege of representation. Any such condition, which tends to make of the congress a kind of Moslem League of Nations, runs too far ahead of present actualities to be practicable. Under the existing conditions, the function of Moslem congresses is to solidarize Moslem public opinion, and for this purpose the essential condition is that the leaders of public opinion in each country shall be free to attend and to express themselves without official restraints, and that they shall subsequently endeavour to guide public opinion in their own countries along the lines or in the directions agreed upon in the congress.

In these respects the Jerusalem Congress of 1931 marked a distinct advance upon its predecessors. At the outset invitations were sent out—in this instance by the Mufti of Jerusalem, who thus stepped into the place vacated by King Ibn Sa'ūd—not only, as usual, to the various governments of Moslem states, but also to the Moslem societies. Owing to an apparently premature report that the Congress intended to raise the question of the Caliphate, all the governments refused to send delegates. The report was authoritatively contradicted, but the only ruling prince whose official delegate actually attended the Congress was the Shi'ite Imām of the Yemen, in South Arabia, though the Egyptian government consented to send a semi-official delegate. On the other hand, and this is the most important feature of the attendance, accredited representatives were present from practically all the organized societies in Egypt and Western Asia, including the Wafdist party and the Y.M.M.A. in Egypt and several other branches of the Y.M.M.A. and the Association of Islamic Guidance in Palestine, Syria, and 'Iraq, as well as from the Khilafat Committee in India, who materially co-operated in the promotion of the Congress. The effect of this was to give increased prominence to the lay element in the Congress, and to make it more fully representative of modern Moslem opinion. " Unofficial " representatives attended from North-west Africa, Russia, Java, and even from Kashgar, in addition to a large number from the other countries already mentioned. During the course of the Congress, the King of 'Iraq, the Amir of Transjordan and King Ibn Sa'ūd, their fears having been allayed, sent messages of support, and the latter even appointed an official delegate, but too late for him to attend.

One of the most striking features was the extent to which the Shi'ites participated in the Congress; in addition to the Yemenite delegate, the Shi'ite *'ulamā* of 'Iraq sent an accredited representative, two Persian Shi'ite delegates attended, and the Mufti of the Shi'ites of Syria sent a message of sympathy (as also did the association of Moroccan students in Paris). The only important Shi'ite group not represented was the Indian Shi'ite community. Though Yemenite delegates were present also at Mecca, it may be said that at Jerusalem (and even for this alone the Jerusalem Congress would be memorable) the Shi'ites for the first time gave expression to their solidarity with the Sunni Moslem world. Never before in Islamic history have the Sunnis and Shi'ites met together to deliberate on common problems, and while on the one hand the fact may be taken to illustrate the weakening of religious inhibitions in political life, it no less truly indicates a growing realization of the common interests of all Moslems in the modern world.

In addition to the general object of maintaining international contacts, the Congress had several immediate practical objects in view, the chief of these being the defence of the Holy Places at Jerusalem against suspected encroachments, the creation of a Moslem University at Jerusalem (and ultimately of other Universities elsewhere), and the organization of Islamic propaganda, with, in the background, the object of enlisting the moral and material support of the Islamic world for the Moslems of Palestine against Zionism. In spite of the unfavourable impression given by the demonstration of a current of opposition within Palestine itself towards the organizers of the Congress, it undoubtedly achieved a very substantial measure of success, and drew up definite plans of action to be pursued in the immediate future. It was, for example, decided to hold the congress every second year, though not necessarily at Jerusalem. A central bureau was established at Jerusalem to direct the work of Islamic propaganda, with local bureaux in the different countries, to report every six months to the central bureau, which itself is to issue an annual report.[1] A scheme of collections for the new University and for " the defence of the Holy Places " was planned; meanwhile, the technical preliminaries for the foundation of the University are to be carried out in readiness for report to the next congress. Amongst other plans approved by the delegates were the establishment of an Arab agricultural bank in Palestine and the creation of an international Arab Academy in Egypt. It remains to be seen how effective these resolutions will prove, and what support they will meet with in the Moslem world generally—above all, whether the project of holding biennial Islamic congresses with continuing committees proves to be feasible in the present circumstances. Since, however, the immediate proposals are both moderate and practical and their execution is entrusted to organized cultural associations, not merely reported to a government and filed in some departmental pigeon-hole, there is every likelihood that they will have practical results of some kind. If this should be so, we may regard it as certain that the congress movement will

[1] The Central Bureau has now been constituted with a Persian Shi'ite of Arab descent as President.

steadily gain in strength, and that its work for the maintenance of cultural unity will assume decisive importance.

It will be observed that so far the congresses have set cultural objects in the foreground and have avoided all direct interference in political affairs. At the Mecca Congress, indeed, King Ibn Sa'ūd expressly forbade the delegates from " dabbling in international politics or the differences which divide certain Moslem peoples from their governments," adding that " these are local questions whose interest is limited to the peoples concerned." Nevertheless, political preoccupations could not be entirely excluded. Even at the Caliphate Congress in Cairo, a resolution of protest against the bombardment of Damascus was carried, and at Mecca a protest against the annexation of 'Akaba and Ma'an to Transjordan was introduced under protest from the Egyptian, Turkish and Afghan delegations. The Jerusalem Congress was even more directly committed to political action by its anti-Zionist resolutions, though its deliberations on the Hijaz Railway (which was considered also at Mecca) were strictly within the range of Moslem cultural interests, the Hijaz Railway being admittedly a Moslem religious endowment. The desire of the Congress organizers to prevent the Congress from being identified with any political programme was shown by the fact that, while advantage was taken of the presence of so many delegates at the Congress to reaffirm in the most solemn manner the full political programme of Pan-Arabism, this was done at a separate private gathering, expressly dissociated from the Congress, and limited to the representatives of the Arab countries. It is unlikely, however, to say the least, that if future congresses are held they will continue to avoid dealing with political questions; on the contrary, the political aspects of many of the problems with which the Moslem peoples are faced will of necessity intrude more and more into the discussions.

In our general survey of the influences which the European West has brought to bear upon the Moslem peoples and the manner in which the sentiment of Islamic solidarity has reacted to their pressure, we have now reached a point where it is possible to state a definite conclusion. In spite of the opposition which still persists in certain circles between the old conceptions and the intrusive western ideas, the general tendency is clearly in the direction of harmonizing them by the ideal of a family of Islamic nations, independently organized under civil governments, but all conscious of their heritage of Islamic culture, and by virtue of that common bond of sentiment and interest maintaining some sort of association with one another —an Islamic Commonwealth, uniting all in the pursuit of the common good, rather than an Islamic

League of Nations, seeking to adjust mutual differences.

Even if it is assumed that Islam may at length find along these lines the means whereby to utilize to the best advantage the vast reserves of power which its peoples possess, it by no means follows, of course, that these hopes will be realized through the mere machinery of congresses and the like, or within any measurable period of time. Not that the time factor should be overstressed; it is a too neglected feature of movements of all kinds in Islamic society that they mature with astonishing rapidity—that, as Professor Massignon has already pointed out, their existence is scarcely suspected before they blaze up and take the world by surprise. The crucial question is that of leadership. When Islam finds a new Saladin, a man who combines exquisite political insight with a deep consciousness of his religious mission, the rest will solve itself.

It remains to touch briefly on some immediate problems which are raised by the confluence of these currents of thought. The first of these concerns the position of the non-Moslem citizens in the national states of the future, if they are to retain an Islamic basis. Shall we see a repetition on a vaster scale of the brutal and ridiculous Greco-Turkish interchange of populations? Not unless European intervention furnishes the same pretexts as served the purpose of the Turkish nationalists. In Egypt and Western Asia the problem of the indigenous non-Moslem minorities is relatively simple. Once the mediæval conception of the political relations to be maintained between Moslems and non-Moslems has been set aside, as it is set aside to-day everywhere outside Arabia (and in Arabia there are practically no non-Moslems), and religious profession has become a matter of personal observance and private jurisdiction, not affecting civic status, then the obstacles in the way of forming homogeneous national units are entirely removed. There is no such cultural cleavage between the Moslems and the Eastern Christians and Jews as there is between the neo-hellenized Greeks and the Turks, or between the Indian Moslems and the Hindus. Historically, Islam, as a social phenomenon, is closely connected with Judaism and the Oriental Christian Churches, and in the Middle Ages both Eastern Christians and Jews made important contributions to Islamic culture and were themselves fully identified with it. Their modern evolution has proceeded simultaneously with the evolution of Moslem society, and the same influences have acted on both with similar effects, as is shown more especially by the part played by Eastern Christians in the development of modern Arabic literature.

The growing sentiment of national unity in the Arabic-speaking lands has already succeeded to a very considerable extent in bringing Moslem and non-Moslem into an organic relation with one another. On every political and cultural organization in Egypt from Cabinet to charity bazaar (except, of course, those organizations which are affected to purely denominational objects) Moslem and Copt co-operate. The same feature may be seen in the public life of Palestine, of Transjordan, in the greater part of Syria, in the relations of the Jews and most of the Christians of 'Iraq with the Moslem population and government, and those of the Zoroastrian community in Persia with their Moslem fellow-countrymen. It cannot be denied that exceptions exist. The Maronites of the Lebanon are not yet prepared to co-operate with the rest of Moslem Syria, the Zionist Jews in Palestine and the Armenian refugee colonies in Syria form unassimilated and perhaps unassimilable groups, and the Assyrian Christians are uneasy about their relations with the Moslem majority in 'Iraq. The position is complicated in Syria and 'Iraq by the presence of sectarian differences within the Moslem ranks. Yet the general impression which is left by a survey of the possible causes of disunity in Western Asia is that the present movements of opinion are in a fair way to solve all of them, except those which are exacerbated by the presence of strong semi-racial, semi-social antagonisms, irrespective of religious creed. The orthodox Moslem Kurds may prove as great a stumbling-block to the organization of a national 'Iraqi state as the Jewish immigrants to the organization of a national Syro-Palestinian state.

However these difficulties may be met in the long run, it is undeniable that the prevailing tendencies are strongly in the direction of maintaining the Islamic basis of the new national units, and that the non-Moslem minorities have generally reciprocated the breaking down of the traditional Islamic pale by accepting and supporting the state recognition of Islam. In the Arabic-speaking areas of Western Asia, Arab national sentiment has undoubtedly been attracted to the ideal of Moslem Arab unity by a revival of national pride in the historical background of the Islamic movement, and the Christian journals are even more zealous than the Moslem journals in preaching the gospel of Pan-Arabia. It was a Greek Orthodox organ which opened a leading article on the Jerusalem Congress with the words : " Welcome to those who have come to lay with sound judgment the foundation for a restoration of the days of 'Omar, the builder of the glory of Islam, upon the lines of his master, Muhammad son of 'Abdullah—upon him be the peace and mercy of God ! " More significant still, possibly, is the fact that the Greek Orthodox Congress in Palestine, which happened to be in session at the same time, sent a deputation to convey its greetings to the Islamic Congress.

WHITHER ISLAM?

It is quite comprehensible that in Turkey and Persia the nationalist motives for maintaining the Islamic religious basis of the state are less cogent. Yet Persia at least seems to be aware that at the roots of its corporate existence lies the cultural tradition of Islam. Even in " irreligious, atheistic Turkey," what spiritual forces are there to be found in the soul of the people but the forces of Islam? Though the present governors of Turkey have disestablished the Moslem church organization, they show a jealous care in protecting the Islamic elements in their social life from the interference of other religious teachings, and so long, at least, as the head of the Turkish republic bears the Moslem epithet of "Ghazi," it appears paradoxical to maintain that Turkey has ceased to be a Moslem state. How far, on the other hand, the conception of Moslem national states can be applied in the exceedingly complicated cases of India and Indonesia the future alone will show. It may be, after all, that in those regions where Islam has not succeeded in permeating the social structure with its own culture and ideals, it will be forced, as it has already been forced in the Balkan peninsula, to resign itself to the diminution of its territorial extension, to the benefit of those other societies which have proved themselves too strong to be assimilated, and eventually also of its own powers of cohesion and solidarity.

The secularist view which is at the bottom of the

conception of national states has been the chief agent in bringing about this altered relationship between church and state. It would be difficult to find anywhere in Western Asia outside Arabia any considerable support for the mediæval theory, which until a few years ago was represented by the Ottoman Caliphate. But this change of view as to the place of religion in the state, which has followed from the acceptance of western political theory and practice, involves a serious breach with the traditional religious conceptions of Islam, and it is impossible to leave untouched the further question whether the same influences which have affected Islamic thought in this field may not also have affected or may affect in the future Islamic thought in the more strictly religious field. This too has an obvious bearing upon the whole problem of the Islamic world. If religious allegiance is to continue to serve as a uniting factor, it would appear to be essential to the firmness of the bond that a relatively uniform religious outlook should be maintained, and that if it develops under the pressure of new ideas, it should develop by the adaptation of similar elements in a more or less equal manner. Otherwise, religion may come to be, as it has almost become in Europe, a dividing rather than a unifying force, and Islam will split up into so many " national churches." Incongruous though the suggestion may seem, it is neither inconceivable nor unprecedented.

WHITHER ISLAM?

For four centuries Shi'ism has borne all the characteristics of a national church in Persia, and Wahhabism came near to giving Arabia a third national church, competing with the Ibādite creed in 'Omān and the Zaidi creed in Yemen.

We come back therefore to the question asked at the very beginning of this book. Whither Islam, as a religion? In more explicit terms : How is the religious thought of Islam reacting to the changes introduced by western education? It is a difficult question, and delicate ground for the non-Moslem, when even the Moslem might hesitate to give an assured answer. Yet it is a question that cannot be shirked.

In the first place, then, it would appear that the great Moslem masses are so far unaffected by western religious influences, and that the bulk of the theological opinion of Islam remains attached to the traditional theology. But this is not the whole truth. In reality, unobserved by theologians and laymen, the religious teachings and outlook of even the most conservative adherents of Islam have been slowly evolving within the last century. It is not so much that any new factual element has been introduced, as that by laying new stress on some points and thrusting others into a less prominent position the whole balance of doctrine and of ethical teaching is shifting, and shifting in a direction which brings it nearer to the modern western ethic, represented also in the current ethical teaching of the Christian church.

Here again, however, it is not to the masses but to the leaders that we must look if we are to judge of the present tendencies in religious thought. And the leaders, indeed, have gone much farther than this. It is true that most of them, however modernist their views, are opposed to the public raising of religious questions. They hold, and rightly, that it would distract attention from what they regard as more immediate tasks, and might bring about ill-will and divisions both within each region and between the Moslem peoples in general. Yet in spite of this there are in every Moslem country—always excepting possibly Arabia, Afghanistan, and parts of Central Africa—definite movements, varying in strength and intensity, towards a reinterpretation or revision of the religious doctrines of Islam. The school of Shaikh Muhammad 'Abduh with its offshoots has long since worked openly towards this end, and even more advanced views have been put forward by individual scholars, especially in India, but it is rather under the surface that the principal adjustments are being made, by the younger intellectuals in particular. One very remarkable feature of these movements is that in method the extreme reactionary reform of the Wahhabis coincides with the advanced modernist attitude. Both reject the accumulation of mediæval teachings which threatened to stifle the life of Islam, and preach a return to the doctrines of the primitive community. It may thus prove that Wahhabism has a decisive part to play in the renovation of religious thought, since by means of the influence which it exerts over widening circles within the conservative body of Moslem opinion, it may close the gap which now threatens to open between conservative and modernist. At the same time this " Protestant " reaction in itself does not solve the problem of the modernist interpretation of Islam, which can hardly make substantial headway until the methods and principles of theological training have been radically altered. Once the mediæval philosophy with which Islamic theology has hitherto been bound up is discarded, the adaptation of its primitive doctrines to the bases of modern theism offers less difficulty than appears at present on the surface.

It has frequently been pointed out that the theological situation with which Islam is confronted to-day is not unlike the situation which arose more than a thousand years ago when it was confronted with the philosophic legacy of Hellenism. In that struggle, however, the outcome of which was the existing theology of Islam, it was to the conservative side that victory ultimately inclined. May it not happen once again, so it is argued, that the conservative spirit, while adapting to its purposes such elements in the new thought as it finds congenial, will prove too strong to allow the thoroughgoing modernist views to establish themselves in the main body of Islam? The argument overlooks the essential difference between the two situations. Then, Islam was in the ascendant and the conflict was confined to a narrow circle of theologians; now, it is on the defensive and has to reckon with an increasing and influential body of lay opinion which has emancipated itself from theological control. Already, while in India, for example, the mass of Moslem opinion still seems to be strongly conservative, modernist views have gained such a hold in Egypt, to say nothing of Turkey, that they can hardly be uprooted without endangering the whole fabric of Moslem society.

Though the possibility of an ultimate schism in Islam cannot, in consequence, be discounted, there are several factors which may intervene to prevent the Moslem world from following too closely the disastrous precedent of the Reformation in Europe. One is the absence of a priesthood, and the power which this gives to the educated "lay" population. In the recent conflicts between the secularized leaders of public opinion and the theologically trained shaikhs, the victory has so far rested mainly with the former, who have, on the other hand, generally preferred to follow a moderate evolutionary policy rather than the Turkish example of radical and violent change. The absence of a single doctrinal authority is also

WHITHER ISLAM?

responsible for another of the conciliatory tendencies of Islam, the " catholic " tendency, which admits of differences of opinion, and is averse from excommunicating any but those who seek excommunication by the narrowness of their own sectarian zeal. Within the body of Sunni Islam differences have always existed, not merely the trifling differences of the various " schools " or rites, but such fundamental differences as distinguished the orthodox theologians from the adepts of the mystical path. Yet in spite of centuries of controversy they have never led to schism.

A third factor is the keen awareness of the whole Moslem world of the vital importance of religious unity in face of Europe and of India. Already this has brought about a striking diminution of sectarian feeling even between groups which have maintained an attitude of mutual hostility for a thousand years. We have seen the manifestation of solidarity of the Arab and Persian Shi'ites with the Sunni " orthodox " given at the Jerusalem Congress, and the part played in Indian Islam, not only by " majority " Shi'ites such as the late Amir 'Ali but even by the ultra-Shi'ite Aghā Khān, is familiar to all observers of recent political movements in the East. The width of Moslem tolerance seems to be increasing in all directions, and may be expected to extend still farther when religion in the narrow sense no longer plays a directing rôle in the national political life of the

Moslem peoples. The danger may still exist that religion will become so weakened as to lose its influence altogether, but we have seen that this danger is less menacing now than it was twenty years ago. Rather should we expect that out of the interaction of the various religious forces now active in Islam there will come a deepening and broadening of religious life.

Finally it must be asked what the general position of the Islamic society, and in particular what its relations with the other human societies, are likely to be in the future world-order. As Professor Berg has pointed out, it depends entirely on the attitude of Europe to the Moslem world and to the East generally whether the Moslem peoples will throw their weight on the side of the East or of the West. At the same time Islam cannot deny its own foundations and live ; and in its foundations we have seen that Islam belongs to and is an integral part of the larger western society. It is the complement and counterbalance to European civilization, nourished at the same springs, breathing the same air. In the broadest aspect of history, what is now happening between Europe and Islam is the reintegration of western civilization, artificially sundered at the Renaissance and now reasserting its unity with overwhelming force. The student of history, though fearfully conscious of the pitfalls of analogy, cannot help recalling two earlier (though even then not the earliest) moments in this secular process of creative interaction between the two halves of the western world. It was the glory and the greatness of the Roman Empire that it united them under its *imperium* and that from that unity were born the spiritual forces which have governed the course of western history ever since. Halfway between that age and ours occurred the first great intellectual adventure of Islam, when it absorbed the heritage of Hellenism and brought it to a new flowering, the seeds from which contributed to the Renaissance in Europe.

The process could not end there. It is going on before our very eyes, on a wider and vaster scale, though the contrast offered by the Islamic world as a whole to the amazing technical progress of Western Europe may still blind us to it; and it may be that the sequel will be the same, that we must wait upon the Islamic society to restore the balance of western civilization upset by the one-sided nature of that progress. Perhaps in the long run it will appear that the bulwark of the Ottoman Empire was the salvation of Islam, that by keeping it isolated, it held it back from sharing in the exaggerated development of European nationalism and becoming " balkanized " —the fate which seems paradoxically to have befallen Turkey itself, as the legacy of its politically Byzantine rather than Islamic past. At all events Islam stands side by side with Europe in distinction from the true

Oriental societies of India and the Far East. The notion of a general "Oriental League" of Islam, India, China and Japan is the fantastic outcome of resentment at the temporary economic domination of Europe. For the fullest development of its own cultural and economic life Islam cannot do without the co-operation of European society; for the fullest development of *its* cultural life, particularly of its spiritual life, Europe cannot do without the forces and capacities which lie within Islamic society. Only by a restoration of that interaction which they enjoyed under the Roman Empire can both recover and exert their full powers.

Within the western world Islam still maintains the balance between exaggerated opposites. Opposed equally to the anarchy of European nationalism and the regimentation of Russian communism, it has not yet succumbed to that obsession with the economic side of life which is characteristic of present-day Europe and present-day Russia alike. Its social ethic has been admirably summed up by Professor Massignon : " Islam has the merit of standing for a very equalitarian conception of the contribution of each citizen by the tithe to the resources of the community; it is hostile to unrestricted exchange, to banking capital, to state loans, to indirect taxes on objects of prime necessity, but it holds to the rights of the father and the husband, to private property, and to commercial capital. Here again it occupies an intermediate position between the doctrines of bourgeois capitalism and Bolshevist communism."

But Islam has yet a further service to render to the cause of humanity. It stands after all nearer to the real East than Europe does, and it possesses a magnificent tradition of interracial understanding and co-operation. No other society has such a record of success in uniting in an equality of status, of opportunity, and of endeavour so many and so various races of mankind. The great Moslem communities of Africa, India and Indonesia, perhaps also the small Moslem communities in China and the still smaller community in Japan show that Islam has still the power to reconcile apparently irreconcilable elements of race and tradition. If ever the opposition of the great societies of the East and the West is to be replaced by co-operation, the mediation of Islam is an indispensable condition. In its hands lies very largely the solution of the problem with which Europe is faced in its relations with the East. If they unite, the hope of a peaceful issue is immeasurably enhanced—but if Europe, by rejecting the co-operation of Islam, throws it into the arms of its rivals, the issue can only be disastrous for both.

INDEX

'ABD AL-HAMĪD I, 36
'Abd al-Hamīd II, 42, 45, 61, 120
'Abd al-Hamīd Bey Sa'īd, 105, 106–7
'Abdul-Mejīd, 138, 140, 226
Achèhnese, 261, 294
Afghanistan, 13, 58, 101, 125, 169–70, 215, 222, 228, 322, 326, 337, 357, 372
Afghans, 180
Africa, Moslems in, 11, 13, 15, 337, 353–4, 372, 379
Africa, North-west, 57, 79–98, 124–6, 129, 155, 159, 324, 336, 341, 357, 360. *See also* Morocco
Africa, South, 13, 98, 354, 357
Africa, West, 13, 15, 79, 87, 89, 93
Afridis, 228
Agha Khan, 180, 183, 375
Ahl-i-Hadīth, 200
Ahl-i-Qur'ān, 200
Ahmadīya, 87, 184, 214–19, 287–8, 309, 353
Alexander the Great, 17
'Alī 'Abd ar-Rāziq, 141–2, 151
Aligarh, 66, 69, 192–3, 195
American schools, 51
Amir Ali, Sayyid, 201–2, 375
'Arābī Pasha, 62–3, 70
Arabia, 16, 18, 58, 72, 154, 181, 259, 321, 336, 337, 366, 370, 372
Arabic language and script, 20, 95, 96, 102, 124, 133, 159, 167, 251, 333
Arabs, 25, 79, 158–60, 180, 205, 223, 236, 268, 333, 368
 in North-west and West Africa, 81, 91–2
 in Indonesia, 240, 256, 260–1
 See also Nationalism
Armenians, 240, 367
Army, political rôle of, 60–2
Asia, Central, 13, 15, 57, 205, 337, 360
al-Azhar, 63, 69, 106, 113, 139–40, 141, 142–3, 150, 268, 269

BAHA'ISM, 169

Bali, 243, 249, 294, 297
Balkans, 11, 15, 369
Baluchistan, 174, 176, 178, 235
Barakatullah, 143–4
Bengal, 13, 176–8, 182, 212
Berbers, 80, 81, 91–2
 Customary Law of, 91, 95, 124–5
Borneo, 242, 243, 249

CALIPHATE, 36–7, 133, 137–44, 169, 219, 252, 253, 285, 307, 355, 359
 of King Husayn, 138–9
 Ottoman, 35, 37–8, 40, 42–3, 92, 262, 344–5, 370
 Abolition of, 138, 207, 224, 225
China, Moslems in, 11, 13, 125, 378, 379
Chinese, 240
Christianity, Relations of Islam with, 16, 24–6, 32–3, 35, 160, 310, 366, 371–2. *See also* Missions
Christians, Oriental, 17, 24–5, 122, 146, 160, 162, 164, 366–8
Commerce and Economics, 19, 26–8, 31–2, 96–7, 119, 133, 153, 155–6, 191, 258, 260–1, 263, 273–4, 277–8, 281, 323, 324–5, 344, 348, 362
Communism, 283–4, 285, 310, 325, 378–9
Congresses, Moslem, 93–4, 139–41, 158, 225, 226, 285, 307–8, 355–64
 in India, 93, 195, 230, 235
 in Java, 285
Crusades, 26, 306, 308

Dār al-harb, 175, 221
Dār al-Islām, 20, 21, 222, 240
ad-Dardīrī, Dr. Yahyā, 105, 114–16, 119
Dutch, 29, 52, 239, 243, 260–2, 272–81, 286, 289, 291–3, 303, 305–6, 311

EDUCATION, 47–8, 49–52, 60, 63, 66, 92, 95–6, 133–5, 148–9, 156, 166–7, 192–4, 208–12, 233, 251, 257, 279, 281, 287, 289–94, 297, 298–9, 308, 329–30, 334, 361

INDEX

Egypt, 18, 20, 32, 44, 45, 47, 52, 57, 60, 61, 62–4, 67–71, 74, 79, 97, 101–65, 170, 207, 267–8, 297, 299, 321, 323, 325, 327, 330, 336, 339, 341, 344, 350, 359, 366, 367, 374
  Leadership of, 59, 63–4, 88, 97, 102, 128, 268–9, 332, 339
Egyptian University, 139, 149–50
England, English (British), 29, 30–1, 63, 65, 120, 173–230
Europe, Commerce of, 28–32, 156, 273
  Expansion and Colonization, 29, 31–2, 98, 160, 240, 272, 275, 277–8, 308
  Interrelations with Islam, 16–17, 308–10, 376–9
  Moslems in, 11, 24–5, 128, 357
  Precarious basis of dominance, 78, 264
  Preponderance of, 44, 263–4, 307, 344
  See also Moslems; Westernization

FRANCE, MOSLEM STUDENTS AND WORKMEN IN, 80, 324, 360
Policy of, in Morocco, 91, 124–5
  in Syria, 156, 157
  suggested concordat of Islam with, 89, 94
French, Moslem propaganda in, 86, 88
French Revolution, 49
French schools, 51
Fulas, 81, 354

Gam'īyat ash-shubbān al-muslimīn. *See* Y.M.M.A.
al-Ghazzālī, 54
Ghulām Ahmad, Mirza. *See* Ahmadīya
Ghulām Allāh, 89, 94
Greek schools, 51

Hajj, 19, 79, 102, 174, 177, 226, 251, 261, 303, 351
Hellenism, 16–17, 373, 377
Haykal, Dr. Muhammad Husayn, 151–2
Hijaz, 221, 230, 356
Hijaz Railway, 43, 133, 220, 363

Hinduism, Hindus, 17, 25–6, 43, 73, 175–6, 177, 180–1, 184–9, 191, 195, 207, 210, 215, 218, 223, 224, 228, 230–4, 240, 246–7, 249, 250, 267, 297, 319, 346, 349, 353, 366
Hindu-Javanese culture, 243, 247–9, 253–7, 296–7, 342
Hormuz, 30
Husayn, King, 138–9, 141, 152, 158
Hyderabad, 176, 182–3, 189, 194, 226

IBN SA'ŪD, King 'Abd al-'Azīz, 139, 154, 356, 359, 360, 363
ijtihād (mujtahids), 67–8, 206–7, 267, 268, 271
India, 11, 13, 15, 17, 28, 29, 40, 43, 52, 53, 57, 66, 69, 73, 87, 93, 139, 140, 173–236, 241, 246–8, 252, 258, 259, 266–7, 319, 325, 333, 337, 346, 353, 360, 369, 372, 374, 375, 378, 379
  Southern, 176, 182, 211, 212, 222–4
Indonesia, 11, 13, 15, 17, 25, 29, 40, 52, 57, 74, 102, 126, 239–311, 319, 324, 325, 337, 339, 341, 353, 354, 360, 369, 379
Paganism in, 244–6
Partai Nasional, 277, 281, 295
See also Hinduism, Nationalism
Industry. *See* Commerce and Economics
Iqbal, Sir Muhammad, 204–8, 225, 235–6
'Iraq, 58, 72, 109, 110–11, 112, 154–7, 188, 337, 342, 357, 360, 367
Islam: Character of, 11–12, 16–17, 21, 24, 378–9
  Expansion of, 15, 24–5, 39, 205, 252, 354
  Political Structure of, 38–40
  Political Theory of, 24–5, 36–7, 205–6
  Race Problem in, 306, 341, 379
  Reform Movements in, 44–52, 67–9, 87–9, 94–5, 114–17, 129, 147, 169, 192–4, 198–9, 236, 266–72, 286–8, 299–301, 372; conservative opposition to, 53–4, 58, 64, 94, 200, 269, 271, 320
  Religious Law (Sharī'ah), 46, 72, 91, 94, 95, 124, 147–8, 166, 183, 206, 232, 271, 335, 350, 354
  Religious Orders, 19, 88–9, 90, 92, 129, 167, 183, 184, 350, 375

INDEX

Islam—(*contd.*)
  Theology of, 12, 16, 67–8, 206, 232, 250–1, 370–6 ; modern Apologetic, 67, 78, 86, 89, 95, 142, 175, 201–5, 213, 300, 353
  See also Ahmadīya, Europe, France, Missions, Moslems, Nationalism, Pan-Islamism, Westernization
Islamic Civilization, Unity of, 14–21, 37–8
  Inequalities in, 55–6, 58, 185–7, 336–8, 348
Islamic Nations, Suggested League of, 133, 359, 364–5
Ismā'īl, Khedive, 45, 59
Italy, Italians, 51, 85, 90, 127, 263

JAMAL AD-DĪN AL-AFGHĀNĪ, 42, 118, 120, 170
Japan, Japanese, 240, 279, 378, 379
Jats, 180
Java. *See* Indonesia
Java War, 274, 276
Jews (Judaism, Zionism), 16, 17, 97, 122–3, 157, 160–1, 361, 363, 366, 367
jihād ("Holy War"), 78, 89, 215, 220, 261, 262, 325, 344

KABYLES. *See* Berbers
Khilāfat Committee, 221–4, 233, 234, 360
Khudā Bakhsh, Shaykh, 202, 225
Koran, 11, 88, 114–15, 134, 135, 167, 191, 198, 199, 200–1, 271, 350
Kurds, 367

LEBANON, 367
Libya. *See* Tripoli
Literature and the Press, 59–60, 63, 87–9, 96, 102, 105, 114–20, 133, 134–5, 141, 142, 150–2, 153, 160, 162, 196–8, 204, 258, 262–3, 276, 331–4, 344, 349, 366, 368

MAHDI, MAHDISM, 93, 214–15, 276–7
Malay language and literature, 244, 258, 259–60, 271
Malay Peninsula, 13, 258
al-Manār, 69, 88, 153, 268–9, 271, 334
al-Manfalūtī, 151
Mappillas, 211, 222–4
Metternich, 42

Missions, Christian, 121–2, 135, 157, 161–5, 195, 261, 286, 287, 297, 302–6, 311, 353
Schools of, 51–2, 109, 111, 305
Missions, Moslem, 24, 86, 89, 153, 175, 176, 195–6, 234, 240, 251, 287, 352–4 ; Ahmadīya, 217–18, 287–8
Mongolia, 13
Mongols, 37, 39, 174
Morocco, 15, 40, 93, 124–6, 129. *See also* Africa, North-west
Moslems, Attitude to Europe of, 24–34, 55–7, 72–3, 84–6, 154–5, 160–1, 165, 202, 215, 261, 264–5, 275, 294, 308–9, 339
  Attitude to Hinduism of, 25, 175–6, 184–8, 224, 229–34, 254, 267, 366
  Character of movements amongst, 77–8, 284, 365
  Leaders of, 58, 63–4, 158–60, 182, 265–6, 283, 337, 358, 365
  Political quietism of, 34, 40, 49
  Solidarity of, 37–8, 43, 55, 73–4, 120, 130, 132–3, 161, 220, 234, 251–2, 284, 315–17, 333, 344–55, 361, 364
  Statistics and Distribution of, 11, 13 ; in India, 176–8, 180, 183
Mughal Empire, 28, 176, 183, 184–5, 189–90, 192, 219
Muhammad, 11, 24, 142, 151, 199, 254, 350–1, 368
Muhammad 'Abduh, 68–9, 70, 153, 170, 268, 343, 372
Muhammad 'Alī (Indian), 158
Muhammadans. *See* Moslems
Mujtahids. *See* *ijtihād*
Mustafa Kāmil (Egyptian), 71, 117, 161
Mzab, 94

NATIONALISM, 70–4, 85, 90, 107–8, 151, 154, 207, 235, 265, 282–3, 303, 307, 325, 338–42, 346–7, 378
Berber, 91–2, 341
Indonesian, 248, 272–88, 294–5, 297–9
Pan-Arab, 72, 92, 97, 120, 156, 333, 341, 364
Negroes, 81, 98
Nigeria, 81, 87, 89

383

INDEX

N.W. Frontier Province (India), 178, 179, 212, 228, 235

OMĀN, 371
"Oriental League," 81, 142, 378
Oriente Moderno, 332
Ottoman Empire, 25, 28, 39-40, 43, 52, 72, 377

PALESTINE, 79, 109-10, 112, 122-3, 126, 131, 139, 140-1, 154-61, 359-63, 367, 368
Pan-Islamism, 40-7, 59-60, 64, 66, 70, 72, 129-30, 207, 230, 262-3, 344, 354. *See also* Caliphate, Ottoman
Paris, Moslems in, 81, 83-4, 89, 360
Persia, 16, 21, 28, 29-31, 39, 40, 58, 60, 71-2, 74, 101, 168-9, 188, 327, 337, 341, 367, 369
Persians, 169, 180, 202, 207, 360, 362
Persian language, 190, 196, 204
Persian Gulf, 29
Philippine Islands, 13, 240, 273
Poland, 128, 357
Press. *See* Literature
Punjab, 178, 210, 228, 235

RAJPUTS, 180
Roman Empire, 377
Russia, 11, 15, 35, 57, 128, 174, 205, 279, 283, 318, 337, 346, 357, 360, 378

SAINT WORSHIP, 183-4
Sarèkat Islam, 279-80, 284-6, 288, 304
Sayyid Ahmad Khan, Sir, 66, 192-3, 194, 195, 196-9, 208, 210-11, 228, 343
Scouts, Moslem Boy, 109, 118, 134, 155, 334
Senegal, 90
Senussis, 89-90
Shakīb Arslān, 97, 127, 162
Shi'as, 39, 41, 67, 93, 183, 194, 220, 359, 360-1, 362, 371, 375
Siberia, 11, 13, 15
Sikhs, 188-9, 218, 228
Sind, 178, 189, 190, 235
Social Reforms, 64, 70, 94-5, 118, 119, 134, 147, 152-3, 156, 163, 287
Societies, Cultural, 81, 103, 153, 156, 193-4, 195-6, 229, 285-7, 334, 352-4, 360. *See also* Y.M.M.A.

Spain, 15, 84-5
Sufiism, 206. *See also* Islam, Religious Orders
Sumatra, 240, 242, 243, 249, 252, 257-8, 260, 270-2, 287, 294
Syria, 58, 63, 72, 79, 109, 119, 139, 154-7, 325, 337, 360, 367

taqlīd, 68, 206, 271
Transjordania, 138-9, 152, 360, 363, 367
Tripoli (Libya), 85, 90, 127-8, 263, 349
Turkey, 35, 44-7, 57, 59-62, 63, 70, 74, 101, 128, 138, 147, 159, 164, 166-8, 181, 207, 213, 220-1, 225, 318, 322, 325, 326, 327, 333, 336, 338-41, 344, 346, 350, 351, 357, 358, 366, 369, 373, 377. *See also* Ottoman Empire
Turks (Central Asian), 180

'ULAMĀ, ASSOCIATIONS OF, 125, 135, 193, 195, 285, 352-3
United Provinces (India), 178, 179, 186, 227
Urdu language and literature, 182, 194, 196-8, 204, 233

WAHHABISM, 58, 88, 183, 206, 267, 371, 372-3
Waqfs (*awqāf, hubūs*), 94-5, 128, 287, 351
Westernization, 44-53, 55-74, 84, 90, 94-7, 153-4, 166-9, 181, 193-4, 202, 265, 270, 289-94, 307, 319-38, 349. *See also* Army, Education, Literature, Nationalism, Social reforms, Societies, Women's movement
Women's movement and education, 64, 94, 96, 149, 211-13, 334

Y.M.M.A., 103-37, 144-6, 149, 154, 155, 162, 354, 360
Branches outside Egypt, 109-12, 131, 360
Covenant of, 133, 136-7
Islamic defence organized by, 121-8
Review of, 114-20, 126-8
Yemen, 326, 359, 371

ZOROASTRIANISM, 16

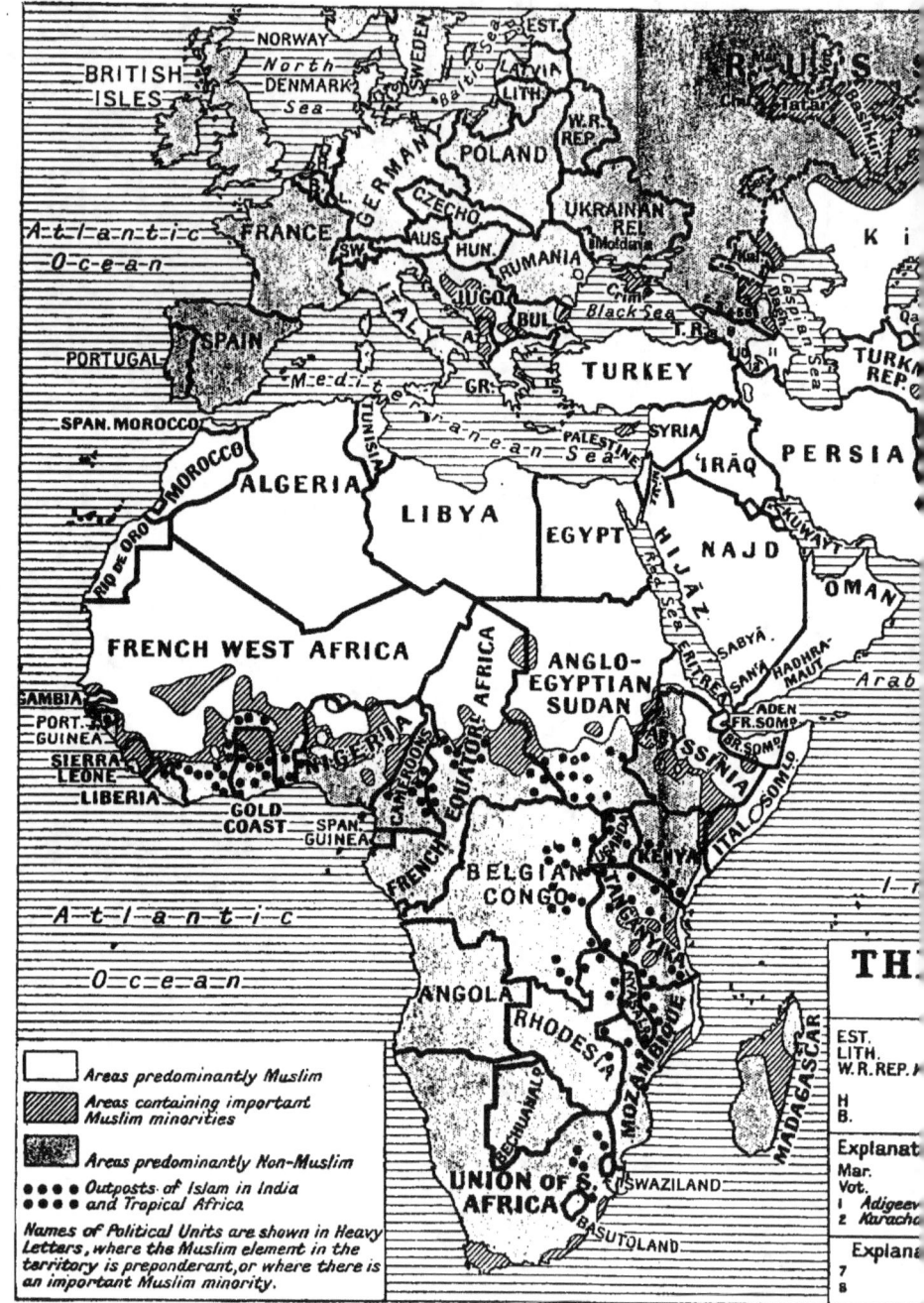

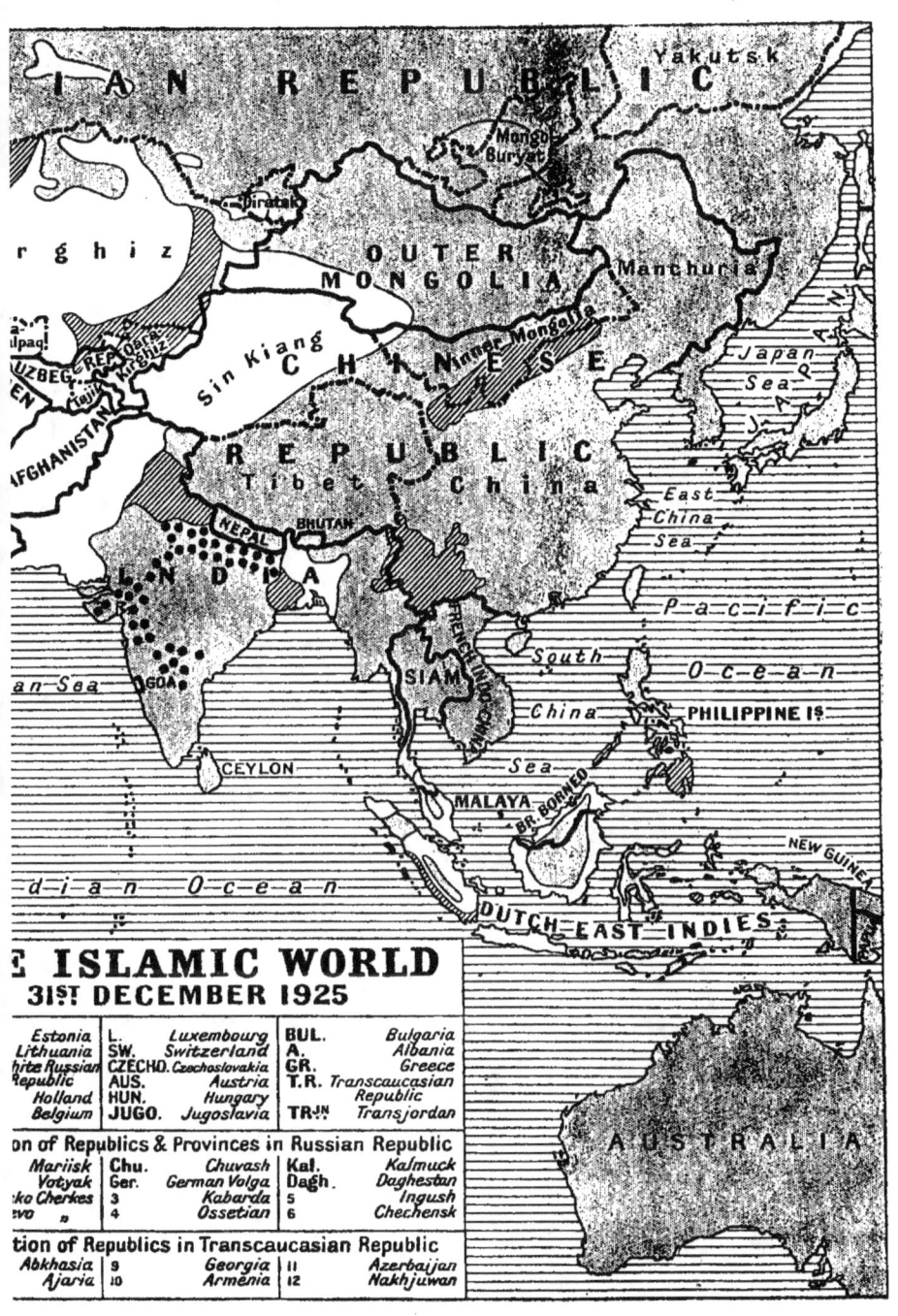

For Product Safety Concerns and Information please contact our EU representative GPSR@taylorandfrancis.com
Taylor & Francis Verlag GmbH, Kaufingerstraße 24, 80331 München, Germany

www.ingramcontent.com/pod-product-compliance
Lightning Source LLC
Chambersburg PA
CBHW070722020526
44116CB00031B/1103